Joseph Orton Kerbey

On the War Path

A Journey over the Historic Grounds of the Late Civil War

Joseph Orton Kerbey

On the War Path
A Journey over the Historic Grounds of the Late Civil War

ISBN/EAN: 9783744745079

Printed in Europe, USA, Canada, Australia, Japan

Cover: Foto ©ninafisch / pixelio.de

More available books at **www.hansebooks.com**

ON THE WAR PATH

A JOURNEY OVER THE HISTORIC GROUNDS OF THE LATE CIVIL WAR

BY

MAJOR J. O. KERBEY

U. S. CONSUL AT PARA, BRAZIL, S. A.; AUTHOR OF "THE BOY SPY

CHICAGO
DONOHUE, HENNEBERRY & CO.
1890

DONOHUE & HENNEBERRY, PRINTERS AND BINDERS, CHICAGO.

PREFACE.

I do not write books for a living. This statement will be no less gratifying to the reading public than it is to myself.

For some years, I have been a Washington news-gatherer, trained to telegraph special facts to the press in the fewest possible words. Recently becoming one of the grand army of office seekers, I have availed myself of some of the abundant leisure always afforded these gentlemen, to jot down, in the form of personal reminiscences, some of the actual experiences and incidents coming under my observation, which have never been printed in the newspapers, and which are herewith submitted without any pretense to literary embellishment.

The only motive that prompts me to this work springs from an honest and sincere desire to put in permanent form, for the master-builder or future historian, some straws that may be used in the mortar that cements the coming monumental history of this period.

It will be apparent to the most casual reader that, in telling so many things that are sure to displease, the writer must at least be trying to be truthful, even at the sacrifice or at the expense of judgment or discretion.

Nor has there been any feeling of bitterness or resentfulness; not even the slightest disposition to "get even" with anybody. I confess, however, to an inborn inability to obey the scriptural injunction to turn the other cheek. And, though enjoying the reputation of an inoffensive citizen, it is my nature, without much regard to consequences, to strike back at any one who may attack.

Mr. Blaine, with whom I have had the distinguished honor of a long personal acquaintance, when I applied to him for a United States consulate, very kindly said to me that he intended to do something in that direction, his only difficulty being in finding a suitable place, or, as he put it: "We have more pegs than holes to put them in; but I'll find a hole some place in which to stick you." I had faith in the promise, and waited some time for my turn. He religiously kept his word and found a hole.

I was nominated by the President as United States Consul to an important port at the mouth of the Amazon River, in the new Republic of Brazil, the object, as the Secretary said, being to afford me facilities for writing up for a press syndicate the possibilities of business for American manufacturers in Central and South America. During my absence from the city, the newspaper-row ring of Washington insidiously attempted to defeat my confirmation, by resorting to some of their usual underhand tactics. Their animus will become apparent to the reader of these pages, and needs no further comment. However, the Senate, after hearing their false statements, fully endorsed me by confirmation, and then, for the first time since my enlistment as a soldier, I subscribed to the oath, received a parchment, and again became a servant of the Government.

THE AUTHOR.

WASHINGTON, D. C., July 23, 1890.

ON THE WAR-PATH.

THIS is not a War Story—

I succeeded in publishing one* in which I told everything that I knew about the war—and more too—and have, in consequence, a double-edged appreciation of that proverbial aphorism of Job's, "My desire is * * * that mine adversary had written a book." That venture in book-making on the war question induced the belief that war writers find their principal adversaries in the ranks of comrades, where they expected friends.

Probably any statement of minor army experience, however well fortified by official record and the testimony of surviving witnesses, is liable to be disputed, or at least provoke controversy. Instead of "fighting them over" in a spirit of fraternity and charity, we fight *over* them, too often with a feeling of bitterness and resentment.

This *substantially* true narrative of *some* of the actual experiences of a boy during the rebellion served to bring forth hundreds of pleasant testimonials from influential sources, establishing every important statement of fact, as well as some positive denials and numerous corrections.

The singular fact was demonstrated that the fiction was almost universally accepted as truth, while the actual experiences were disputed. In some instances voluntary

*"The Boy Spy," by J. O. Kerbey.

corroboration was tendered for minor events that did not occur at all.

Through this source, attention was directed to numerous disputed historical events, and much valuable information furnished which tended to throw new light on old subjects.

With a view of further developments, the author of "The Boy Spy" recently undertook another scout in Dixie, visiting all the important points on the war trail from Fortress Monroe via the Peninsula to Richmond and Fredericksburg, interviewing, as a newspaper scout, a great number of ex-Confederates, who unconsciously gave some interesting testimony from the "other side" that has not heretofore been made public. Our own side has been somewhat overdone.

From Fredericksburg the writer drove, in a buggy, over the exact ground covered by the Army of the Potomac in its historic march to Gettysburg, in 1863, accompanied by an artist and a photograph outfit.

We traveled for days via the upper fords of the Rappahannock to Manassas and Ball's Bluff, thence over the Potomac at Point of Rocks to Frederick, Antietam, South Mountain, Gettysburg, etc.

It is of this recent scout, through the enemy's country for later information, that we propose to tell in this *brochure,* and perhaps relate some interesting stories gathered *en route* from all residents as to their experiences and remembrances of those "unforgotten days."

That the reader who may accompany us on this trip should have a better understanding of its purport, it seems necessary to briefly make a *resume* of the preceding publication.

Fully conscious of the appropriateness of the comment of Disraeli, that the author who speaks of his own book is almost as bad as the mother who talks of her own baby, I venture to offer the review of the official journal of the Military Service Institution, New York, January, 1890, so ably conducted by a gallant cavalry officer, who has, in these days of peace, wielded his pen, as a military author, with as much honor and credit to himself and his country as he did his sword in times of war.

I beg to present my army father and captain, under whom the Boy Spy served at the front in the famous 2d United States Cavalry, Gen. T. F. Rodenbaugh, now a retired general, well known in military as well as in literary circles, and who is probably better qualified in every way to speak a word for me than any of the other many kind friends who have tendered their good words and wishes.

I have not had the pleasure of meeting my dear old captain since the war, but his kindly letters, bearing the 2d Cavalry motto, "*Toujours Prêt*," are always most welcome.

"The war for the Union is remarkable above all human conflicts for the number of pens that have sought to preserve its history. Realizing, as it seems, that the materials—the bricks and the mortar—must be gathered together before the master-builder can begin his work upon the great historical edifice, each soldier has brought forward his 'own story' of skirmish, or battle, or campaign, and in imagination lays it at the feet of the coming Homer who shall immortalize American valor. One of the latest and most important of these 'literary bricks' is 'The Boy Spy' —a title hardly worthy of the mass of valuable information contained in its 500 pages; for it is not a juvenile work, nor does it consist of the lurid trash too often, under similar caption, unloaded upon an indiscriminating community. Between its lines, descriptive of the author's personal experience, first as a wild youth rushing into the enemy's country from pure love of adventure, and afterward taking his own life in his hands as an experienced soldier and scout, may be read the shaping of the policy of a great government; the slow awakening of a great people to the public danger; the rude methods at first resorted to in organizing masses of armed men, and the intrigues attending the appointment of their leaders; glimpses of the personality of Presidents Lincoln and Davis, cabinet ministers, commanding generals of both armies, flag officers and legislators, in moments of perplexity or triumph, as words fell from their lips in the confidential atmosphere of the army telegraph offices, or under the strong excitement of the battle-field.

"Commencing his adventures with the first mutterings of the storm in 1861, and with the aim of winning his spurs by some deed of daring and special service to the Government, we find the 'Boy' at the Confederate Capital, Montgomery, watching the gatherings and growth of the secession flame. Immediately after the fall of Sumpter, slipping through the lines in front of Fort Pickens with important information which undoubtedly prevented its capture; detained on board Admiral Porter's war vessel as a suspicious character, but eventually sent North as a friend of the Union; at once re-entering the enemy's country in Virginia. Imprisoned in the Old Capitol—as he says—for no other offense than having fallen in love with a pretty little girl who wore short skirts, low neck dresses, played the guitar sweetly and sang Dixie; who lived between the two armies at Fredericksburg. Escaped, and was enlisted in the regular cavalry; detailed on special service before Fredericksburg, at Burnside's headquarters, and taking part in the Stoneman raid as a scout and expert telegrapher and signalist.

"IN TENNESSEE AND CUMBERLAND GAP.—A thrilling experience at Gettysburg. Mingling with leading Confederates at Richmond, and anon with senators at Washington. Unconsciously treading the tortuous, dangerous path of André and Nathan Hale, with the possibility of a long rope and short shift at the end.

"In the action of this true tale, the reader is reminded now of Defoe, then of Verne, and again of Charlie King, although it lacks the literary smoothness of those writers.

"The author writes as he acted in war times—quickly and intuitively, as well as fearlessly, without much attention to grace of diction. As he expresses it, he fires low to hit the masses, and he calls a spade a spade. He builded better than he knew. Through the coarse web of privation, wounds and war, runs the silken thread of the tender passion, giving the story a touch of romance so often omitted, when our battles are fought o'er again in our dignified, grandsire moments.

"Besides its historical data, this book contains interesting biographical material, especially regarding Abraham Lincoln, Jefferson Davis, Andrew Johnson, John Covode, Simon Cameron, Edwin M. Stanton, Ben Wade, Parson Brownlow, Generals Hancock, Howard, Fitz-John Porter, Doubleday, Burnside, Hooker, and the cavalry service of the Army of the Potomac."

We tip our fatigue cap with grateful thanks; our old uniform bulges out with pride, as we request the General to please stand to one side 'till we fling another "literary brick" at the master-builder and "t'other fellows" who have been throwing mud and mortar.

CHAPTER II.

IF the readers for the time being will individually consider themselves members of a "Travel Club," corresponding to the recent social gatherings organized for mutual entertainment, and, in imagination, accompany a congenial excursion party over this most historic ground in America—permitting me to act as guide—I shall esteem it a pleasant privilege, and endeavor to point out and describe the many interesting features, as we go along.

The professional guide of Washington, who tenders tourists his valuable companionship at fifty cents per hour is usually fortified by a large brass breast-plate as a badge of his authority, in addition to the brass he carries in his face. My only license will be that granted by your kind indulgence, while I attempt to act as lecturer, for this personally-conducted tour.

We will swing our club around Washington one day, before carrying it to the front.

As every tourist desires to see the White House first, we shall make that a starting point.

The home of all the Presidents since Adams' day, has been pictured even in the school-books, so that it will be recognized by all, and a description is unnecessary. It is probably the only building remaining, that will be at all familiar to the old soldier. The magic hand that has so wonderfully transformed the city, has not yet soiled its white walls by the touch of modern improvement.

Its tall, white pillars that seem to stand as ghostly sentries over the portals of the white sepulchered tomb of a long line of dead Presidents and buried ambitions, remind me of the early morning long ago, when I, as a solitary horseman, with uncovered head, was one of a few who witnessed the body of the assassinated Lincoln being borne through the gates.

The night previous, I had been roused from sleep by an order to take charge of a scouting party on the Tennellytown, or Rockville Road, and arrest every person whatever might have been his representations, who should be found attempting to leave the city in that direction. I was then a Cavalry officer, detailed on special signal duty, and the order addressed to me was supplemented with the startling intelligence that an attempt had been made an hour previous to assassinate the President at Ford's Theater. The messenger did not understand that the shot had been fatal.

After a night of restless anxiety in the saddle, scouring the country in the vicinity of Fort Reno—which is in the neighborhood of ex-President Cleveland's summer house, Oak View—being anxious as to the result, and with a nervous desire for later intelligence, in the early morning I galloped my horse across the northwest section, now occupied by the palatial residences of the ultra fashionable people, reaching this part of the avenue, just as the hearse turned into the west gate, followed only by those who had been at his bed-side, perhaps less than a dozen persons on foot, with heads uncovered.

Standing near the gate may be seen, perhaps, a greater

number of points of historic memories than any where else in the city.

In that plain-looking old-fashioned brick, well known as the Sickles-Key house, the wounded Secretary of State Seward, then resided. It is now the home of Secretary Blaine. His next door neighbor being Senator Don Cameron. The corner house, for a long time the home of the famous Commodore Stephen Decatur, is now a club; diagonally opposite was Senator Sumner's bachelor home, now an annex of the Arlington. Close by is Zack Chandler's, where, perhaps, the political campaigns were planned during reconstruction days.

The little adobe structure around the corner that looks so like a Spanish mission chapel, is the celebrated St. John's church, where it is said some of our Presidents were attendants because the rectors did not bother much about politics or religion, but are quite exacting as to the respectability and endorsements of those seeking fellowship in that fold.

John Hay, the private secretary to Lincoln, built that elegant house on the next corner. Sandwiched between him and the philanthrophist banker, Corcoran, is one of the descendants of the Adams family.

On the opposite of this little park in front of the White House, which is said to contain a greater variety of shade trees than any other like area in America, is the plain-looking home of General Beale, where, it is said, General Grant walked over from the White House every morning to see his intimate friend. Near by was the home of Colfax. In fact the walls of every house on all sides of this square might tell some interesting stories.

In the great review of 1865, it was my good fortune to be located on the east side directly under the window of the second house from the avenue at which the venerable General Winfield Scott was privately seated, with glass in hand, reviewing in retirement, the grand parade of a victorious army he once commanded. It so happened that General Sherman, after refusing to shake hands with Secretary Stanton in the grand stand, angrily mounted his horse with flushed face, dashed by us, and in attempting to force his way out of the crowd, created something of a sensation to the intense amusement of General Scott. When the handsome Custer at the head of his gallant cavalry men approached the reviewing stand, the salute of the drum corps frightened his wild horse, and becoming unmanageable, dashed past the assembled dignitaries at a run-away gait, his long hair streaming behind—Custer, notwithstanding the scare, saluted with his sword as they passed.

But I might go on in a reminiscent strain *ad infinitum*. We will go around the corner and pay our respects to one of the last of the living heroes of the war, Admiral David D. Porter.

The gallant old Salt is always at home to a veteran and many needy shipmates leave his presence with substantial remembrances from the "old man," as "tars" will persist in terming their captain.

He is quite well preserved, physically; and, perhaps, mentally, has done more work toward preserving the Naval history of the war, than all the other officers combined. He has a room fitted up in his house resembling a captain's quarters aboard ship—the walls covered with books and charts, and the tables, around which are seated secretaries busy writing, are piled with papers. The Admiral recognizes me as the "boy" aboard his ship at Pensacola, and in a jolly way expresses his regret that he had not thrown me overboard because I described my first impressions of his appearance as resembling a "model pirate with black whiskers and a devilish uncertain eye."

Though his black beard is now white, and his wicked eye somewhat dimmed, the Admiral preserves, in a remarkable degree, his old-time vigor. During my visit, desiring to show me a book of reference, he climbed upon a chair to reach a top shelf and jumped down as lightly as a boy. Admiral Queen, who also remembers the boy very well, lives on the ultra fashionable avenue on which reside the Ambassadors of the Russian and British governments, as well as lesser foreign representatives, and here are located the two Naval statues to Farragut and Dupont.

The one thing that will probably impress the old soldier of the Army of the Potomac, on revisiting the city, is a feeling of neglect and ingratitude toward the residents of the National Capital and especially of Congress, at the entire absence of any statue commemorating the valor and gallantry of the commanders of the Army of the Potomac. The most available locations are now occupied by fitting tributes to Generals Thomas and McPherson and others of the Western armies.

Perhaps the societies of the Army of the Potomac are responsible for the neglect. At Arlington, which may be seen from the rear of the White House, there sleep in their last sleep, an army of twenty thousand who died in defense of this Capitol. The only monument to these dead heroes being the stone erected to the memory of the 1,300 unknown dead, whose bones were gathered from the battlefields in the surrounding country after the close of the war.

Admission to the White House is accorded visitors at certain hours, though only to the East Room, which, in general appearance, somewhat resembles one of the large carpeted halls devoted to ice-cream parlors. In this historic room have been gathered, in past years, perhaps a greater number of distinguished people than in any like area in the country. It is probably safe to estimate that everybody, great or small, known to American history, as well as their families and friends, have, since the Adams administration, been in the East Room, as also distinguished visitors from other lands. It was my privilege, as a boy, to have attended Buchanan's last *levee* as well as Lincoln's first, and those of every President since. I may, perhaps, venture the opinion, from close observation, that the two Democratic ladies, Harriet Lane, of Pennsylvania, and Mrs. Cleveland, have been the most popular first ladies.

Taking advantage of the license accorded a newspaper scout, we slip up-stairs and present to the pleasant Private Secretary Halford a card bearing this inscription and name, asking its presentation to the President, to secure an open sesame:

"A Federal and a Confederate soldier desire to pay respects to the President."

The courteous Secretary looks sharply at my companion, but takes the card in, returning with a smile, inviting us to the Library. This is the semi-circular room on the south side, directly in the center of the building, overlooking the Potomac, which the Presidents occupy as the offices where public business is transacted. We found probably a half-dozen persons seated in the room. President Harrison is standing by the window, his arm raised and fingers playing a tatoo on the glass, as he talks vigorously to a certain Western senator, whose ignorance and arrogance are only exceeded by his money. With the proverbial big ears, I overheard the President say, in tones so decided that I, as a newspaper man, should have felt rebuffed: "I tell you I won't do that, Senator, and I told Mr. —— the same." When the senator attempted to discuss the subject further, the President deliberately turned his back and walked over toward "the next," which happened to be the Rebel and the Yankee. I had reported for a Western paper the President's debates on Dakota when in the Senate, and in this way became personally known to him. He shook hands and cordially greeted my Rebel friend, who was made to feel quite comfortable in the White House. The President was probably glad to see us, because we did not stay long.

But we shall have to hurry along. As our time in Washington is so limited we will next go to the top of the monument. It takes but nine minutes for the elevator to travel the 500 feet, and upon that elevation we shall be able to see more in the ten minutes than in a day down below.

Toward the north is the White House that resembles a tiny toy. Beyond are the hills, which were fortified during the war. With a glass the remains of Fort Stevens may be discerned. This is the point Early directed his raid on the city, when the 6th corps came up the river and discouraged any further attempts in that direction. Lincoln stood on the parapet of the fort when the skirmish was going on. To the west is the Arlington National Cemetery; beyond may be seen, on a clear day, the heights of Centreville, with probably a distant view of Bull Run Mountains. To the south lies the beautiful Potomac, winding like a ribbon to the sea. Right below us one may get a proper idea of the magnitude of the importance of the reclaiming of the river flats. Close by is the Bureau of Printing and Engraving, where the paper money is manufactured.

In the east lies the beautiful park, known as the Mall, extending in a broad expanse of luxuriant verdure to the Capitol Grounds a mile distant.

In this park are located the Agricultural Department and its experimental gardens, the Smithsonian Institute building, which is said to be the most graceful bit of architecture in the city. It looks quite ancient and foreign with its towers and gables, being covered with clinging ivy, adds very much to its attractiveness. In the rear of Smithsonian is the nucleus of the projected National Zoo Gardens, which are intended to preserve specimens of all American species.

Close by is the National Museum. This is a centennial exposition somewhat condensed.

I am not considered a competent guide here. In fact I have been charged with purposely losing visiting friends in this place. It's simply immense and must be seen to be appreciated.

The Medical Museum which adjoins is another interesting place for those who like to see horrible things preserved in alcohol—bones, skeletons, plaster casts of war wounds, etc.

The Botanic Gardens contain everything in the way of flowers, and under its glass roof one may, in the depth of winter, imagine one's self in a tropical land.

Hurrying along up Capitol Hill through this grand park we encounter a solitary tree on the South side growing in the middle of the broad walk. This is known as the Henry Clay tree, and the woodman's ax spared it because old Simon Cameron, then a senator, threatened to shoot any one that would destroy the tree that was Clay's special admiration.

On the east side of the Capitol, directly opposite the Senate, may be seen one of the old landmarks, the *Old Capitol* Prison once used as the Capitol and during the war famous as a prison for "suspects"— or disloyal subjects. What wonderful stories these old walls might reveal if they could but tell one-half of the sorrows and troubles that have been buried in their depths.

I never pass it without looking up to "My Window" expecting to see the ghost of my former self looking out. I recently took a photograph of this building, and to those who may be curious as to the place, I shall be glad to supply copies to the club.

It is soon to be torn down to make room for the new Supreme Court building which is to occupy this cite, corresponding to that of the new Congressional Library on the opposite square.

The old building was remodeled into a block of fine residences, in one of which Senator Spooner, of Wisconsin, is now living.

It is of course luxuriantly furnished, but I recently told the laughing Senator that I wouldn't sleep inside of his house. Nothing could ever efface from my mind the feelings that the very walls are permeated with the army "bug" that I know once infested its walls as numerously as grains of sand in the plaster on its walls.

Belle Boyd whom I knew in Old Capitol Prison, recently wrote me in regard to identification. She is now lecturing before G. A. R. Posts throughout the country on her experience as a Rebel Spy. Enclosing a photograph of herself disguised in the costume of a Confederate Cavalry officer. She wrote beneath it: "You see I pants for fame." There is no doubt of her identity, or of the fact that she did good service for the Confederates.

The following is a copy of an autograph letter from Belle Boyd, the Rebel Spy:

"LIBBY, PENN., Feb. 25, 1889.

"*Dear Boy Spy.*—Your letter was received amid the tumult of battle—is my heart and head ever right—over my identification being mixed with Bell Starr's death, hence apology for delay in writing. I remember you in the old Capitol, as I recall you having rather curly hair, a slight mustache and dark blue eyes, rather a handsome fellow. Am I right? And I remember Buxton, Frank Lacy Buxton, of Buxton Hall, England, our English friend. I will write you a letter at earliest leisure.

"BELLE BOYD, REBEL SPY."

A description of the Capitol building need not be attempted. Its magnificent proportions are familiar to every American through the illustrations in school books and histories.

The grand stairway approaches to the Grecian portals of the Senate and House rotunda, on the eastern or real front, are seldom used. Instead of entering through the massive bronze doors, we will follow the crowd into the dungeon-like passage beneath the grand steps, and grope our way in the dimly-lighted interior through the crypt to the rotunda.

Here we will find seated in an arm-chair, on the south side, a fine-looking old gentleman, with gray hair but erect military bearing, in blue uniform, whose genial countenance invites the tourist to propound questions.

This is my old friend, General P. H. Allabach, for a long time chief of the Capitol police force, who in his courteous way will detail you a suitable guide to the building, and relieve me of that tiresome duty.

Because of a striking resemblance in personal appearance to Capt. Bassett, the familiar Sergeant-at-Arms of the Senate, these two officials are known as the Capitol Dromios.

It would be difficult to find, however, any two persons who were more unlike in other respects. General Allabaugh is the veteran of two wars, and enjoys the distinguished honor of having personally led the last desperate onslaught of Burnside's army on Marye's Heights, during which he lost 700 men and had his horse killed.

While quite undemonstrative and modest, the old hero has quite decided convictions on the war question as well as of matters of current events, and is not afraid to express an opinion when called upon. When disorderly visitors or innumerable cranks, that are daily attracted to the building under his charge, give his force too much trouble and annoy members, he does not hesitate in obeying orders, and fires them out unceremoniously. If he does not talk much, perhaps he thinks in a profane language sometimes.

On the other hand, Sergeant-at-Arms Bassett, who enjoys the same military title of Captain, has been an employé of the Senate for fifty-nine consecutive years, and in that time three wars have come and gone, which did not disturb for a day the serenity and repose of this faithful government employé. He has also passed safely through all the administrations from the days of Polk. He has known by personal contact all the senators from Webster to the present, and been a witness on the Senate floor and in Executive Session to all the stirring events that have occurred in these years. Yet this mild, courteous old official has never been known to express an opinion, and a news-gatherer would as soon think of appealing to one of the statues in the niches of the Senate walls for an item of news, as to approach Capt. Bassett for an idea.

He has been a consistent member of the Presbyterian Church for sixty years. It was my pleasure to have sat at the same table with him daily for a long time, and the only words that escaped from him were the reverential grace he was accustomed to offer.

Both of these officials are Democrats, their positions are outside the protection of the Civil Service, yet a Republican Senate and House have wisely and considerately retained them in service.

After a hurried walk we will take a front seat in the Senate gallery, for a rest. It is the most restful place in the big building, and a few moments here will serve to soothe your nerves after a visit to the distracting House galleries.

The Senate is quite dignified, and we shall have to be quite decorous in its august presence.

Yes, I think I know them all by sight, and can point out those most prominent. I should be glad, however, to answer any questions (by mail), as I find that to be most satisfactory to visitor and guide.

I was a boyish attendant in this gallery during the last days of the session preceding the war, when Douglas occupied that seat now filled by a Delaware senator, and John J. Crittenden had the corner that Mr. Frye, of Maine, holds down. Mr. Seward, I think, had the seat on this side which was afterward filled by Sumner and Conkling.

There was a good deal of excitement in those days, when the leading Southern men, like Jeff. Davis, were almost daily seceding.

The gentleman in the chair is not always the Vice-president, who is the presiding officer by virtue of his election by the people. The waspish gentleman with a large head and glasses and thin waist is Mr. Ingalls, the Republican President of the Senate *pro tem.*, by choice of Republican senators. He looks as if he were excessively bored by the duties. I presume they honored him with this place to keep him from talking too much on the floor. He is a buzz-saw when he gets started.

To the right of the chair is the Democratic side. The venerable-looking man in the front row, who reminds me of a Mormon elder, is ex-Gov. Jo. Brown, of Georgia. By the way, the Southern States have a practice of sending their ex-governors to the Senate, even if they were governors of the Confederate States. The senator nearest Brown is Harris, of Tennessee, who is probably the best parliamentarian on the floor, and promptly comes to their rescue when in a tangle on some point of order, a discussion of which, by the way, seems to consume half the time.

The handsomest man on the floor sits next, Gen. M. C. Butler, of South Carolina. He lost a leg at Brandy Station, in Virginia, where I happened to be also, but on the opposite side. He is a most courteous gentleman, and, although an ex-Rebel and a fire-eating Democrat, he and the Republican Don Cameron, of Pennsylvania, are intimate friends. The English-looking person, Gen. Wade Hampton, of South Carolina, with iron-gray side-whiskers, reading a paper on the back row. Alongside of him is Governor Vance, of North Carolina. a jolly, good-natured ex-Rebel; General Ransom, his colleague, was on Marye's Heights when Allabach's brigade charged.

The tall, fine-looking man with long black hair is General Walthall, of Mississippi, a typical ex-Confederate who succeeded Mr. Lamar. That gentleman going along on two crutches is Mr. Berry of Arkansas. He left the other leg in the Confederacy.

I believe, without exception, every senator from a seceded state, was either a Confederate officer, governor, or legislator.

Mr. Reagan, of Texas, whom I knew in Richmond, was Jeff Davis' Postmaster General, while Vest, of Missouri, was in the Confederate Congress at the same time. My observation and experience have shown that these "rebel" senators are invariably clever men, personally, and, if the time should ever come, they will be the first to take arms in defense of the whole country, either from attack without, or insurrection within the re-united States.

On the Republican side, the Union soldiers are becoming thinned out. Since Logan's death the only two prominent ones are Generals Hawley, of Connecticut, and Manderson, of Nebraska.

Col. M. S. Quay, whom everybody wants to see, is in poor health and seldom in his seat, was an officer at Marye's Heights. He is a most unobtrusive, kind-hearted gentleman, who suffers in silence the bitter attacks from those who, by his good management, have become disappointed sore-heads.

In personal appearance I imagine he is about such a looking person as Ben Butler may have been at his age.

They are quite dignified down there on the floor, and a looker-on might imagine, from their savage manner and stinging speeches, that the sections were about ready to go to war again; but if you could get into these cloak rooms under the galleries, or peer behind the scenes into committee rooms, where a "Rebel and a Yankee" may be found almost any time, sampling Congress water, or lounging on the elegant sofas, smoking and telling humorous stories of the war, you would become impressed with the truthfulness of the Shakespearean quotation, "All the world's a stage," and senators, like other human beings, are only actors.

Attention is diverted to the reporter's gallery by the loudness of a few occupants, who, by frequent exhibitions of their ill manners annoy and abuse the courtesy of the Senate, which grants to the press at large the exclusive privilege of this convenient gallery over the Vice-president's desk. In the minds of some of these conceited news manufacturers there is a greater aggregation of wisdom and statesmanship, honesty and purity, than is assembled on the floor of the Senate. They are so like buzz flies and crickets that I am constrained to suggest a sentence from Edmund Burke, which seems so generally applicable to both their methods and their work: "Because a half-dozen grasshoppers under a protecting fence make a field ring with their importunate chink, whilst thousands of great cattle repose or chew the cud and are silent, pray do not imagine that those who make the noise are the only inhabitants, that after all, though many in number, they are other than the little, hopping, loud and troublesome insects of the hour."

There is also provided for the press a large room in the rear of the gallery, which is furnished handsomely, gratuitously supplied with every convenience: stationary, messengers, pages, telegraph offices, etc., where the news-gatherers assemble to exchange lies, or abuse each other, ventilate their personal grievances, put up jobs and file their "specials" at the telegraph office, which are daily published as "reliable" by the sensational press throughout the country.

I venture the opinion that the average "well-known correspondent" is a mighty uncertain quantity, and, generally speaking, a bad lot and devilish unreliable. I ought to know, as I have been one of them myself. Where he is "well known" no especial honors are attached to this generic gentleman. I have parted with my aspirations in this direction and retired to private correspondence. For many years after the war I was in charge of the press telegraph business in that room, and in addition to the regular proceedings of the Senate, I handled all their "special" copy, and subsequently got into the swim as a "regular."

The correspondents became pretty "well known" to me, and I might, perhaps, be able to relate some "good stories" about them that they are so eager to print about public men.

The representative of a New York daily, upon being requested to correct his statement confounding Senator John Sherman with a real estate agent of the same name who was engaged in the Washington real estate boom, declined, because, as he said, "It was a pity to spoil a good story." The same reporter published matter of a sensational character relating to a certain Western senator's family affairs, but promptly made a correction, after the senator made a brief call upon him, in which he quietly remarked, "You can publish anything you choose about myself as a public man, but if you ever mention my family again, I will kill you precisely as I would a rat,"—and he meant it. This reporter is well known as a henpecked husband; the talk was that his wife dictated such matters, and he had to go to bed when she said so.

Of course there are very many honorable gentlemen

who represent first-class journals, whose characters are beyond question, and who confine themselves to legitimate journalism; but these are the exceptions.

One of the oldest in years, as well as in continuous service, enjoying the honors as the Nestor of the press, has earned quite a reputation as a fearless exponent of the wrong doings and intents of public men. He is a hard hitter through the columns of the paper, which has promoted, to the fullest extent, the development of this crank. Yet before the ink may be dry in a wicked attack on a public man, the same pen will rush to the unjust defense of any one of the newspaper ring whatever may be the charges against him. His sins of "omission" are not recorded in this world.

No one cares to provoke controversy alone with an enemy surrounded by friends, who has unlimited facilities for attack, and no opportunity is afforded to repel.

His integrity and purity of personal character are unquestioned, though it is known that General Sherman, upon being assailed by this knight of the pen, abruptly retorted that "he believed this correspondent would slander his own mother for money." An attempt to involve the old hero in an official action for this charge resulted in failure. When an effort to compromise or to secure a retraction, was made by a conciliatory remonstrance which was more courteous than the original attack had been, to the effect that "it was a pretty hard thing for the General of the army to publicly accuse a man of a willingness to slander his mother." Old Tecumseh replied, "Yes, it is a hard thing to say; but I believe it of you."

Though at the head of the Washington Bureau of a prominent Republican newspaper of Cincinnati it is notorious that during the Blaine and Logan campaign, he was a most bitter and virulent enemy of the head of the Republican ticket, probably because the wives of these two gentlemen were not congenial.

Though nominally at the head of the paper here, he has been relieved of a portion of his duties by a brilliant unmuzzled pen. He now amuses himself by writing letters to his paper after the manner of the old ladies who subscribe themselves "constant or indignant reader," who complain of fast driving on the street, or protest against the dust, object to the crowing of chickens too early in the morning, or find fault with the flavor of the water supplied the city.

As he is physically incapable of personally gathering any of the facts relating to the numerous charges of a public character, it follows that some official sore-heads furnish the material, using this method to ventilate their personal grievances as a sort of sewer. He may be seen accompanied by a little shepherd dog who is used to round up the stray sheep.

His next-door neighbor on newspaper row, was the Washington manager of a Chicago Republican daily, who claimed to control its policy, as well as edit its pages by special wire from Washington. This person also did everything in his power to embarrass the campaign, because of a personal antagonism to the second man on the ticket.

General Logan had threatened to club him for an unlimited libellous attack of a personal character.

As a reward for his "special services" in behalf of Mr. Arthur's nomination at Chicago, this correspondent was appointed to a position of "disbursing" agent for a junketing commission.

When the question of confirmation subsequently came up in the Senate, Mr. Logan objected on the ground that this Republican correspondent of his home paper, had offered to furnish the chairman of the Democratic campaign committee with material to be used against Logan in the canvass. The General appealed to Senator Gorman, Democratic chairman, who, rising in his place, stated that Logan's charge was true, and the name was turned down. This little item of executive sessions the correspondents were not so eager to publish.

The gentlemen of the press became as greatly agitated as a swarm of bees whose hive had been upset, and at once began buzzing around the senators to their great annoyance, printing all sorts of criticisms for hesitating to accept one of their number who had been proven treacherous to his party and friends.

Subsequently, during the absence of Logan, he was confirmed, made the tour with *one* of the three commissioners, and on his return disbursed $11,000 in payment for a house.

That ghoulish-looking, hard face is protected by a rhinocerous skin. He has objected to every new-comer that has presumed to invade the exclusive precincts of Washington journalism, and was himself dismissed from a Chicago Republican paper for his arrogance and jobbery, and now has a merely nominal connection with a

Chicago Democratic paper, under the protection of which he continues his vocation of lobbyist.

It was my fortune to have attended, as an expert press telegrapher, all of the great National Nominating Conventions.

It was undoubtedly the machinations of this cabal, then existing, that succeeded in defeating Mr. Colfax, and precisely the same influences have sought to prevail against Mr. Blaine.

There will probably always be a newspaper ring in Washington. A new-comer, who is objectionable or does not soon conform to the existing conditions, is soon made away with in a business sense.

Ben: Perley Colon Poor and his contemporaneous journalists have disappeared. The jewish-faced gentleman who wears his bustle in front, is his double successor. It is said he married the Boston paper. No one ever accuses this accomplished journalist of any sort of jobbing, though he is said not to deceive his looks, and is so stylish that he wants the "airth"—what to him is the newspaper world? When relieved of a prominent Chicago paper, sometime since, all the "boys" united in protesting against the outrageons interference of a managing editor in Chicago with the Washington Bureau, and a plot was deliberately formed to "freeze out" the worthy young gentleman sent here to do the work. It was, however, peppered to suit the taste of the manager, and became so hot here that the ice was thawed and the inevitable accepted.

As I said previously, there are many honorable

exceptions. I am not attempting to describe the rule. Perhaps all of us have our price. I have known some of them to accept bribes from both sides. That conceited fellow's tolls to Boston are one dollar a line.

The official proceedings of the Senate are reported for the record verbatim by Mr. Dennis Murphy and his accomplished assistant stenographers, who occupy tables on the floor of the Senate, immediately in front of the clerk's desk.

A reporter for the Associated Press is also on the floor alongside, who condenses the doings of every session, which you see published in the daily press everywhere.

Though there are ostensibly *two* organizations, known as the Associated and the *United* Press, that are apparently rivals, they are, in fact, under one general control. It is understood that the older and more influential associated gobbled its vigorous young rival by securing a control of its stock. As long as there can be no established opposition to the monopoly of the Western Union Telegraph Company, it will be seen that *two* press associations can not exist.

Whatever may be said to the contrary by the friends of the telegraph company, I record it as my testimony, as an expert, that, in effect, Jay Gould can now, through his agents, indirectly control or muzzle even the Associated Press organization, in his own interests.

These associated press organizations being composed of papers of all shades of politics, throughout the entire country, require of their agents brief statements of *fact* and items of general news only, and no opinions or comments.

By the employment of a large force of competent reporters in Washington, they are able, in a systematic way, to cover the entire ground, whether general, legislative, committee work, executive or general news.

By reason of this improved service there remains but a limited field for the special, whose principle duties are now confined to manufacturing opinions and comments, or in looking up items of local interest. A good deal of this work is now performed by department clerks, principally ladies.

The personnel of the well-known Washington correspondent has, in consequence, suffered. Prominent newspapers do not now have their best men in Washington to do exclusive work. They have adopted a clearing-house system for the exchange of news through bureaus, by which a New York, Chicago, and Cincinnati paper use the same matter. This has been followed by a system of small newspaper syndicates, which manufacture and sell news. The correspondents of these are usually composed of the numerous newspaper hacks and deadbeats, who attach themselves as barnacles or suckers to the press, using it as a cloak, or convenience, to better enable them to ply their real vocation of blackmailers, lobbyists, claim agents or stock gamblers.

There are a number of such men with a nominal connection with a newspaper, who do not pretend to gather any news, and whose only reports are those made up from the premature intelligence they may be thus able to gain of proposed legislation, which they telegraph by *special wire* and by special privilege of the telegraph companies to their correspondents *direct* to their offices on Wall street, before it is possible for others to do so. I am not flying opinions, but recording *facts* that I know to be correct and which may be established easily.

It is both unfair to the general public and the press that Congress should provide and foster such trusts, and permit the telegraph companies to thus discriminate.

Great injury and injustice is in this way done, under the protection of Congress, and the same facilities are used to better enable the professional lobbyists to further the interests of their agents in procuring legislation.

The "special wire" privilege can be enjoyed by the few to the exclusion of the many, as the person who leases a wire and operator for so many hours each day has the exclusive control of it. May not *all* available wires be thus leased, at least for the time being?

It was my duty to have handled alone the Message of ex-Secretary Boutwell, that announced a change of policy on the selling of gold, that caused the celebrated Black Friday calamity. If at that time special wires had been in use, millions would have been made and lost by the extra facilities now afforded gamblers for manipulating government action. The dispatch I held in my hand might have netted me a million dollars if I had chosen to *delay* it, and send ahead a private message to a confederate in New York, giving this important information. As it was, it did leak out in New York, through the sub-treasury agent, as shown by an investigation by a committee of Congress, before whom I was examined. Hon. S. S. Cox, then Chairman complimented me highly and called attention to the fact, that *no oath* was required of this operator, as to the inviolability of the many important secrets that pass through his hands, as was the case with the sub-treasurer of New York. "A more faithful performance of duty has been exhibited by this poorly paid operator."

By courtesy of the committee on rules of the Senate, the press gallery is under the control of a committee of correspondents who nominate their own doorkeeper whom the Sergeant-at-Arms appoints.

The representative of the correspondents now acting as a guard over closed doors—between the executive sessions and the reporters room—enjoys the distinction of having stolen a President's message from the government's keeping and sold it to the press for publication in advance of its delivery.

It is not charged that any of the employés are responsible for the leaks from the executive session. I presume the senators generally understand without the farce of an investigation, that whatever information is given out, is furnished by one or more of their own number. They not intentionally reveal the secrets of Executive Session, but in an indifferent way submit to being interviewed. Some of the reporters boast of their intimate relations with what they familiarly term "My Senator." Each of these will cross-examine his man, probably *assume* certain things to provoke a denial which furnishes a clue—then they will assemble in their clearing house, exchange notes and make up a report—that is not as often correct as they make out, but as no denials can be made, the public is led to believe it is correct.

When employed at the main telegraph office at night, it was my duty to receive from the correspondents their copy, record and count it. In this way I handled for years and saw every word of all matter filed, and became quite familiar with the handwriting and style of each of the gentlemen of the press.

During the sessions of the high joint commission of the celebrated Alabama claims, the greatest anxiety was shown to learn something of the proceedings and prospects of a peaceful settlement or of a possible war with Great Britain. I kept myself awake at nights, in attempting to translate the cipher dispatches that were sent by cable, through my hands, as receiver, to be transmitted to the London foreign office. No words were used, but figures, arranged in groups of four—similar to this, 1889, 1981, 1776, 1865, 3632, etc. I was successful only in ascertaining that the first figure of each group of four, referred to a page in the government cipher book, and the remaining three corresponded with a word or sentence written or printed in that book, so that it will be seen that the cipher code of the British government is practically unlimited in resources and almost past finding out.

The gentlemanly representatives of the New York *Tribune*, Messrs. White and Ramsdell, succeeded in getting a copy of the treaty after it had been sent to the Senate for ratification, filing it with me for transmission. It was published in New York to the consternation of the officers of both English and American governments. It will be remembered the senators became quite indignant and demanded that the newspaper men should account to them for the manner of obtaining it. Of course they declined, were arrested for contempt and imprisoned in a committee room.

Failing to obtain any satisfaction and as the copy had been withdrawn after sending, I was summoned before the Committee to testify as to my knowledge of it and especially as to the handwriting of the copy used.

I received instruction from President Orton and Manager Tinker to give to all questions the stereotyped reply,

"I respectfully decline to answer."

Though cross-examined by Matt Carpenter and Roscoe Conkling, I was able, to their disgust, to "respectfully decline" to be interviewed. For this offense, I had the distinguished honor of being called before the bar of the Senate as a recalcitrant witness, and by the orders of that august body, I was relegated to the charge of the Sergeant at Arms of the Senate. I have related these matters here that you may the better understand some more interesting events of a recent date that follow.

We have been in the Capitol too long, the club is tired and no doubt hungry. I shall be glad to escort you to Harvey's, one of the old time Maryland restaurants, where we may enjoy the best of oysters, and over our coffee and cigars, I'll tell you a little story of a recent conspiracy.

CHAPTER III.

WASHINGTON "CLUBS"—THE "GRIDIRON PRESS" CLUB—THE TRAVEL CLUB DINE—AFTER-DINNER CONFIDENCES—THE CONSPIRACY TO PAY THE CONFEDERATE COTTON LOAN.

The club practice in Washington is developing to a remarkable degree, not only the physical, but the mental, social, religious and wicked as well as business tendencies of the habitues of the Capitol.

Among the innumerable societies of this character is one organized by a coterie of correspondents, ostensibly for social gatherings of the press gang, known by the odoriferous title of the "Gridiron Club."

It is notorious that the Washington correspondents do not dwell together in harmony; on the contrary, there is a lamentable dearth of sociability in the guild, for the sufficient reason, perhaps, that success in their business of news-gathering hinges largely on the "beats" of a rival reporter for a contemporary, and a "scoop," or exclusive item, results in creating envious feelings and excites daily questions of veracity and unfair dealings.

The gatherings of the Gridiron are, therefore, limited to occasional assessment dinners, to which a member may invite a friend as guest—on the principle, perhaps, of supplying seasonable "game," which may be broiled upon their gridiron in the presence of the members, being well basted with wine, and, when done, picked to the bone.

Your guide invites the "Travel Club" to become his guests at an oyster supper at Harvey's old house, familiar to the old boys during the war and to the visitors to the capital ever since.

We will have some blue points on the half shell, or, if you prefer, low neck clams, as a basis, saddle rocks fried in bread crumbs, a bushel of steamed, with all the accessories.

If you do not know how to enjoy oysters, try some of the terrapin in Maryland style, which is a specialty of this house, or perhaps a luscious canvas-back duck with home-made Virginia currant jelly and a baked sweet potato would suit the ladies. And by the way, John, bring us a decanter of that sherry from the cask imported from Cadiz. What are you hesitating about, you grinning Fifteenth Amendment? Do you suppose I am going to fill this crowd up on common beer?

I hope all will feel perfectly at home, and be able to enjoy an hour in this communion of comradeship, while we, in imagination, eat from the same old stump and drink from the same canteen, while I with a feeling of confidence relate some experiences of a conspiracy relating to some facts of the war.

There are rings within rings, or wheels within wheels that are connected by an intricate system of cog-wheel mechanism, that go round and round overriding not only the will of the masses, but crushing like the car of Juggernaut, any obstacles that are in their path.

It is probably safe to say that every important private or corporate interest has its representative at the Capitol.

The average newspaper man, being shrewd, popularly supposed to know everything, and by reason of his press connection, having an open sesame to official quarters becomes the favorite choice as the Washington agents to look after the interests of the great corporation. Of course they do not openly make any such contracts. They cover this outside business by working through attorneys. Through an exchange or combination of interests the correspondents are supposed to be able to manufacture public opinion, commenting upon measures either favorably or unfavorably, as they are interested, or perhaps uniting in systematic denunciation of any public man who may be opposed to them.

It will be seen that statements of fact or the comments of the average Washington "Special" may through this influence be unreliable. The intelligent newspaper reader, however, is not greatly influenced by the assertions of newspapers, unless supported by facts. He is rapidly being educated to form his own conclusions. As Sairy Gampe says, "facts is stubborn things which wont be druv mutch."

But the sin of omitting to do the whole duty as a chronicler of public events, may be even greater than that of committing an injustice.

To black-mailers silence is frequently golden. In thus relating some personal observations and experiences with lobbyists in Washington it will be seen that, personally, I have nothing to gain and everything to lose.

Perhaps in a business sense it would pay better to submit this story to some interested parties for "revision" rather than tell it to the club.

It is the motive which gives character to any act or deed. My object is simply a desire to put in permanent shape for record some actual experiences and observations to which I involuntarily and perhaps providentially became a witness.

I might appropriately put it in the legal form of a last will and testament, or in the deposition of an ante-mortem statement, realizing that "my sands of life will soon run out."

I was for some years engaged with the *Inter Ocean* bureau here, as a reporter and the operator of a special or exclusive telegraph wire, which originated in the *Tribune* office in New York, and run, via Philadelphia and Baltimore, to the Washington office in Newspaper Row. In the same room were also located the reporters' desks of the Philadelphia *Ledger*, Cleveland *Leader*, and my Pittsburgh and Salt Lake City papers, and some others who are popularly known as "The Sisters," probably because they are weak and dependent upon their associates for all they get.

This wire extended directly west to the Chicago *Inter Ocean* editorial rooms, and also reached the St. Paul *Pioneer Press*.

It will be seen that there were unexcelled facilities afforded me for the study of the *modus operandi* by an intimate association with these gentlemen of the press during some years.

I made a study of short hand, and it become one of my regular duties to take "dictation" from the managers, or to collect my own notes in this form, and to telegraph direct from them instead of transcribing.

By this remarkable system of telegraph short-hand, I was able to transmit, by the use of logarithms and arbitrary signs and contractions, press matter at more than double the speed of the ordinary method.

It became my habit to "take down" in notes all matters of interest, which enable me to better relate now, with a degree of exactness, matters that have been preserved in this way.

* * * * * * *

There arrived in Washington during the session of Congress the first year of Mr. Cleveland's administration, an old gentleman who was universally recognized an one of the shrewdest Wall street operators. His immense dealings and bold operations, as well as his clever sayings, had made him quite famous in his way. Though his name is as familiar as a household word, and he is not at all sensitive as to its publicity, we will, for convenience, call him Uncle Remus. In a quiet way he had engaged quarters at one of the up-town European Hotels, affected by professional lobbyists on account of its privacy and superior table.

His arrival was not announced in the press.

The first move of the professional lobbyist on reaching Washington, is to entertain his intended victims at a dinner or supper, just as I am using the club as an illustration.

This wily operator did not wait for dinner, but at once invited the "boys" of the press to a breakfast. During this preliminary sitting he took occasion to explain that his presence in the city was purely for social recreation and amusement, at which the boys seemed to see something funny enough to create a laugh.

He inadvertently observed that, as he had not brought his secretary along, and had an immense correspondence to answer, he would like to engage a temporary amanuensis, for whose services he would pay five dollars per day, and asked the boys to send him a reliable person.

It so happened that I was warmly indorsed by the correspondents as a proper person, as being familiar with "ways and means," and fully capable of doing his work.

I was at once engaged, and became the confidential secretary of the great lobbyist.

The following morning I reported for duty. Though it was nearly 10 o'clock, the old gentleman was yet abed and to my knock at his door, he growled from under the clothes, "Get out," instead of "Come in." I knew something of his ways, and instead of retiring indignantly, I laughingly made myself known, when he responded more politely, though quite indifferently, "I'll see you later."

When I called later, about noon, I found my employer entertaining some friends.

There were seated about a centre table, on which were a number of glasses and some ice-water, or lounging on sofas, smoking the finest cigars, a number of gentlemen, who, like myself, had probably reported for duty. Among these were a couple of the "well known" correspondents, an ex-congressman, now a member of the third house, one of those retired by their constituents who remain in Washington to practice law; also, one of the many "hotel sitters" used as a sort of copper or roper in.

To my offer of services as his clerk, my uncle good-humoredly observed that as he was very busy, the best way to serve him just then was to "take a walk," or if I preferred it, to go get a carriage and have the bill sent in here. "You might come in again in the evening," he continued, laughing, "and let him know how you are getting along."

In the evening I found a senator and a United States judge dining with this king of lobbyists.

Several days were thus spent in reporting for duty, merely to be excused, because the presence of even a private secretary was not always desirable when surrounded by visitors, surreptitiously discussing "private enterprises of great pith and moment."

To some suggestion that I should feel more comfortable if permitted to do some work, that I might earn the salary, he replied, brusquely, "You are getting your five dollars a day, aint you? What are you kicking about, say?" I did not growl any more, but with a broad smile took another walk to meditate on "the ways that are dark and the tricks that are vain."

It will be readily seen that this voluntary offer of five dollars per day for doing nothing, was in some way a bribe. Trying to find out just what was to be expected or accomplished is the only thing that occupied my time.

The accomplished lobbyist does not personally haunt the lobbies of the Capitol. As a matter of fact, my uncle was not to be seen publicly. Like an official who manages great interests, he sticks to his headquarters, and through the agencies he employs he moves his men in a mysterious way on the Congressional checker-board.

Congressmen who have access to the floors and can reach the ears and prompt members at the proper moment and thus precipitate their interests are the favored agents; or it may be a newspaper man, who may, through his recognized press connections or legitimate quest for news, have access to committee rooms, and in many ways be able to forward his employer's purposes.

One of the most accomplished gentlemen of the Washington press is that elegant-looking person whose military bearing and suave manners impress every one favorably. He never antagonizes any one; is popular everywhere; yet he is, in fact, the most successful lobbyist in Washington, and one whose services are eagerly sought by such men as our uncle. He is a veritable Mephistopheles. I confess to a personal attachment and a disposition to shield rather than expose him.

Through persistence, perhaps, I succeeded in impressing my services on Uncle Remus during part of each day, reading aloud the financial items in the New York papers, and in taking from him "dictation" in matters of finance to submit to the press boys as "special" of interest for their several papers. His "interviews" were generally accepted, being quite readable from the well-known spicy flavor of the old man's sayings.

It was satisfactorily established to me by the correspondence I was called upon to personally handle, that Uncle Remus was in turn only an agent in Washington of a well-known New York capitalist, who controlled telegraphs and railways, and wielded a greater one-man power than the President of the United States.

I make the assertion boldly, though there may be no way to prove it, but the facts are, Uncle Remus was in daily and hourly communication with the secretary of this capitalist *by a special wire* direct to his office; and if an examination of the record could be made it would be shown that this New York party supplied by telegraph transfer the funds to the Washington agent. But great is the special wire privilege, of which no record is made of its illegitimate transactions.

I was soon admitted to the rooms as a regular attendant, and became apparently so deeply immersed in the private papers before me that my presence was not regarded by the numerous callers. It might make interesting reading, but it is not my purpose to divulge the general character of the business to which I had access as confidential secretary, except in the one particular in which the question of a treacherous conspiracy against the government which I, with hundreds of thousands of comrades, had served years to uphold, become involved.

One day, in the exercise of my duty, I was required to reply to a letter addressed to my employer as the agent, dated, 80 Coleman street, London, England, and signed officially, "Gabriel Lindo, Solicitor and Secretary to Confederate Bond-holders' Committee."

The correct name and address is given.

The purport of this original letter, which I held in a hand trembling with suppressed indignation, was to this effect:

An English syndicate, in which the German Rothschilds were interested had been established, that held as a nucleus the bonds of the ex-Confederate cotton-loan of ninety-five million pounds sterling, or four hundred and fifty million dollars United States greenback currency.

This letter was an official proposition from this syndicate to their American agent proposing to pay him certain instalments of so many thousand pounds each, upon his succeeding in having certain action taken by Congress looking toward the *eventual* payment of this cotton-loan.

The letter indicated that there had been previous correspondence on the subject, wherein the American agent had offered his services and expressed the opinion that the matter was entirely feasible because of the recent election of a Democratic President.

There is no suggestion of politics in this story. No ex-Confederates make an appearance amongst the latter-day conspirators. It is solely a conspiracy for gold, in which a prominent Wall street broker, a lobbyist who was bred and born away down in Maine, is the principal agent.

The English secretary's letter further stated that in the event of having their bills referred to certain committees, they would supply funds to bear the expense of argument before these committees.

In replying to this communication, Uncle Remus bade me write in effect, that he had already introduced bills looking to the establishment of a Special Court of Claims, to which all such questions were to be referred for final settlement, and before which they were now ready to bring their argument.

"Write that word 'argument' plainly," said Uncle

Remus, with a sly twinkle of his eye, "so they will not misunderstand it."

He further detailed to his English employer the steps that had been previously taken; that he was spending his time in Washington on this special business, and had succeeded in "interesting" some of the most influential parties in his scheme.

The unfolding of this latter-day conspiracy, on the part of its professed friends, to rob the Government of the results of the war that had cost hundreds of millions of dollars, hundreds of thousands of lives, served to rouse any latent patriotism in my heart, and awakened some of the old-time scouting fever in my blood. I concealed my feelings, however, determined in my own mind to follow it up.

Apparently indifferent on the subject of the letter he was dictating, I ventured to lead my uncle into a discussion of the matter, and while seemingly jotting down the notes for the formal letter he was to sign, I "got him down" inshorthand, and transcribe herewith *verbatim, ad literatum* the exact words used:

"Why, Mr. R., I thought there was a constitutional amendment that forever prohibited the payment of the Confederate debt?"

"That constitutional amendment is not constitutional," said Uncle R., as he lighted another 50-cent cigar, and between each whiff ejaculated some of his sharp sayings.

"The Supreme Court decided that the Rebel States were never out of the Union, didn't they?"

"Yes, I believe so; but——"

"Well, but me no buts! Don't that scripture say that

three-fourths of the States must ratify any constitutional amendments?

"The Southern States, according to the highest court, not being out of the Union, were entitled to a vote, but they never 'ratified' anything, did they?"

To my observation that they didn't, but had the chance and neglected their opportunity, and further venturing the opinion that there would be another war if an attempt was made to pay the Rebel debt, the Wall street statesman, in his characteristic manner, blurted out:

"Who the devil was talking about paying any 'rebel' debt. Don't you get the words 'rebel debt' in this correspondence. We don't want to use the word *Confederate*, either. It's the '*Cotton-Loan of the Southern States*' we are talking about and 'War Claims.' The facts are," he continued, as he walked up and down the floor, "the Southern States negotiated a loan with capitalists of a friendly nation, giving as security the cotton crop. This became known as the 'Cotton-Loan,' which was the *first* placed on the market. Well, the United States Government seized and appropriated to their own use this cotton, upon which this lien had been previously placed, and, of course, became responsible for their property thus confiscated, as the States were, according to the Supreme Court, in the Union. I'm no lawyer; we buy our law in New York ready made, or to order, and it's the opinion of the ablest attorneys that the war was only a big riot, and the Government is responsible for the damages done by the rioters, as was established later in the Pittsburgh riots."

Becoming interested, and, perhaps, indignant, I replied,

somewhat boldly, "Congress will not dare to pass a bill for the payment of the English and Dutch Jews who supplied Rebels the money to help destroy the Government."

Uncle Remus halted abruptly before me, and with a half contemptuous and amused glance, fired back:

"Well I supposed that any body who had been in Washington as long as you have would have learned something." resuming his walk with a marked sigh of resignation:

"I told these fellows I wanted a man to do my work that knew something and not a damned fool.—

"Why," he continued, as he brought his fist down on the table and upset the ink-bottle, "don't you see there is four hundred million dollars here to start with?"

Afraid to again speak my mind aloud I nodded affirmatively, when he took my breath away by the significant words, that I saw were only too true:

"Why man, we can do *anything* where there is that much money behind us."

"But that won't buy *the people*."

"We don't want to buy the people; all that is necessary is a few Congressmen to go along with the Solid South."

"All we ask is the passage of a little bill of ten or twenty lines 'establishing a Court of Claims.'

"It is cheaper to buy seven judges than the whole of Congress," said my Uncle, laughingly.

"The word *Confederate* or Southern War Claims, does not appear in the bill, which is so worded that *all claims* of whatever character may be referred to it.

"This will eventually get all these matters before the Supreme Court, which is precisely what we want."

I recall with a vividness that startles me now, in the light of subsequent events, this prediction *made and recorded* at that time, 1886.

"We will get the Supreme Court."

Mr. Lamar, in the year following this was placed upon the bench.

It has been my pleasure to know Mr. Lamar personally as a most courteous gentleman whom no one can accuse of any dishonorable motive; yet it must be conceded that this Judge in the Supreme Court, represents the dry bones of the Confederacy and recalls the scriptural text:

"And shall these dry bones live?" Chief Justice Fuller was also opposed because of his early antagonism to reconstruction. Subsequently a bill drawn up by myself from Uncle Remus' dictation was introduced in Congress. referred to the proper committee before which arguments were made in favor of its passage.

I am not offering legal opinions on this question—merely submitting *facts*.

One of the ablest jürists in the United States, Judge Fullerton of New York, made the argument before the committee of Congress. * * * *

The projectors do not expect immediate results. They claim that their only expectation is to secure a legal standing, of the Confederate bonds of all denominations by this agitation in hopes of a future realization.

A number of interested parties have been quietly gathering them up at nominal prices.

I realized that the scheme was dangerous, only in the way that Uncle Remus had put it.

"We can do *any*thing where there are hundreds of millions of dollars behind us."

It haunted me, not only in my waking but in my sleeping, like a ghost of the dead Rebellion.

I dreamed that the spirit of a murdered President stood before me, holding in a ghastly skeleton hand a scroll, upon which, like the handwriting on a wall, I read the words of my war commission:

"Know ye all men by these presents. Having special confidence in the honor, valor, patriotism and fidelity of ——, I hereby appoint him —— etc."

To this were attached the autographs of A. Lincoln and E. M. Stanton, with the War Department's red seal attached, like a dreadful wound.

I wakened with the feeling that the commission, resigned so long ago, was, in a manner, yet in effect, and I determined to do what I felt to be a duty, and, as of old, I became a scout for the Government, in trying to defeat the schemes of the latter-day conspirators.

It will be remembered that I was able to keep the secrets of my employers, in relation to Black Friday telegrams, where millions were at stake, and, being brought before the bar of the Senate, failed to produce certain papers that I had handled in confidence. I did not want to violate the privacy of the papers I had seen while acting as a private secretary. It is apparent that there was no selfish object to gain by doing so. It was, therefore, through a sense of duty to my country only that led me to quietly seek

General John A. Logan, then senator from Illinois, in his retired home at Calumet place.

I found the General laying on a lounge in his library. After his cordial "Why, how are you?" I handed *the original letter of the English secretary* and a copy of the reply.

After reading them over, his black eyes snapping at me over the top of his glasses, he said:

"Where did you get this?"

I detailed the entire matter, explaining fully my connection with it as secretary, and that my only object was a sincere desire to thwart the schemes of these men, and that I had come to him in confidence for his advice and suggestions, knowing that I could rely on him.

It was Sunday afternoon. Mrs. Logan was present, and Parson Newman says, Senator Logan, was a good Methodist and we all know he is in Heaven; but the strict regard for truth which I have been trying to follow in this, compels me to say that the Senator swore; indeed John cursed roundly, and acted so wickedly that Mrs. Logan felt compelled to interfere to quiet him.

"Why," he said, rising from his seat and shaking the papers in his hand, "it's a meaner conspiracy than anything enacted by the Rebels here in Washington just before the war."

After expressing his thanks to me for giving him my confidence he went on:

"I had heard something of it; but like a great many others was disposed to pass it by as impracticable; but here are documents in black and white that prove conclusively that there is an organized attempt in that direction—which is bad enough, but the meanest part of it is that it shows traitorous schemes in our own ranks."

As a matter of policy, and in order that I might watch further developments, it was arranged between us that the whole matter should be kept in strict confidence, to use his own words,

"It is better not to open fire on them yet; you watch this thing closely and report everything to me."

The General bade me a grateful good evening, holding my hand warmly as we walked to his front gate he said:

"The Government owes you something handsome for this."

In the weeks and months following, during which I continued to act as the secretary for Uncle Remus, whenever he came to the city, I collected and filed with General Logan all the further evidence I could gather.

I wrote and had mailed, in different parts of the South, decoy letters, representing the writers as being holders of Confederate bonds, which were addressed to this general secretary at his London office. The replies to these fictitious letters were of value as indicating their purpose, and were filed with General Logan.

We were also able to develop the fact, that a Washington newspaper man was an accredited agent of the syndicate and had made trips to Europe and the South in furthrance of these schemes.

I had frequent consultations with General Logan and directed his attention to bills that had been introduced in the House.

I am inclined to think he conferred with some of the Republican Senators on the subject, probably Mr. Edmunds.

Soon after the unexpected death of General Logan, I addressed a note to Mrs. Logan requesting her to prevent these private papers falling into the hands of any one, to which she graciously replied that "all of her dear husband's private papers should be sacredly preserved." This letter, bordered with the deep mourning bearing date of the month of his death, is in safe keeping and in the light of subsequent events would make a startling page, establishing the fact of the beginning of the work that has slowly but steadily, step by step, moved forward—and the end is not yet.

Feeling it incumbent to put the matter in the hands of some one for safe keeping and if necessary to be used in case of my death, I concluded that the most appropriate depository would be with the Commander-in-chief of the G. A. R., as the preserver of the rights for which this comrade died. This grand organization may be depended upon to not only preserve but make the proper use of it, if the occasion should ever rise.

With this object in view, I consulted in confidence an ex-commander-in-chief, well and favorably known all over the United States, as a decided, but most conservative working member of the order.

He heard the story with astonishment and received for deposit such papers as I had, with a written statement as above narrated, also the letter of Mrs. Logan acknowledging the papers in her possession,

This gentleman agreed that the matter was of a startling character and he fully realized its importance and expressed the opinion of an attorney, that this interest might, in time, "plant themselves" here so firmly that they would be able to carry out their nefarious designs.

Being about the time of the flag episode, he observed further:

"If this question should be presented to the Annual Encampment of the G. A. R. about to assemble it would raise such a whirlwind and "norther" compared to which the flag incident would be but a mere zephyr."

WASHINGTON, D. C., June 21, 1887.

J. O. KERBY, ESQ., 23 Seventh street, New York.

Dear Sir and Comrade: I have received and read with care your favor of 20th inst., with its enclosure. Further reflection confirms the opinion in which we both agreed on yesterday, that the time has not arrived for any public exposure. My own judgment is, that to make an attack now would not serve any good purpose, either general or personal, and that great circumspection ought to be observed in order that knowledge either of facts or suspicions be not too largely confided, as you know there are but few who are capable of suppressing their own tendency to talk. The necessary thing now, as you have indicated, is to get proofs and fix the facts. As it is, I don't see very clearly how this is to be done; but certainly if there is any agitation of the waters the oyster will shut up tight, and steps will be taken to discredit what is already known. You speak of being willing to make affidavit, etc. I venture to suggest that it might be wise and well for you to make up a circumstantial account of your whole knowledge and connection with the matter, including a statement of the fact and circumstances of any communication you have made on the subject to other persons. A copy of this paper you would wish to deposit in trustworthy hands. The fact that there is an English agency which has undertaken the task of getting recognition of the Confederate bonds is known in a general way—the *concrete fact* that they are in earnest about the matter, and are securing agencies in this country and among Americans having place, prominence and power, is the thing to be *proved* and made known in due time; and, if proven, will be the nucleus of a hurricane to which the flag wind will seem a zephyr. My advice to-day is not to confide your facts to any impecunious person who might sell them, or to any politician who would try to help his own ends by their use. Fraternally,

S. S. BURDETT.

As additional evidence I am induced to record this gentleman's testimonial herewith.

WASHINGTON, D. C., NOV. 4, 1889.

DEAR COMRADE KERBEY:

I have been reading over the "Boy Spy," and must give it as my opinion that in many respects it is the most remarkable and interesting narrative to be found in the considerable body of literature dealing with the events of the War of the Rebellion. That you have not refrained from saying things likely to displease, as well as those sure to please, proves that your book is as you claim, "a history of events occuring under your notice, and not merely a fancy sketch." I can the better understand and believe your narrative of personal encounter and escape, because of my long personal acquaintance with you here in Washington, where, as I know, you have kept the field as a "newspaper scout," *and have since the war been able to do the State service.* I don't know of a more interesting book for a winter's evening reading than the "Boy Spy," especially for the old soldier boys and their families, most of whom will find in its pages some familiar fact and incident. Fraternally yours,

S. S. BURDETTE.

I had not given the matter to any one else, except a brief statement to the editor of a soldier's paper with whom I was then associated. I assumed that the manager of a paper published ostensibly in the interest of soldiers, and claiming to be the especial friend of the dead Logan, would preserve in strict confidence such matters. I have the reason to believe, and do believe, that my confidence was violated, and that one of the newspaper fiends to whom this editor was under obligations, and who was interested, was made acquainted with the fact that I was "on to their scheme."

This has naturally resulted in some bitter antagonism, in which the attempt has been made to deliberately kill off, in a business sense, so troublesome a person. It is the policy of the interested parties to do this, of course, but I do not require any assistance, or even sympathy. As General Burdette says, "I have kept the field as a newspaper scout."

It would have been better policy to have "stood in" with the gang.

During the recess of Congress the matter remains seemingly dormant, but is revived at each of the sessions.

In pursuance of a sense of duty, I had these papers "handed down" to the different commanders of the G. A. R., as may be seen from the following official correspondence:

NATIONAL HEADQUARTERS GRAND ARMY OF THE REPUBLIC,
KANSAS CITY, MO., October 26, 1888.

MAJOR J. O. KERBEY, Washington, D. C.

Dear Sir and Comrade: Major Warner, commander-in-chief, desires to acknowledge the receipt of the confidential communications, and directs me to thank you for the patriotic motives which inspired them. He intends to keep the subject-matter thoroughly in mind, and, should occasion offer demanding the official action of the G. A. R., your services will not be forgotten.

Very truly yours, in F., C. & L.,
EUGENE F. WEIGEL, Adjutant General.

Subsequently, Gen. Weigel writes from St. Louis under date of November 21, 1889.

* * * "My official cape having fallen on the shoulders of Col. George H. Hopkins, of Detroit, Mich., the papers you refer to are all in his possession, having been duly sealed by me and marked "very important." This, I took it to be carrying out the spirit of your previous letters. * * *

[*Copy.*]

COMMANDER-IN-CHIEF—RUSSEL A. ALGER.

HEADQUARTERS G. A. R., DETROIT, MICH., Dec. 21, 1889.

MAYOR J. O KERBEY, P. O. Box 293.

Dear Sir and Comrade: In reply to yours and letter from Col. Weigel, the confidential papers referred to were duly transmitted and are safely on file in this office. I have read them with a great deal of interest. * * *

I return herewith letter of Gen. Alger.

Sincerely yours,
GEO. H. HOPKINS, Adjutant-General.

I have given only a brief outline of *facts*, omitting an under-current of rumor and surmises that might be more interesting.

I have asserted that there is a wide-spread organization to accomplish the eventual payment of *all* the Confederate debt.

That the matter is not dead, nor even sleeping, may be proven by the following extract from the *Washington Post* of October 9th, 1889.

I beg to remind the reader that editorial notes may also be "seasoned," and that in apparently denouncing a scheme, the writer attempts to avert antagonism.

Editorial, Post, Oct. 9, 1889.

THE CONFEDERATE BOND SCHEME.—"The story published last week in the *New York Herald* in regard to the arrival of the agent of a syndicate of English Confederate bond holders, whose mission is to urge forward some payment of those bonds, if only to the amount of one per cent, shows such an amount of ignorant assurance on the part of that agent and his syndicate, as to pass all bounds of rational belief. It is true that the British islander rather prides himself of knowing very little about matters belonging to the outside of his insular confines, and that the Englishman in his self-satisfied and unapproachable superiority of the people of other countries is a veritable podsnap. But all this is very different from averring that he is absolutely the animal characterized by the prophet Jeremiah, "as sniffing up the wind at his pleasure."

"The egregious simplicity and stupidity that would now undertake to realize upon a Confederate bond is so great that it is simply incredible. The whole of that transaction belongs to the ancient history. One might as well attempt to collect payment on a French *assignat* of 1793. *No one can be found who has the slightest financial responsibility or indebtedness in connection with the Confederate loan.*

* * * * * * * * * * * *

"The Englishman's hallucinations and delusive hopes in this matter rest less on forgetfulness of events than on ignorance of our institutions. He knows that certain States were sometime since in rebellion, and that in a kind of a way they were connected with their loan.

He also knows that these States still retain their autonomy in the re-constructed Union. It seems to him just, therefore, that these States should assume part of the obligation for which he gave his gold".

* * * * * * * * * * * *

"It is said that advantage is to be taken of some of the rising enterprises of the South, and that paying something on the Confederate will be made a condition of their obtaining any loans from England. Doubtless there are enterprises in the South and elsewhere that would be very willing to pay a reasonable bonus for assistance in the way of English money, but it is beyond all doubt that no corporation can be found that will furnish such a bonus in a manner to imply any sort of legal responsibility for the Confederate loan."

The italics are mine. I simply wanted to call attention to the fact that we have found persons of the greatest financial responsibility in connection with this scheme.

This editorial, with that of the New York Herald, establishes the fact that I have endeavored for five years to impress upon G. A. R. commanders that there *exists* such an organization, which has planted itself here, and is steadily and rapidly growing. Whether it may be successful or not, is an open question.

As tending to indicate the "policy" of the same paper that prints the above, I attach herewith a recent editorial note, dated May 3, 1890, bearing indirectly on the very point that Uncle Remus denies, *i. e., a court* to which all such matters may be referred:

"Mr. William Wheeler Hubbell, in a communication to *The Post* this morning, suggests a "bill of rights to a court" as presenting a constitutional and practicable way of disposing of the private calendar. That is, a certification to the Court of Claims of all bills reported and remaining on the calendar at the adjournment of Congress, without limitation. By this means the just compensation of claimants, it is argued, will be facilitated, and what now seems to be insurmountable barriers to their rightful recognition be permanently removed."

THE PRIVATE CALENDAR.

A PRACTICABLE AND CONSTITUTIONAL WAY OUT OF THE DIFFICULTY.

Editor Post: Your excellent articles on the duty of the United States to its creditors, showing the great injustice done to citizens, the destruction of their labors, and reduction to poverty of those dependent on them, and the dishonesty, in violation of the Constitution to fix a limitation on claims due from the Government and none on claims of the Government, are doing much good, in awakening politicians to the fact that the great chart was made for citizens "to pay debts" as it declares, and "not to take private property without just compensation."

Forty years ago I attained the honor of admission to the Supreme Court bar, and for about that time have had experience with Congress as a creditor, and have only obtained a small fraction of justice. The great evil lies in the fact that, for the purposes of an election before the people, the republic principle of a majority rules, but when in Congress, inside of the Capitol, the despotic rule of "objection" prevails. The present Congress has attempted to modify this to some extent, but the neglect of the private calendar is quite as bad and unjust as the turning of the majority power into a despotism multiplied by the number of members inside of the Capitol.

There is one legitimate constitutional way out of the difficulty, however, and it is one adopted by the British monarchy and some other powers in Europe—it is a bill of right to a court.

At the end of every Congress, let all bills reported and remaining on the calendar, be certified to the Court of Claims, which shall give the court jurisdiction to hear and determine each case on principles of equity and justice, irrespective of any limitation as to time, and give judgment on the principles expressed in the Constitution, so that just compensation shall be rendered to every man according to his inherent merit. This course would make prosperity instead of bankruptcy, and the Government itself would share, by greater revenues, in the general prosperity that such a course would create. The principles of the Constitution would then be practically fulfilled, and the success of a republican form of government be no longer "an experiment," as stated by Washington, but would become a successful practical realization; the calendar of every Congress would be cleared, and business on it finished.

WM. WHEELER HUBBELL.

Washington, May 2.

CHAPTER IV.

THE TRAVEL CLUB TO THE FRONT, VIA THE POTOMAC TO OLD POINT, AND UP THE JAMES RIVER AND PENINSULA TO THE CONFEDERATE CAPITAL.

THE one day allotted to Washington will barely suffice to give the Travel Club a foretaste of that which may be expected during a sojourn of many days in the Capital. We will now, as they say down South, "carry" our club to the front, hoping we may be able to spend another day there on our return.

After our hasty spin around the City of Magnificent Distances, all will be tired; and, after the club dinner, a rest will be appreciated.

Instead, however, of going to an expensive hotel to be packed into a stuffy 8x10 room, we will jump on a cable car, reaching the 6th street wharf at 4 P. M., and board one of the elegant steamers that sail every evening for Old Point and Norfolk.

The fare is but $1.50; a stateroom suitable for two persons, or even four, in a pinch, may be secured for an additional dollar which, altogether, about equals the sum a first-class hotel will charge the same number of guests for a back room on the top floor.

From the deck of these steamers the tourist may enjoy, during a pleasant evening's ride, a series of historical views, which will pass before him like a moving panorama developing scenes that can not be shown anywhere else in America.

The Washington Monument should be viewed from the water level to be properly appreciated. The visitor is apt to express surprise that the tall shaft should not have been located on higher ground, forgetting that at the time of its inception the principal entrance to the city was by the river, so that its location was probably selected with a view of impressing the approaching travelers, as in the case with the Statue of Liberty in New York Harbor.

To me the monument grows more beautiful every time I look upon it. Its strikingly grand and at the same time simple proportions rising to the unsurpassed height of 555 feet from the green turf, should be seen from the sea-level basis. From the rear deck of the steamer as it leaves the pier, you are surprised to see that the dome of the Capitol, which seemed to be the highest from the streets of the city, becomes quite dwarfed by the tall shaft.

A beautiful view is also to be had of Arlington: The setting sun beyond it bringing out in a most effective manner the pretty white and red bars of the old flag that waves so gracefully in the evening breeze that sighs through the tree-tops a constant requiem over that bivouac of the dead, who died that the flag might wave over them.

The island or river park that has, like magic, been literally raised up from the bottom of the river, will astonish the old soldiers, who will only remember a nasty marsh below the well-known long bridge that at every low tide showed its loathsome features and dispensed an offensive malaria-breeding air over the city. Now all this is rapidly becoming a beautiful park, with elegant drive-ways, encircling lakes of clear water.

To the left, as we glide by, is the arsenal grounds and barracks, the boat passing so close to the stone sea-wall that even the swell of the waves do not drown the happy voices of hundreds of ladies and their escorts who promenade as well as children who gambol on the green while the bands of the regular artillery play their evening serenades.

In one of the finer looking houses, or officers' quarters, the court convened, which tried and convicted the Lincoln conspirators. Inside of this enclosure they were all hung, and beneath the stone slabs along which the regular sentry's beat was located, and over the stones of which walked hundreds, daily, without knowing it, lay secretly buried not only their bodies, but also that of J. Wilkes Booth, until resurrected some time after and delivered to their separate friends.

The eastern branch of the Potomac comes in here; a short distance above will be seen the ship houses of the old Navy Yard, or perhaps in the stream, may be laying a Monitor or torpedo boat. They have a daily target practice out this way, but we will probably succeed in running by safely.

The fine building and extensive environments on the Maryland Hills, opposite is St. Elizabeth's Government Insane Asylum. The flat land below is Giesboro point, used during the war as a recruiting depot for Cavalry horses. At Alexandria just six miles below, a stop is made, perhaps long enough to permit the eager tourist to go ashore and run up into the main street of this old town.

The first visitor will be struck with the marked difference between the North and the South by this quaint ancient looking town lying so distinctly between the "Old line" of civilization.

Here Washington and Lee worshipped in the same church in which may now be seen on one side of the chancel, a tablet to Washington and another to R. E. Lee. Most of our soldiers will remember it as a starting place in their Virginia campaign, and children seem to think its only interest attaches to the sad death of Col. Ellsworth, at the beginning of the war.

On the back grounds of almost any of these views may be discerned against the horizon, the broken outlines of some of the old earth-works on forts erected for the protection of the Capital.

After an hour's pleasant ride in the gathering twilight, we glide past Fort Washington, garrisoned now by a single ordnance sergeant: The tolling of the steamer bell announces that we are passing Mount Vernon, the home during his life, and in death of him who was first in war.

No boats were permitted to land passengers here except the regular packets that belongs to the regents of the estate. It is assumed that every visitors to Washington has been to the tomb of Washington.

The tolling bell, served to bring up a general discussion among some passengers of our great father, one old river man declared that in years gone by, a British war vessel that had ascended the river, permitted a number of their crew to go ashore here. By some means they had been provided with a too plentiful supply of grog, and in a spirit of devilish ghoulishness desecrated the old tomb and robbed the coffin of the skull and took it away. It is said that the replaced skull may not have been that of Washington.

One of the passengers, evidently a member of the real estate syndicate now mapping out the entire country about the capital into lots, declared that Washington was one of the shrewdest real estate dealers the country has yet produced, and he seemed to be able to support the assertion by quoting items from Washington's book-keeping, which indicated quite clearly that the original George Washington had a very keen foresight.

All of the veterans will remain on deck to get a glimpse, through the darkness, of the ruins of the once well-known landing at Aquia Creek. At this point was embarked all of the Army of the Potomac, that once occupied the thirteen miles of country between here and the Rappahannock in front of Fredericksburg, during 1862-63. Here also, and from the adjoining landing at Belle Plains, were brought the wounded from Spottsylvania, The Wilderness and Mine Run to be treated in the temporary hospitals or sent away by boats.

A little below this, we reach Matthias Point, and instead of the Rebel battery once located there, that was so annoying to our Potomac Flotilla, we discover the first light-house on the river erected by the Government, that now flashes, out from the darkness, caution and protection to the navigators instead of gun flashes of defiance and destruction.

The river now begins to widen until the receding shores

are almost lost to sight in the fast-gathering darkness. Except for the frequent camp-fires of the numerous shad fisheries that are located along the banks, one could scarcely tell where the water leaves off and the shores begin.

During the season these shad and herring fisheries are an important industry on these waters. I have no doubt the interior reader will imagine it a fish story to be told that they catch fish by steam here; yet it is a fact, that in the largest stations, the immense seines are drawn by portable engines, and in a majority of cases, horse-power is used to operate the windlass that hauls in the great masses of fish that are dumped into the holds of schooners very like they handle coal in other sections.

The fact that all the fish are caught on the Virginia shore is one of the curious features that not even the oldest fisherman could explain.

One of my numerous trips down the river happened to be in the company of the once-familiar Congressman, Hon. Mr. Belford, of Colorado, the genial and companionable gentleman who was proud of his distinction as the "red-headed rooster of the Rocky mountains." Mr. Belford was reared in that part of the "rowdy West" where water was scarce. This being his first visit to the seashore, he became greatly impressed by this "great waste of water" that was being extravagantly exhibited before his eyes, and kept the entire boat in a hilarious mood by his quaint observations.

In reply to a hint that it was time to retire, the Congressman blurted out:

"No; I am not going to bed to-night. Why, my great heavens, just look out there at the water, will you? Great Scott! it's on the other side of the boat, too. It's all around us, ain't it?

"You must remember that I am from Colorado, where they haul water around in barrels and sell it. No, I'm going to stay right here and take it all in while I have a chance."

At his invitation all hands went below to sample the water, after which the Western Congressman lighted a cigar, went out on the "back porch," as he termed the afterguard, put his feet upon the "fence" or rail, and, with head uncovered, remained there long after all the rest of the crowd had turned in to be rocked to sleep on the bosom of the fair Chesapeake.

The proper thing for the first visitor is to rise early that you may have a view of the sun coming up "out of the water"—the boat being out of sight of land on the eastern side, and quite a ways off the western or Virginia shore.

Daylight will reveal, here, a most beautiful picture of early morning at sea. Ships of almost every description with white sails spread, or steamers, leaving a dark ribbon of smoke as a wake in the air, may be seen going and coming in all directions, either outward bound or from distant ports for Baltimore and the cities and rivers of the grand Chesapeake Bay.

The steamer runs under the guns of Fortress Monroe, the massive dark walls of which look so low from the water that we come upon them suddenly and look into the grim-throated guns with a fear that they might go off unexpectedly and a wish that they were pointed the other way.

We land at the Government Pier and take breakfast at the sumptuous Hygeia Hotel—one of the finest perhaps, on regular table fare, to be found anywhere.

We will take the Fort first that we may see the guard-mount of the regular garrison. They have their drill and execution pretty nearly perfect. It is witnessed by hundreds of lady visitors daily, so that there is considerable incentive to keep up the practice.

Hours may be spent upon the ramparts, gazing alternately out to sea or looking down upon the beautiful interior, which, with its handsome officers' quarters, beautiful gardens and plants, profuse in rich colors and fragrance; numerous laughing children and ladies moving about leisurely; officers and soldiers in their bright uniforms present a most peaceful, almost a holiday picture. Except for the piles of cannon balls and great guns there is no warlike aspect in the enclosure. Its immense walls, as seen from the rampart, rather suggests a heavy stone fence enclosing beautiful homes.

Fortress Monroe covers eighty acres of ground; the walls are of granite, thirty-one feet high, surrounded entirely by a moat of seventy-five to one-hundred and fifty feet in width, and eight feet depth of water. The armament of the old fort is about five hundred guns, and inside its walls an entire army may be protected from siege.

It cost the Government over two million *before* the war and probably as much since in completing and repairs.

Yet Fortress Monroe would practically be of no service whatever in a time of war with a foreign nation.

This conceded truth does not speak well for the skill or foresight of our regular engineer officers, who planned, located and spent Government apppropriations year after year upon this useless war relic.

It is so located that guns could not reach an enemy who might choose to sail past out of range, toward Baltimore or Washington. And for protecting the James River and Norfolk, its massive walls are not nearly so useful as were the Rebel sand batteries nearly opposite, at Sewell's Point, which did protect the Confederates for years, enabling them to build in security, and almost within gunshot, the Merrimac.

A little distance out toward the front is an abandoned fort that, at great expense, was literally raised out of the water. It is known as the Rip Raps.

From the rampart may be seen, off Newport News, the battle "ground," on the waters of Hampton Roads, on which occurred the most remarkable naval fight of the age—that between the Monitor and Merrimac. Had this Rebel ship escaped the little Monitor and run by Fortress Monroe to Washington, she could have destroyed everything in her path to Washington and Baltimore.

Very many stories might be told of Fortress Monroe and its environments. Around its grim old walls cluster many pleasant memories, as well as some that, like disagreeable ghosts, haunt its dark, damp casements.

The one spirit that will not down is that of the imprisoned President of the Confederacy, who was confined here after his capture. His cell was the first casement to the right of the entrance, a disagreeable, dark, repulsive-looking hole. In that dungeon the iron was forced into the proud heart of Jeff. Davis, and it was said by himself that, when the order to put irons on him was executed, he resisted violently, hoping the guard would kill, rather than manacle, him.

The extensive Hygeia Hotel, erected on this Government ground within a hundred yards of the fort, is crowded with guests, especially during the winter and spring months. Here gather, to recuperate during Lent from the excesses of "the season" at Washington, the ultra fashionable society people of Washington, Baltimore, Philadelphia and New York. The interesting invalids, in their migration from Florida to the North, also delight to stop over at Old Point.

The waters of the bay and numerous adjacent rivers supply the choicest of oysters and fish. The surrounding marshes and lowlands are the favorite haunts for ducks and game, and the sportsman is happy in the pursuit of that pleasure. The rich soil of the back countries produces, in abundance, the earliest of vegetables and fruits.

The hotel provides sumptuously and artistically for the inner man—and woman. This accounts for the regular attendance of so many rich papas and mammas. The principal attraction, however, to the daughters, seems to be in the well-fitting fatigue coats and trousers worn by the officers from the fort. There are a number of these military gentlemen stationed here. They generally mess at the hotel; the proprietor having an eye to the fitness of things, no doubt making it an attractive feature all around.

There is usually a ship of war or two lying in the roads, either of our own or of some other government, the officers from which are permitted to come ashore to mingle with the "army"—and the ladies. In an architectural view the hotel is not pleasing to the eye. Beginning with a mere country tavern, it has grown, from year to year, by additions and annexes, into an immense hostlery, that resembles, from the outside, a large infirmary, where the invalids are protected by the glass fronts that enclose its broad verandas, when the sea breezes blow too fresh for the hothouse plants.

The dining-room and dancing pavillion, standing by themselves, are beautiful structures, resembling in general outline two large canvass tents. They are built of finely-finished native pine wood. An immense chimney, in the middle of the dining-hall, rises like a center-pole of a tent, and supports the arch, or turtle-back roof. In cold weather four "fires on the hearth," of crackling hickory wood, cast their cheerful shadows and warmth over all who are so fortunate as to come within their genial influence.

Being located within a few rods of the water's edge, one may sit at a table, and under the stained-glass windows almost feed the fish that are tempted to come within sight.

The dancing pavillion, immediately adjoining, being similarly constructed, is, indeed, artistically beautiful. A dias at one end contains the band of the regular artillery, who play in the afternoon, during dinner, when children may dance—be seen and not heard—while their fond parents dine. Every evening is a dance, and it goes, without any further attempt at description, that a more delightful day and evening may not be enjoyed anywhere—than at Old Point Comfort.

One may promenade on the broad walks surrounding these halls—the ripple of the tide almost touching your footsteps, while out to sea, the ships riding at anchor or sailing in or out, seemingly try to keep time with the music or dance in unison with the gay assemblage inside.

There are many pretty ladies, in gorgeous and elegant costumes, whirling in the arms of handsome officers, over the broad floors, to the seductive music of the band, or in bevies or groups, talking and laughing together. Seated around the walls are distinguished-looking men or comfortable-looking women.

Every body seems to be happy and if any of the club contemplate matrimony I advise them, by all means, to take in Old Point Comfort on your bridal tour.

Of course the officers are the favorite partners for the dance and, as a rule, the regular officer is a good dancer, and always a gentleman. It is part of his military education.

But there are plenty of dancers who do not wear the uniform *now*, but have in days gone by; and one of the pleasant features of this pleasant place is, that so many gentlemen with gray mustaches and perhaps gray bangs, but, withal, an erect military bearing, are able, on the floor, to eclispse the "cubs"— as the younger officers are familiarly termed.

And now before we leave Old Point, I have a special request to ask of the lady members:

Will you not, while I sit down and rest, please play that beautiful waltz song, I first heard at Old Point—that is such a general favorite in the South whither we are bound:

"I am going back to Dixie," or "Ise gwine back to Dixie."

A few minutes' walk will take us into the beautiful grounds of the National Soldiers' Home, located at Hampton, directly across the small inlet that separates Old Point from the peninsula proper.

The old veteran will be interested here, and doubtless the first impression will be that they would rather live here than at the stylish Hygeia Hotel.

There are over 2,500 old soldiers quartered at the home; every one of whom wears the same fatigue blouse, cap and pants, so familiar to all that were around here twenty-five years ago. They seem to live in quiet comfort, the Government providing everything that is necessary to make them contented and happy; in addition to good clothing, they are well fed, comfortably quartered, and furnished good spring beds, promptly doctored, and otherwise well cared for. The climate is salubrious, the grounds extensive and pleasant; buildings, new, larger, and more elegant and convenient than the Hygeia. They have nothing to do but to answer roll-call, and no marching orders, except to follow the bugle and drum calls to rations. The waters afford most excellent boating facilities and good fishing. Yet, with all this, after spending some hours among the old inmates, I was reminded rather of the hospital feature of army life, and but a little contact creates the impression that it savors rather of an asylum for old army cranks. I came away with the feeling that I'd rather turn my toes up under six feet of gravel than be compelled to exist on top of the handsomest plot of ground in America, in this style.

Close observation satisfied me that a majority of the inmates are of foreign birth, the preponderance seeming to be with the German element, who smoked their pipes of peace and growled in their native tongue, while they lounged about on the beautiful grassy lawns, or held down comfortable arm-chairs on the broad verandahs of the hospital.

The officials say, that with barely an exception, their free boarders are kickers to such an extent that it has become chronic, and is tolerated by the officials as a disease.

They average a funeral a day at Hampton, which gives the band belonging to the place and the non-commissioned officers plenty of opportunity to keep up their parade practice.

The superintendent of the cemetery calls attention to the miscalculation of the managers in allotting so small a portion of the extensive grounds for the reception of the dead. In time it will probably all become a soldier's cemetery, which is in fact the soldier's only home.

It is the desire of the authorities to increase the capacity of the Hampton Home, and plans are now being considered, looking to the eventual concentration of all the soldiers at this location. In the course of nature the inmates of each of the branches will decrease. Those remaining may be better cared for here, where the climate and surroundings are so well adapted for the comfort of the old and infirm.

Directly adjoining Hampton is the training school for Indian boys and girls, and also the Colored Normal Institute. The colored and Indian boys mix indiscriminately, without regard to color, race or previous conditions. The long, straight hair of the "one, two, three little Indians, four, five, six little Indian boys," as well as the short, curly wool of the colored boy is cropped so short that it is sometimes difficult to distinguish them. The schools being conducted on the military principle, all are dressed alike in the same uniform.

The town of Hampton is one of the earliest settlements of Virginia. A church may be visited in which the colonial settlers worshiped. In our war this town became familiar as the place from which Gen. B. F. Butler dated his official communications.

We will not linger here, but take the little steamer that starts from its old wharf and which will convey us across Hampton Roads, over the place where the Merrimac sank United States wooden frigates that are yet buried beneath the water—the flag at the topmast only remaining above water—and after a pleasant ride of ten or twelve miles, are landed at Norfolk, Virginia.

Much may be said of Norfolk and Portsmouth, the twin cities by the sea. They are such quiet, dignified towns, and have been here so long, they impress the visitor with a feeling of respect due to old age. They had the advantage of New York and Brooklyn in an earlier start in life, and in the superior water and harbor facilities, as well as being the nearest, geographically, to the great Ohio and Mississippi Valleys. Just why they stopped growing a hundred years ago is left to the club as a text for an essay on the subject. Norfolk is now the pea-nut market for the world.

It may truly be said of these two cities that they observe too well the precept, emulation without envy. Even the school-books recite their ancient history, and tell of their early settlement, of the Gosport Navy Yard at Portsmouth, of the numerous great occurrences happening heareabout, of the visits of the colonial governors; also of Washington, of La Fayette, and others. They have also been visited by the yellow fever and cholera—but not mentioned in the books—as well as by British ships on hostile errands, Confederate as well as Federal soldiers.

To my mind, however, the most interesting of the distinguished foreign visitors was that of the poet Tom Moore. It was on the occasion of his stay in the old town that he penned the beautiful poem, "The Lake of the Dismal Swamp."

The Club will not care to go into this terribly desolate-looking canal country back of Norfolk, in which is located the truly dismal swamp. In lieu of an attempt at a description of it, I beg some one to recite the poem of Moore, which so graphically portrays the scenery and expresses, in his poetic language, feelings that only one who visits there may experience.

I believe the story of the poem is, that a young English

nobleman and the daughter of one of the colonial governors were betrothed. The lady died in Norfolk, of cholera, and her burial place was, for sanitary reasons, kept a secret. The young gentleman's mind becoming unhinged by the blow, he imagined his bride was lost in the Dismal Swamp. In search of her, he entered, alone, the fastnesses, and following the light of the *ignis fatuus*, that is nightly displayed in such places, he was lost in its fastnesses, and never again heard of.

THE LAKE OF THE DISMAL SWAMP.

"They made her a grave too cold and damp
For a soul so warm and true;
And she's gone to the Lake of the Dismal Swamp,
Where, all night long, by a firefly lamp,
She paddles her white canoe.

"And her firefly lamp I soon shall see,
And her paddle I soon shall hear;
Long and loving our life shall be,
And I'll hide the maid in a cypress tree,
When the footstep of Death is near."

Away to the Dismal Swamp he speeds,
His path was rugged and sore,
Through tangled juniper, beds of weeds,
Through many a fen, where the serpent feeds,
And never man trod before.

And when, on the earth he sank to sleep,
If slumber his eyelids knew,
He lay where the deadly vine doth weep
Its venomous tears, and nightly steep
The flesh with blistering dew!

And near him the she-wolf stirred the brake,
And the copper-snake breathed in his ear,
Till he starting cried, from his dream awake,
"Ah! when shall I see the dusky lake,
And the white canoe of my dear?"

He saw the lake, and the meteor bright
Quick over its surface play'd—
"Welcome," he said, "my dear one's light!"
And the dim shore echoed, for many a night,
The name of the death-cold maid;

Till he hollow'd a boat of the birchen bark,
Which carried him off from the shore;
Far, far he followed the meteor spark,
The winds were high and the clouds were dark,
And the boat return'd no more.

But oft, from the Indian hunter's camp,
This lover and maid so true
Are seen, at the hour of midnight damp,
To cross the lake by a firefly lamp,
And paddle their white canoe!

The nice little steamer Ariel leaves Norfolk on alternate days at 7 A. M., for Richmond via the James river. The fare for an entire day on the most historic stream in America is but one dollar. Good meals are served aboard at fifty cents each.

I might fill the pages of a good sized book about this trip up the James river, but shall merely outline the journey, leaving it to the readers to fill out when they come out this way on their bridal tours.

The school boys and girls may take the history of the country as their guide book, and, perhaps, follow along in imagination the feelings and thoughts of those tempest-tossed mariners of the seventeenth century—Captain John Smith and his party—as they sailed up this river in 1609, and also the thrilling stories of the decades that have followed since that time.

The New England writers who furnish our histories and school-books, seemingly desire to dwell upon and keep to the front the Pilgrim Fathers and Plymouth Rock, and leave untold the entire story of the Cavaliers in Virginia. The facts are indisputable, however; the first settlement of America was made at Jamestown, Virginia, fifty miles up this river. That it was not more successfully and permanently established resulted from the fact that these first colonists comprised four mechanics,. twelve laborers, fifty gentlemen and not a woman. Just how Mr. Smith expected to build up and populate the new country, is another problem submitted to the club for further discussion.

There is no settlement at Jamestown now. The boat touching at the croaking and shaky remains of an old landing, dump us into what seems almost as lonely a spot as that at which the colonists were landed nearly three hundred years ago. There is not a sign of human habitation. The farm house of a lady near by will afford the tourist shelter and entertainment until relieved by the return of the boat from Richmond.

The river at this point is three miles wide. On the opposite shore is a fine range of bold and beautiful hills.

There is no vestige of the ancient town, except the small ruins of a church portal or steeple, and a disordered group of tombstones.

It is charged that the hordes of relic hunters have carried away, one by one, more than two-thirds of the few remaining bricks.

One enterprising Yankee, it is asserted, sent off to New England two hundred of these relic bricks in one lot.

One wonders if they desire to transplant this original landmark and rebuild it upon Plymouth Rock.

Surely the historical societies of the State, or better, perhaps, the general government should interpose to protect from the despoiling hands this only remaining ruin of the original settlers.

In these days of lavish centennials, might not a few hundred of the many millions being appropriated for celebrations, be used to establish at this point a Government reservation?

The site is an island separated from the main land by a very narrow body of water. It was on account of the protection thus afforded from attacks by Indians that the location was selected.

What a place for lugubrious meditation! But it is not my forte nor genius to write in the style of Young's Night Thoughts. I would rather be dancing at the Hygeia than meditating up here.

On one of the tombstones I succeeded in making out an inscription following an obliterated name, declaring him to "have been a great sinner who had died in the hope of a joyful resurrection."

This, however, is an early record of the acknowledgment of the boundless mercy of Heaven, and gives a backward and upward glance at that divinely consoling proclamation to so many who have traveled their weary ways on this peninsula, "Come unto Me all ye that labor and are heavy laden, and I will give you rest."

On one of the tombstones we will rest, shaded by the bough of a tree whose trunk has embraced and grown over the head stone of another. And, as better expressing the situation to-day than can be given by any of our modern travelers, permit me to read to you an extract from the writings of the celebrated "British Spy."

These famous papers, which appeared anonymously over a half-century ago, created throughout the English-speaking world an interest similar to that excited by the letters of Junius.

The author of the "British Spy" papers was William Wirt, the Attorney-General. He visited this spot about 1838, and found it a ruin at that period. His description at that time is strikingly applicable to the present. It expresses my sentiments on a recent visit so graphically that I am constrained to ask the indulgence of the Club.

The ruins of the steeple mantled with ivy only remains. It is difficult to look at these awful proofs of the mortality of man without exclaiming in the pathetic words of Shakespeare:

"The cloud capped towers, the gorgeous palaces,
The solemn temple, the great globe itself;
Yea, all which it inherits shall dissolve;
And, like this insubstantial pageant, faded,
Leave not a wreck behind."

Whence arises the irrepressible reverence and tender affection with which I look at this ruin? Is it that my soul, by secret subtile process, invests the mouldering ruin with her own powers imagines it a fellow-being—a venerable old man—a Nestor or Ossian who has witnessed and survived the ravages of successive generations, the companions of his youth and of his maturity, and now mourns his own solitary and desolate condition and hails their spirits in every passing cloud?

Whatever may be the cause, as I look at it, I feel my soul drawn forward, as by the cords of the gentlest sympathy, and involuntarily open my lips and offer consolation to the drooping pile.

·Where is the busy, bustling crowd who landed here 200 years ago? Where is Capt. John Smith?—that pink of gallantry, that flower of chivalry. I fancy I can see their first, slow and cautious approach to the shore; their keen and vigilant eyes piercing the forest in every direction to detect the lurking Indian with his tomahawk bow and arrow.

Good Heaven, what an enterprise, how full of the most fearful perils, and yet how entirely profitless to the daring men who personally undertook and achieved it.

Through what a series of the most spirit-chilling hardships they had to toil. How often did they cast their eyes to England in vain, and with what hopes of deliverance, day after day, did the little famished crew strain their sight to catch the white sail of comfort and relief. But day after day the sun rose and set and darkness covered the earth, but no sail of comfort or relief came. How often in the pangs of hunger, solitude and disconsolation did they think of London—her shops, her markets groaning under the weight of plenty, her streets swarming with gilded coaches, bustling hacks, with crowds of Lords and Dukes and Commons, with busy, contented, healthy faces.

But now where are they all; the little famished colony which landed here and the many-colored crowd of London—where are they?

Gone where there is no destruction. Consigned to common earth.

Other generations have succeeded them—which are just as busy and bustling as those before—have sunk into the same nothingness.

Another and yet another billow has rolled on, each emulating its predecessor in height and curling its foaming honors to the clouds, then roaring, breaking and perishing on the same shore.

Is it not strange that familiarly and universally as these things are known, yet each generation is as eager in the pursuit of its earthly objects, projects its planes on a scale as extensive, and as laborious in their execution with a spirit as ardent and unrelaxing as if their life and this world were to last forever?

It is curious to reflect what a nation has sprung up and flourished from that feeble, sickly germ which was planted here.

It is but a step from the sublime to the ridiculous, and involuntarily I feel like singing out across that river of oblivion "Hello Smith!" as one does to a ferryman to come and take us "over the river."

That reminds me of once yelling myself hoarse repeating the customary signals, the words "over, over" to call a sleepy ferryman's attention to the fact that I wanted to get over to his side. Finally he heard my call, and growled back, "you are over, you durn fool."

It seems like a rude attempt at iconoclasm to spoil the pretty Pocahontas story, that all American boys and girls have enjoyed as a pleasant episode in their dull school-books. But a strict regard for truthfulness of details require that I record the tradition gathered from several days spent in the country, interviewing the oldest inhabitants. Rather reluctantly I concluded that her reputation was not good. I got the impression that "Poky" was considered to have been a great fraud. She is talked of by the old people living about there as being a pretty fast young Indian flirt. It is said she attended all the high toned Indian balls, and excited the envy of her companions by her superior gyrations. She excelled in dancing the can-can, and at the fashionable watering places on the James, then frequented by her select crowd of princes and princesses, her bathing costumes were regular stunners.

She seems to have made a mash on John Smith, and through her attractive charms led him into the forest, and this accounts for the trouble he got into by straying off from the colonists. I venture the opinion, that there never was any trouble ancient or modern but there was a lady concerned in it.

Old Powhattan, the father of Poky, got on, as they say now-a-days, and would have clubbed his would-be son-in-law, but for the interposition of the daughter.

It is undoubtedly true that Pocahontas subsequently reformed and married Mr. Rolfe, and as a necessary preliminary to this step, she was baptized into the Church of England. I touched the rough stone font from which she was baptized. It may be seen in the old parish church at

Williamsburg. When she visited England, John gave her the shake.

Many of the proudest F. F. V.'s trace their ancestry to Pocahontas.

The history of the colonies record, however, that twenty young women of humble birth, but pure life, were subsequently imported by a Dutch vessel and sold to the planters for wives, the payment being made in tobacco. I have not been able to hear of any who traced their ancestry to this more prolific source.

Here were also landed the first slaves, along with that other twin relic of barbarism—tobacco; both of which have been a curse to the advancement of Virginia.

As a striking historical coincidence, it may also be noted here, that on this same historic peninsula almost within sight of their first landing place, the slaves were first made free, by General Butler's famous contraband of war order.

On this narrow neck of land, which is only about twelve miles in width, between the James and the York rivers, occurred the beginning and the ending of the colonial and revolutionary epochs which closed with the surrender of Cornwallis at Yorktown.

The colonists subsequently moved six miles into the interior, establishing their capital at Williamsburg.

Very much may be said of interest about "Ye Ancient Colonial Capital."

Here may be seen the tombs of Lord Botetort, as also a statue in the campus of the William and Mary college, one of the earliest institutions established in America. The remains of a curious round brick building is pointed out as the "powder horn," that Patrick Henry led his company of militia from Hanover to seize, compelling the governor to take refuge aboard an English vessel in the York river.

The old church remains in a good state of preservation. This was established during the reign of the earliest colonial governor. The silver service presented by Queen Anne, is preserved and used. I believe that King George, the three times, presented the bell which has called to worship for hundreds of years the flock within its hearing.

Williamsburg is worth a visit. It is situated on the ridge, or only high ground on the peninsula, the waters from each side flowing into marshes or low ground connecting with either the James or the York river.

The only highway leading to Richmond passes through the one long street of the straggling old town. The principal promenaders on sidewalks are the town cows.

The court-house is a trifling, ill-arranged affair, built after the design of Sir William Wren, the celebrated architect.

Along the main street marched, in glorious array, after the battle of Williamsburg, on May 5, 1862, McClellan's magnificent army of 60,000.

A pleasant lady resident took great delight in relating, to me, how gallantly the Federal veterans advanced, of their boasts of going straight to Richmond, and then laughingly told of the disorderly return after their repulses on the Chickahominy. As her story, so charmingly told at my expense, seemed to please the assembled company, who had listened approvingly, I ventured to modestly remind them of a similar army of 80,000, every one of whom was a veteran—a victorious army led by a chief they adored—who had, in like gallant array, marched through the cities of Maryland, giving the inhabitants the information that they were not only going to Washington but to Baltimore and Philadelphia. But they halted at a little town in Pennsylvania called Gettysburg, and retired in utter disorder, very likely as they had witnessed McClellan's army.

In the church at Williamsburg is a tablet to the Confederates who died in defense of Williamsburg, erected by the ladies of the town, bearing the touching inscription:

"THEY DIED FOR US."

We might linger along on this interesting peninsula and put in as much time as McClellan. There is much to be seen that we have not been able to even glance at.

Here was the birthplace and death-bed of slavery, as well as of Bourbonism. It is now known politically as the black belt, the colored voters outnumbering the whites.

Here the Indian was first taught the white man's way.

In these old homes lived the colonial governors.

Our observations "On the War Path" really begin at ye ancient capital of Williamsburg. It was from this point that the youthful Washington started on his first scout on the war trail to Fort Pitt. As the emissary of Dinwoodie, the British Colonial Governor, Washington went from Williamsburg through a pathless wilderness hundreds of miles. He got there.

It is a singular fact that our proposed war path leads us almost in the footsteps of Washington. After leaving the capital he traveled via the settlement of Richmond, and from thence to Fredericksburg, where he delayed to visit his mother at his home. On leaving Fredericksburg, he traveled precisely the paths since followed by the Army of the Potomac towards Alexandria. In the subsequent journey as a guide for Braddock's army, he led them over the now historic plains of Manassa to Loudon County, and, crossing the Upper Potomac somewhere in the same vicinity as the Army of the Potomac and Confederate armies, he reached "Frederick town," as we do Frederick, Maryland. From there we moved up to Gettysburg, but in going west we follow the footprints of that band, as our dispersed armies did on going to my Pennsylvania home at Braddock's Field.

But we must hurry on to Richmond, without delaying at the Chickahominy Swamps, but go direct to the Confederate capital.

CHAPTER V.

THE CONFEDERATE CAPITAL, RICHMOND, RE-VISITED BY THE TRAVEL CLUB.

THE longest way around is often the nearest; the great Generals who conducted the Army of the Potomac to the Confederate capital found this the best course to pursue. In chaperoning our club, I have endeavored to guide you in their illustrious footprints.

I succeeded in reaching Richmond alone, however, by a shorter and more expeditious route, in the month of August, 1861, nearly three years before the Generals got there. I was not a prisoner, but entered the enemy's capital as a Federal scout, and was free to go about the city for months.

But this is a long story which has already been told. I only mention it here as tending to show some qualification as a guide to the city, earned by this thrilling experience. A lifetime will not efface from memory a single detail of those days when, as a boy, I was in Richmond, not only among strangers in a strange land but in the midst of enemies; in truth "homeless near a thousand homes I stood."

The actual expense in the way of fares by this pleasant water route to Richmond is less than by all rail.

The time by water is twenty-four hours, that by rail five hours. We will stop at Ford's hotel, located on the hill between the beautiful and historical Capitol park and

Broad street from there may be reached within a square or two, nearly all the principal points of interest.

It was at this house, then called the Powhattan, that I lived during my scout in 1861–2, and made the acquaintance of the "Colonel" and Lieutenant Elkton, "my Maryland" friends.

During recent visits I have occupied the same room, and, as may be imagined, lived over again as I sat by the open windows and looked out upon the old scenes that were burned into the memory by the red-hot brand of war.

If I were asked to mention that which most impressed me on my re-visit, I should unhesitatingly say that it is in finding the city looking so very much as it did twenty-five years ago.

There is, indeed, but little to note in the way of modern improvement in the Confederate capital as compared with the great changes that have come over Washington.

It may be accounted for on the hypothesis that as the oldest inhabitants have retired from business, their only occupation is to hold on to the titles and deeds. They are of that self-satisfied class so peculiar to the South that practice too well the hunkidori doctrine, to let well enough alone. They won't do any improving themselves and are only obstacles in the path of others.

During a visit, one of the young men of the new South aptly expressed the situation when he observed to me that Richmond needed, more than anything else, a few first-class funerals.

That portion of the city destroyed by fire during the evacuation, has been re-built so nearly in the old style of architecture that I almost failed to notice any change. The Jewish merchants seem to retain their possession of the business on the main streets.

Jeff Davis' executive office in the old Mercantile building at the foot of the Capitol Square, has given way to a new custom-house and post-office erected on the site by the Government.

The next most noticeable change is that of a fine city hall being erected on the site of the old building, directly across the park from the post-office.

In the winter of 1861-2, Mayor Mayo had his headquarters in an old building here, as also Marshal Winder and his Baltimore plug-ugly refugees. There was a constant friction between the Mayor's authority and that of the despotic provost-marshal, carpet-bagger from Baltimore.

My room in the Powhattan enabled me to see every one who entered that building, and also afforded an outlook on the park through which I saw President Davis walk daily between his home and office.

The Capitol Park remains precisely as of old, except for the removal of the Clay statue and the depositing of a fine statue representing Stonewall Jackson, the gift of some "English gentlemen," as it is inscribed, which, by the way, will remain there, a perpetual reminder and menace to the Northern visitors of the "English gentlemen's" sympathizing sentiments.

The Governor's mansion is located in one corner of the Capitol grounds. During a recent visit it was my privilege to call upon Governor Fitz-Hugh Lee at this home, where I was most courteously received and hospitably entertained as a Federal re-visitor.

Inside the Capitol building everything looks cheerless, rather dingy and neglected. The walls of the chambers are liberally supplied with the portraits of Virginia's favorite son, General R. E. Lee, flanked by his able Lieutenant, Stonewall Jackson. One can not help noticing the omission of that other grand Virginia soldier, General J. E. Johnston, who surrendered to Sherman after Lee.

Cheap portraits of Lee and Jackson sorrowfully posing by a newly-made grave, the imprint on the tombstone of which is "The Constitution"—are quite common in Virginia. One sees them even in colored barber shops, bar rooms and other public places

The first point of interest to which I have always paid my respects was Libby Prison.

The hotel people and the hack drivers and guides say that. without exception, the first point the tourist to Richmond seeks is not Jeff Davis' mansion, the Capitol, or Lee's home, but Libby.

This ugly old brick structure, so sadly familiar to thousands, was the shrine to which the old veteran invariably hobbled the moment he got ashore in the city.

When the question of the removal of this old warehouse to Chicago was being agitated, I gathered the impression that the objection to its removal lay in the fact that the Richmond Yankees very properly felt that, in parting with this old relic for a good sum, they were killing the goose that laid golden eggs.

It was represented that the Western city would not gain by Richmond's loss, as but few of the Western soldiers were interested in this Eastern prison. However, the fact is frequently overlooked that a majority of the old Army of the Potomac have, since the war, helped to build up the West.

The newspaper agitation, however, probably accomplished all that was desired in securing an immense amount of free advertising for the sale of relic bricks from Libby.

The old warehouse proper was a three-story building, say about 150 by 200 feet. Calculating nineteen bricks to the square foot in these walls, one may form an idea of the rich bonanza there was for a while in the supplying of Libby bricks at 50c. and $1.00 each.

Probably sufficient has been distributed throughout the country in this way to rebuild the original structure, somewhere else, if they could be again "contributed."

When I last saw it at its old stand, the ugly old pile looked quite familiar, except that its closed, deserted and almost haunted appearance created in my breast a doubly realizing sense of desolation.

It was an early Sunday morning. The shops were closed, and the streets in the neighborhood more quiet than I had seen them during the war.

The large double doors were closed, and barred on the inside; the windows were shut down. Spiders had woven their webs about the iron gratings, and dust of years had accumulated on everything that would hold it. The little 8x10 panes of glass, remaining unbroken in the sash, were so covered with dirt that I could not see into the old shell. The whitewashed walls outside had been drenched by the rains and storms of twenty-five years, leaving only a few ghastly-looking streaks here and there.

How different from my first visit as a boy, when all was activity. Then in every hole and corner, inside and out, there was life and soul. Now all were gone; only the terrible memories remaining.

It was during August, 1861, shortly after the first battle of Bull Run, that I first stood on the pavement outside, and gazed, with boyish feelings that I could scarcely repress, upon the crowded Federal prisoners inside those walls. All of them seemed to be jolly and happy; most were in what might be termed light marching order in regard to clothing. Their hearty, ringing laughter, that seemed so like defiance to the solemn guards, could be heard squares off. I recall Congressman Ely's appearance distinctly, as he stood near a window, in his shirt-sleeves, in earnest conversation with a group of officers.

I saw them every day. The place had a singular infatuation then, and is full of memories for me. I have preserved an original photograph, taken at that time, copies of which I can supply those members of the club who desire them.

I observed some alteration had been made since the war; on the water-front, an addition of some forty feet of wall had been erected, the roofs had been renewed, and other minor changes made in the interior, which the engineer of the fertilizing works occupying the adjoining property pointed out to me.

The watchman, who had eyed me quite suspiciously while peering about so curiously, thinking, no doubt, I was a relic hunter wanting a chance to steal a brick, became quite communicative when I introduced myself as a former Rebel soldier. He volunteered the observation that, if they did not watch it night and day, the whole concern would be stolen, brick by brick, by the relic fiends. One could scarcely credit the stories told of the tricks resorted to by strangers to get hold of a piece of Libby before it should be taken to Chicago. He pointed to where a brick had been dug out from the wall the day previous, by a respectable-looking gentleman whom they had caught in the act, and took before the Mayor, who imposed a heavy fine.

While the watchman was absent at the station-house, another party climbed to one of the windows on the river front, and cut out a pane of glass. He showed me the putty crumbs then scattered below, which had attracted his attention to this "robbery," as he termed it.

I had made myself so thoroughly familiar with Richmond streets and the habits of the prominent Confederate officials, that, had the Federal cavalry entered the city, in the years following, when I rode with headquarters as a scout, I could then have acted as a guide to that big club, and piloted them everywhere, as I am trying to do now for this club. It was probably with a view of using my experience in this direction that I was so detailed at headquarters, but I have already tried to tell of that experience.

I can not help, however, expressing the opinion that our cavalry might have easily entered the city, and not only released the prisoners at Libby, but probably have captured Jefferson Davis.

The Confederate White House, the residence of Mr. Davis, is on the edge of the bluff or hill overlooking the low ground upon which the railways enter the city. It is but two squares north from the Capitol grounds or our hotel. I walked over there frequently, and, on the occasion of a war reception, was inside of the house as a Federal scout. I could have pointed out even the bed-chamber of the President of the Confederacy, and should have been glad of the command of a detachment to have attempted his capture in his night-clothes.

Gen.. Lee's family lived on Franklin street, a few doors beyond St. Paul's church. The tourist is shown this as the home of Lee, but as a matter of fact, it was only a temporary home for his family.

St. Paul's church, where both Lee and Davis worshiped, looks just as it did during the war.

It was during the first year of his residence in this city that Mr. Davis was baptized and confirmed in this church. It will be remembered that during the church service on the April Sunday of 1865, he received the telegram from General Lee announcing that he could no longer protect Richmond.

I always attend service here when I am in Richmond over Sundays.

The Spottswood Hotel, from the balcony of which Mr. Breckinridge responded to his reception in Richmond, was burned.

The Exchange and Ballard, connected by the bridge or causeway over the street, remain as of old.

The old theatre building below it, where I saw the actress tramp under feet, amid tumultuous applause, the United States flag, is yet a dime museum. The Confederates generally confess that their first mistake was in insulting the flag at Ft. Sumter, and they express regrets that they ever adopted a separate flag, believing they would have fought with greater success had they retained the "Old Glory."

I walked down there and stood upon the same step upon which I was almost paralyzed by being familiarly recognized by an old friend. It was over that hill, on this street, that the colored Federal troops first entered the city. Col. J. B Jones' blockade post-office has been remodeled into a business block. Franklin street remains, as of old, the handsome, aristocratic residence thoroughfare of Richmond.

There are some elegant old homesteads here, occupied by the most cultivated as well as courteous and hospitable families, nearly all of which are surrounded by beautiful gardens. The houses generally, architecturally, present a stately and dignified appearance. One may see here any number of Grecian portals and immense Corinthian pillars to private dwellings. I could not find a single bay window in Richmond. In Washington one can't find a residence that isn't two-thirds bay window from cellar to roof.

Of course I should like to take the boys of our Travel Club around to see "Capitola," the bewitching "Maryland" white slave, whose chains President Davis so dramatically removed for our entertainment, and in which we immediately became tangled.

A peculiarity of Southern homes is that each has a name of its own. Capitola's was called by the boys "Poplar Grove," because one sickly poplar tree stood in front of it. I had no difficulty in finding the house, because I had been there so often, you know. I did not see the pretty, dark-eyed little brunette, "my Maryland," but a hospitably inclined young lady of whom I made some awkward inquiries, cordially entertained me, and in an agreeable manner offered consolation for my disappointment.

While living at Fords, on the Powhattan, a number of Maryland "refugees" being there, it was my privilege to become quite intimately associated with them. As long as life lasts, I shall never forget the songs they sang, especially that pathetically beautiful "Maryland, my Maryland." If the young lady players have not heard this old war song, I advise them to procure it, and while you play and sing, try and realize how it would sound to you as a serenade if away from home—surrounded on all sides by the very sounds and smoke of a terrible war.

We will visit Camp Lee, now the new fair grounds, but during the war the rendezvous for Confederate recruits and conscripts, where I was encamped during the months of November, December, and part of January, 1861–62, as a Federal scout.

It was at this place I saw President Davis, attended by staff, review the cavalry of General Ransom, now the courteous senator from North Carolina; here the Richmond ladies were wont to come to bring to the exiled Maryland refugees their sweet smiles and words of encouragement, or solid comfort contained in baskets laden with dainties and perhaps useful articles of wearing apparel. It was here we "boys" first met the bewitching Baltimore lady refugee, Capitola, with whom we all became so thoroughly enamored through the mutual sympathies engendered by the sorrows of our "banishment" from home.

I mention it as a somewhat remarkable coincidence, that on the occasion of a recent revisit to this old camp, I received from the hands of one of the indentical refugees who had been a companion here, and whom I had not seen or heard from since the war, a letter and package of Baltimore papers containing a two-column attack captioned with display lines, "*The Boy Spy's slanders refuted.*"

I should like to incorporate this entire article here, not that it is at all flattering. On the contrary it is an exceedingly hostile and bitter criticism, which was intended to be quite crushing in effect. The author, who had also been an alleged Maryland refugee, writes with a resentfulness that is evidently fathered by regret that I had not been hung then, but yet felt that he was not too late, if the chance were offered, to Ku-Klux me.

Though printed as refutations, they are in effect, involuntary corroborations, from this Confederate source, of the truthfulness of the Boy's Richmond narrative.

The article admits that I was in Richmond as stated; that my true character was unknown, though there were some suspicious circumstances attaching certain movements at that time. The dates I gave are slightly corrected; but the fact that I was nominally associated with the Maryland refugee battery some time previous to reporting to Camp Lee, was unknown to the writer, whom I did not know personally.

That I was detailed as the company clerk and handled all the papers and had liberty to go as I pleased throughout Richmond is conceded.

Much feeling is shown at the comparison of Maryland refugees in the Confederate army with the more numerous East Tennessee Unionists in the Federal army, a subject, by the way, worthy of greater consideration by war writers.

In replying to the statement that the Maryland refugee business was a source of annoyance and of no especial benefit to the Confederate authorities, as but a comparatively small percentage of refugees were from Maryland, he gives his own case away by saying that of the 125 or 150 men comprised in the 3d Battery of Maryland Artillery twenty were bona fide Marylanders.

This admission, that so small a percentage were Marylanders, is greatly exaggerated, as I was one of these twenty alleged refugees. A greater portion of the remaining were refugees from Ireland and Germany, or deserters from other Confederate organizations. The personnel of this Baltimore battery, as described, is held up to Baltimore Confederates, now, as a reflection on dead Confederates, the object being to cater to a prejudice in that quarter. I have no apologies to offer; as a matter of fact, I am more liable to a charge of finding fault with our own than with the Confederate officers.

In this case I told the truth about the Confederate captain. I did not name him, but he is a brother of the well-known Mayor Latrobe, of Baltimore. He was subsequently cashiered and dishonorably dismissed by the Confederate authorities, and is yet living to defend himself.

Lieutenant Rowan, or Elkton, of the story, became the captain, and was killed beside his guns at Nashville. The "Colonel" was a Sergeant Hooper, of Cambridge, Maryland, who, I have since learned, left the battery in disgust, because the writer of that article cheated him out of his promised and well-merited promotion. He is also dead.

Mr. Buchanan was also transferred from the battery at his own request, and is, I believe, at the present time an employé at the United States Custom-House in Baltimore. I have no doubt that he will bear me out in the statement that the dismemberment of this so-called Maryland refugee organization was threatened while in Knoxville, because of the incongruous and insubordinate material of which it was composed.

The attempt to besmirch the Boy is verified by the writer's own admission, that he was made first corporal and entrusted with the company records—selected as one of the guards at Parson Brownlow's house in Knoxville, and was subsequently detailed to carry the important dispatches to Cumberland Gap, precisely as stated.

I beg the indulgence of the club to these personal explanations, as they say in Congress when a newspaper attacks a member and he wants to reply through the Associated Press and Record.

The Baltimore newspaper which printed this ventilation of personal spleen and prejudice and opinions which they dubb refutations, positively refused to publish a hundred words of reply, because, as they said, "Baltimore is filled with ex-Confederates."

I beg to take this method of putting on record, for the Baltimore Confederates as well as those elsewhere, that, as a Federal soldier and newspaper writer, I never impugned the motives or patriotism of the genuine Confederate veteran.

They had in their armies numerous frauds, bounty jumpers, cowards and skulkers, precisely as we had, and these are their blatant survivors.

As illustrating the point, I refer to page 252, Boy Spy, referring to Confederate officers as follows:

"Our other lieutenant was a Mr. Claiborne, one of the genuine sons of the South, not a Marylander, but a native of Mississippi, and as clever and as courteous a young gentleman as it has ever been my pleasure to meet. I recall my acquaintance with Lieutenant Claiborne, though formed in this surreptitious way, as one of the most agreeable in which I have ever shared.

"If it shall so happen that this writing may meet his own eye, or that of his family or friends—and I have given the correct name—he will understand some of my actions toward him, which were at that time, to say it briefly, inexplicable.

"Lieutenant Claiborne, I think, followed the Confederate fortunes to the end—I am sure he did so if he lived to see the end—for, without a doubt, he was earnestly, though quietly, sincere in his devotion to the cause of the South."

I did not know of his subsequent history when this paragraph was printed a few years ago. It was only since the story has revived the interest in the matter that I learned that Lieutenant Claiborne died beside the guns of his battery, bravely doing his duty—the soil of his native State absorbing his blood the day before the surrender at Vicksburg.

He was a handsome, black-eyed, typical Confederate

officer, who was my companion, my friend and rival, whose courteous, gentlemanly bearing and seductive smiles cut me out of all the girls I was at so much trouble to look up and foolish enough to introduce my friend to, because I admired him so much myself.

I remembered nothing of Claiborne's home affairs, except that he was well connected with the celebrated family of that name in Mississippi.

It was, therefore, most gratifying to receive a letter bordered with deep mourning, through the mails, from his mother.

I have never had the pleasure of meeting this lady, who no doubt symbolized, in courtly grace, the ladies of the old South, as her son did of the younger generation. Among the many letters received from various sources, I esteem this most highly, as testifying to a Federal soldier's voluntary tribute to a Confederate.

March 20, 1887.

MAJOR KERBEY,

My Dear Sir: I shall be delighted to see "The Boy Spy" any time as soon as convenient to him after mid-day to-morrow, and I am truly glad to get this near to him at last. If I were not sick in bed, where I have been for the last five days, I should try to make you understand with what heartfelt enjoyment I read the paragraph which spoke of my son as if the writer had known him always just as all who knew him spoke of him to me. If I had not been sick on Wednesday, my little nephew, Ferdinand Claiborne Walsh, would have taken you a note, begging you to call on me as soon as possible; as it was, I asked a friend to call at your office and tell you how anxious I was to meet you. I found your address in the paper of the 8th inst., and intended sending for you as soon as I should be able to leave my room. To-morrow, should I be well enough, I shall look for you until I see you. It isn't often one has an opportunity of making another (and that other an old lady of seventy-five) as happy as this meeting with such words of commendation of my son and only child has made me; and wherever you spoke of him I noticed it was in the same high terms. Surely the recording angel will blot out many a sin from your record for thus giving comfort to the childless widow. You can understand, then, the pleasure your note received yesterday has given me. I was not able to write until to-day. Hoping I shall see you very soon, believe me I am truly yours,

MARY STANFORD CLAIBORNE.

During my visit to Richmond, letters from this malignant Baltimore Rebel, conspicuously addressed to "The Boy Spy," came to me at the hotel; and marked papers were freely distributed, the object being to identify and annoy me while in Richmond. It failed of its purpose, as it was my pleasure to have been specially invited to visit the armory of the celebrated 1st Virginia regiment, where any Northern visitor interested in such matters may spend an evening most agreeably.

I shall be glad to take the Club to the R. E. Lee Camp of Confederate Veterans, where you will be surrounded by a lot of old Rebs wearing the gray only in their hair, who will, in a most hospitable manner, take each by the arm and escort him around, not as a prisoner, but as a friend whom they are glad to welcome to their battle-scarred old town.

The Confederate Soldiers' Home occupies several acres of rather barren ground in the western suburbs. The main building was, I believe, once used as a school. Seven or eight cottages, each built by the separate donors whose names they bear, are arranged on the flanks, similar in plan, as well as architecture, to our camp-meeting grounds.

There are only 110 inmates, who looked quite familiar in their gray uniforms. The small number seems quite trifling as compared with the 2,500 at Hampton. I understood the percentage of foreigners, however, was about the same.

It is not generally known that this home for the disabled Confederates probably owes its existence to the G. A. R. organizations of their former enemies. The efforts inaugurated by the Phil Kearney Post, of Richmond, secured about $8,000 in cash toward its inception.

On one of the large buildings on the north side of the square the visitor will see the sign, Veterans' Army Association of Blue and Gray; also Phil Kearney Post, G. A. R. Here the veteran may find a comfortable place to rest, and a comrade in blue may be found, no doubt, to act as a guide to the different parts of the city.

During an evening walk, I chanced to see a half-dozen boys in blue standing about the doorway, as if waiting for some one. Taking a good look, to be sure that they were not Rebs in blue that I had been taken in by, in Virginia, on former occasions, I inquired cautiously what was up. A clever comrade replied, courteously, that they were to be received as a G. A. R. organization at the fair then being held at the armory. My curiosity got the better of my surprise, and I made myself known as a G. A. R. comrade, when I was at once urged to join them in their march to the Confederate fair. I had no uniform, not even a bronze button; but the password was sufficient, and I was pressed into the ranks and marched with them, along broad streets, to the music of "Yankee Doodle" and "Marching Through Georgia."

The hall was gorgeously decorated and filled with some

of Richmond's beautiful daughters, who gave the old Yankees their welcome smiles while the band played inspiriting National airs as we filed around through the crowded hall.

It was my pleasure to meet there Gen. Edgar Allen, well known as a prominent attorney and politically as "Yankee Allen," who is commander of the department and a Senior Vice of the entire organization.

It will astonish old soldiers to find that there is, in reality, but little political friction between the Confederates and Federals in Virginia.

Quite a number of ex-Confederates are Republicans, and I was surprised to find my file closer, on this evening, to be an old 6th New York cavalryman and a staunch Democrat. Of the two Republican factions, General Mahone is understood to be the leader of the Confederate Republicans; while his antagonist, John S. Wise, heads the old line Whig, or Civilian Republicans, who object to being "bossed"—as they term it—by ex-Rebels.

Whole chapters may be written about the new industries that are being so wonderfully developed in Virginia since the war. They have the coal for fuel in the greatest abundance, the ores are practically inexhaustible, a most productive soil, and a more congenial climate than that of the great West. Good farms in fair condition may to-day be bought in these fertile Virginia valleys at less than is paid for the unimproved land in the blizzard country. Northern emigration, especially of the farming and manufacturing class, is particularly desired in the South, if accompanied by small capital. The better class of white laborers are also welcome in certain sections.

There is no hesitation, however, on the part of the people living here, in expressing their opposition to promiscuous foreign immigration—they want only that class of workers who do not get pains in the back.

The old fellow, whom I met on the swamp farm on the peninsula along the Chickahominy where the principal crop is bull-frogs, and they say in good seasons the product equals forty bushels to the acre, gave me his views on the labor question while he chewed tobacco savagely and spit vigorously that portion of it that did not leak out the corners of his mouth.

"We doant want no white niggars hyar. I'm ninety year old, drunk whiskey, chawed terbacker and voted the Dimocrat ticket all my life, and I tell you white labor haint reliable. I fit into the war until Mister Grant told us to take our hosses and go home and plow. Waal, my hoss war a mule, and I turned my gun into a plow-share, as the preachers advised. Waal, along one warm May day, soon ater the surrender, I started in to plow, myself—all my niggers had gone off with the Yankees. Waal, gentleman, I plowed, and sweated, and plowed and swore on that day, befo dinner time come mo than I did all endurin the wah. I got demoralized and wanted to quit agin. I sat on my plow-beam all afternoon, and you've heer teel of that Britisher that wished for night or Blucher? Waal, I wished for night or a nigger—no sah, white labor aint reliable."

The principal crop in Virginia has always been tobacco. This product has probably been the cause of more legislation, litigation, internal revenue and trouble generally, than all the other interests combined. The chief industry of Richmond is in the manufacture, packing and shipping of tobacco in its various forms. The most recent is that of the cigarette establishments, where thousands of white girl operatives are employed, but as this branch of the business has been so well advertised in the cigarette pictures, we can check it off.

There is nothing of special historic interest in Richmond that may not be seen in one day, at an expense of, say two dollars. There were no important battles nearer the city than those of Seven Pines and Fair Oaks. I paid five dollars for a drive out there, and would not advise any one to make the trip, with a view of recognizing anything. Quite a heavy growth of young pines has grown up and almost obliterated every trace of the famous battlefields, by the changed aspect of the ground. A little National cemetery embraces the seven pine trees, from which the name was taken. The superintendent's lodge and the few lonely graves, with the flag waving over them, is the only sign of life left upon a field which was, one evening, a scene of the wildest excitement. And we may here say that the city might then have been taken. Does any of the *later*-day soldiers think that the *old* Army of the Potomac was camped in 1862 within *four* miles of Richmond?

On the way out we stopped a few moments at the Union National cemetery, located on this road leading to the North. Though somewhat isolated and located on the opposite side of the city from the Confederate, at Hollywood, it is more beautiful by contrast, because of the greater care that is taken of it by the agreeable superintendent, who, by the way, I discovered to have been an old regular cavalryman, who left one of his arms on this field.

This superintendent volunteered the pleasant information that the Confederates always march out to the Union cemetery on Decoration Day, and strew the graves of the Federal dead with flowers.

I am glad to be able to record my testimony, gathered from an actual observation in late years, as well as by personal contact, that there is a genuine sincerity and good feeling on the part of Confederate veterans toward the Federals, both dead and living.

While in Richmond I witnessed the funeral of a prominent citizen, who had been an active member of several societies. My attention being attracted by the music, I followed. I always follow a band, just as I did when a boy, and on coming up to this procession, I observed with feelings that I may not describe, but which I should like some of our Northern G. A. R. men to have witnessed. The guard of honor on each side of the hearse was composed of the blue and the gray. On one side walked men in the blue uniform of the G. A. R., and on the other, the gray of the Confederate Veterans. Put yourselves, in imagination, in my place in that beautiful cemetery on that May morning of 1887, and have your heartstrings touched by the scene, and surroundings and music, till the old frame vibrates under such influences so violently that all old war-prejudice and animosity is forever shaken out of you.

I am tempted to say that the best part of Richmond is to be found in her beautiful cemeteries.

Hollywood may be briefly described as the most sacred soil in all Virginia.

No one should go to Richmond without visiting Hollywood. It may be reached by street-car lines at a cost of 10 cents. If time is short, mark off everything else on the list of attractions, but see Hollywood before you die.

On my visits I spent part of each day out there. During the beautiful Virginia autumn weather of October and November, 1862, I believe that I walked out to these beautiful grounds every pleasant Sunday afternoon, lounging under the big trees on the hillside overlooking the James river and listening to the roar of the rushing waters over the falls, that I, in boyish dreams believed flowed on towards friends and home, and wishing and longing that like a bubble I might ride on its bosom and it would bear me away safely and surely inside the Union lines. Many prisoners on Belle Isle, nearly opposite, have looked towards these green slopes dotted with the white tombstones, wishing, almost, that they were at rest there instead of enduring a living burial in that prison.

One might imagine from the numerous great rocks that hold their heads above the spray of the dashing waters, that one could step from stone to stone from Belle Isle to Hollywood shore; but a wild, tearing, wicked-looking depth of water dashing against and rushing around the huge boulders, and then frothing with anger, apparently, at the impediment, would deter the stoutest heart from an attempt.

But few of the casual visitors to Hollywood have discovered a little fifteen by twenty-foot private lot almost on the edge of the bluff, enclosed by a plain cast-iron fence, on the gate of which is a tablet bearing the name of Jefferson Davis. There is but one little grave inside, a lonely little grave in the center of the lot, in which lie the remains of the infant son of Mr. Davis, who died from the effects of a fall.

It was during the last year of the war—when Grant was battling around the Confederate Capital—when the little children were innocently playing around in front of the executive mansion, this little pet baby-boy fell from the steps to the ground, dislocating his neck. It was a sad blow to the parents, made doubly so by the surroundings and nature of the fatal occurrence.

The Sunday-school children of Richmond's war days, in their times of poverty, themselves, contributed their mites to purchase this lot, to which, keeping step to the booming of the cannon, in a body they followed the remains of their President's baby.

This little boy sleeps there yet in his long sleep of innocence, the spot having become a shrine for those who were Sunday-school children while we were thundering at their gates; but never for a Sunday disturbing their regular services.

Close by this is the tomb of ex-President Monroe, over which a beautiful piece of iron work has been erected.

In striking contrast with this, is the simple mound in an uninclosed lot, which is the only mark over the remains of another ex-President—Mr. Tyler. It was his request that no stone or mark be placed at his grave. The turf is kept green and the mound tenderly cared for by his Virginia descendants.

On a knoll is a massive but plain slab to the memory of ex-Governor Henry A. Wise and his family.

Lieutenant-General A. P. Hill, who was killed just four days before the surrender of Lee, is resting in a pretty spot. No stone has yet been placed to his grave, the only designation being the name, A. P. Hill, without title, cut on the stone steps that lead into the inclosure.

One of the attractive features of Hollywood as distinguished from all other cemeteries that I have visited, is in its broken grounds, beautifully diversified by hills and little valleys, through which pretty streams or murmuring brooks "go on forever" singing a sadly quiet lullaby to the sleeper, or the watcher who is only waiting.

Near one of these little streams is a tall shaft to the memory of Gen. J. E. B. Stuart. As an old cavalryman of the Federal army, that was often pushed by him, it was my privilege to stand uncovered by his grave, with a sense of the deepest respect for his memory.

Commander Maury is near by; so is Chief Justice Marshall. Indeed, one wanders through these large grounds, finding on the tombstones name after name that is familiar to all readers of American history.

On the other side, farthest from the river, sleeps an entire army of Confederate soldiers, who were killed in battle or died near here. This Confederate section is the Arlington of Richmond, though not to be compared with the Arlington of Washington in keeping and attention. In place of the head-stones supplied to all Federal dead by the Government, we find here small wooden posts—on which are tacked tin tags, bearing, in some cases, the names, but in a majority only a number, almost washed out by the storms—indicating the last resting-place of thousands whose memories are as dear to the bleeding hearts of Southern mothers as are those to our own hearts that are being more carefully preserved by our Government.

Will the time ever come when this great Government will provide alike for the dead soldiers of both armies?

Surely a stone may be given to mark the last resting-place of an enemy, when we give bread to the living Federal pensioner and his dependent family.

A large pyramid twenty feet square at the base and about eighty feet in height, built of Virginia blocks of granite, is the simple but beautiful monument erected to the Confederate dead.

Twining about it and clinging lovingly and fondly all over this huge pile of unmortared stone is the beautiful Virginia creeper, so sweetly appropriate and always pretty; its luxuriant and graceful foliage supplemented by the handsome trumpet flower produces an effect that has yet to be equalled by the most skillful sculptor of similar statuary.

Right by this, and in the same grave with those of his command who died on the field and were brought back from Gettysburg, rests the body of General George E. Pickett. It was his request that he be buried here with his comrades, though the location is not so desirable as others. A suitable monument may in time be erected here.

It is not my purpose to dwell on the fact that the Southern people, though they went from war to devastated homes and have had to labor and toil in the face of opposition of divers kinds, have, notwithstanding their poverty and hardship, bravely succeeded in rebuilding their homes and country without government aid; and, though poor, yet, as compared with the more prosperous North, they have erected to the memory of their General Lee a magnificent monument, while General Grant's body lies almost neglected in the city where his successes in war made the people roll in luxury and prosperity—rich even to surfeit, in everything but gratitude.

We might linger in Richmond for days and weeks.

Trains leave for Fredericksburg at 6 P. M., affording a rest and delightful ride of sixty miles in the pleasant evening through the well-known cavalry fields of Hanover, Guinness Station, Bowling Green and Ashland ; but like the cavalry, we will dash through these places quickly with the train and make our next stop at Fredericksburg.

CHAPTER VI.

FREDERICKSBURG—what a cloud of war memories hangs over this old town! The mere mention of the name awakens the veteran's slumbering interests; like the pass-word, it clears the way, and raises the flood-gate through which rushes down upon us such a stream of reminiscences, that we are almost overwhelmed, and in despair of being able to record them lay down the pen, tempted to get into the swim and float down, like the other chips, through the whirlpools of time into the broad ocean of oblivion.

As long as life lasts there will never be effaced from the tablets of my heart and mind a single event connected with Fredericksburg during the war. To a majority of old soldiers of both armies this chapter, dated at Fredericksburg, may be like a letter from home, written by one of the "boys." I have estimated that every soldier of the Army of the Potomac, as well as that of Lee's Confederate Army of Northern Virginia, has at one time or other, been at Fredericksburg.

We were not here for three days only, as at Gettysburg, which has become the Mecca of American valor to which tourists throng daily, and neglect this more interesting field. We all *lived* here for a couple of years, every day of which was as a year of an ordinary lifetime. It was, indeed, an eventful period in the lives of all. Who will forget the first pleasant occupation of the country by

McDowell in the summer of 1862, the cavalry raids of Dahlgren, the return of Burnside in November, 1862, the shelling of the town on December 11th, the terrible battle on the 13th of December, our sad Christmas on the Rappahannock? How we all lived over the river on those Stafford Heights during the whole of that dreadful winter of 1862–63—the severe cavalry picket duty on the flanks, the mud march and its disappointments, then the Chancellorsville campaign during the leafy month of May, after which we moved off to Gettysburg.

General Grant again conducted the Army of the Potomac back to almost within gunshot at Spottsylvania, the Wilderness and Mine Run, so close that the wounded were brought to town. The ambulance procession is said to have been fifteen miles in length, reaching to Belle Plain. I mention all this in support of my statement that, at one time or another, all of both armies were here. The floating population, aggregated nearly half a million souls, and perhaps all of the survivors and their families and their friends may become members of our club and make this visit with us.

The most disastrous battles of the war, perhaps, that the world ever saw, were fought here, and here repose the remains of 20,000 soldiers who died *at the front*, a majority of whom were slain in the battle, and are buried on the field, yet this Fredericksburg, a beautiful old town so rich in historical memories, and but an hour and a half from Washington City, is almost forgotten by the country, by the tourists who flock to Gettysburg, and Memorial day here is remembered only by a few Confederates of M. F.

Maury's camp who have quietly strewn the graves of Federal and Confederate alike with the flowers contributed by the ladies of the town.

Some statements made herein will, no doubt, be disputed and that I may be fortified, have collected some figures, that I record herewith, to establish the position that within sound of cannon in Spottsylvania county, the greatest battles were not only fought, but the casualties aggregated more than in all the rest of the war. The greatest heroism of the Anglo-Saxon was on these fields displayed. Probably there is not another ten miles square on the entire surface of the earth so replete with history—ancient, colonial, revolutionary as well as rebellion history—as this.

RECAPITULATION.

Fredericksburg, Dec. 13, 1862.

Federal killed, 1180—wounded, 9028—missing, 2145—12353—
Confed. " 579 " 3870 " 127— 4576— 16,929

Chancellorsville, May 1863.

Federal killed, 1512—wounded 9518—missing, 5000—16030—
Confed. " 1581 " 8700 " 2900—14181— 30,211

Wilderness, May 7, 1864.

Federal killed, 5597—wounded, 21463 missing, 10677—37737—
Confed. " 2000 " 6000 " 3400—11400—49,137

Bloody Angle, May 8 to 21, 1864. Spottsylvania C. H. and Minor Engagements.

Federal killed, 4177—wounded, 19687—missing, 2577—26441—
Confed. " 1000 " 5000 " 3000— 9000—35,441

This is not all; but these four battles, make a grand total of 131,718 divided as follows: Federal, 92,561; Confederate, 39,157.

Of this number there are interred in the Federal cemetery on Marye's Heights 15,273; of the dead who died at the front and are buried on the field, 12,243 sleep in unknown graves. Every State, every regiment, and God only knows how many families, may be mourning a son, a husband or a father, who sleeps here, among the "unknown" and who are practically forgotten. Shamefully neglected by the G. A. R., orators, poets, or the multitude who assemble at Arlington every year.

There is very much of interest about Fredericksburg, besides its war history. Only a little ways over on the peninsula, lying between the Rappahannock and the Potomac rivers, known as the northern neck of Virginia, in "Wes'molan," as they abbreviate Westmoreland county, George Washington was born, and they tell me the stump of the cherry tree George haggled is pointed out to those who visit the old homestead. I have seen a rusted bit of iron that a Virginia Yankee tried to make me believe was the genuine hatchet used by George, while other enterprising countrymen offered a cane cut from the tree.

Not many of the boys who lived in the dug-outs of winter quarters on Stafford Heights, below or nearly opposite Fredericksburg, knew that the Army of the Potomac was then encamped on and that they were burning the fence-rails from the original farm of Mrs. Washington, the mother of him who was first in war.

At the point where the center pontoon was laid by Burnside, just below the old mill leading to the rocky road, marks also the spot where the youthful George beat the record and astonished the other boys by his ability to throw a stone clear across the river.

I have a good photograph of this pontoon landing, showing the old mill, the wheels of which still go 'round and 'round, and the mill-race, through which I proposed laying my sub-marine cable, runs on forever.

No soldier who crossed this pontoon can forget it, and they will recognize the old mill that yet stands by the destroyed railroad bridge. The rocky road, or lovers' lane, leading up to the main street over which so many bleached and trembling souls trod that day, looks precisely as of old.

Mrs. Washington lived on one of the hill streets of the town. The house is still standing in a fair state of preservation—nearly as she left it. The visitor will be cheerfully shown through the rooms in which she lived and where she died, by Miss Moon, the pleasant as well as cultivated and pretty daughter of the present owners.

It will be remembered that Washington, while en route to the capital to be inaugurated President, visited his mother at her home here. The garden in which she is described as meeting him so indifferently—scarce stopping her planting of onions to greet her distinguished son—is, at the present time, still growing onions and "garden sass." La Fayette, as well as many other distinguished people, visited Mrs. Washington during her life-time.

Mrs. Washington is buried on the outskirts of the town. The old soldiers will all recall the unfinished monument. It stands yet, precisely as it did during the war—a crumbling shaft that has marked, for years, a nation's neglect of the grave of the mother of the father of his country.

There is a prospect that through the recent agitation of this shameful neglect, the women of the entire land may unite in the movement inaugurated by the ladies of Fredericksburg to redeem not only the grave, but. perhaps, the home of Mrs. Washington, as they did Mount Vernon, the tomb and home of the son.

I always spend an evening out there; it's a pleasant walk to a pleasant spot, and I love to sit on the same ledge of rocks, under the big trees, where I spent so many happy hours with Geno.

The love story is coming, boys and girls, but we will not tell it at this tomb.

Near the tomb is a venerable old square brick building, known as "Kenmore," built nearly 150 years ago for Betty, the sister of Washington, then the bride of Colonel Fielding Lewis. This time-honored house is now the property of W. Key Howard, Esq., a courteous gentleman who will conduct us through the house, explaining its interesting history and describing its beautiful ceiling decorations.

One medallion in plaster, over a mantle, was designed by Washington, and it evidences fine artistic ability. The lover of the antique may find, in this old burg, some rich specimens of the curious and unique, in both design and execution, that may not be equalled by the modern imitator. There are huge, if not massive, hinges and locks on the old oaken doors of many houses here that would delight the connoisseur. Door-knockers, with hangers over a foot long, are quite common. The study in old roofs and corners, or gables, would interest the architects who build the modern Queen-Anne houses. Here are some original specimens of genuine Queen-Anne architecture.

There is an absence of sameness in those old homes, both in exterior and in their inner parts, that is quite a relief to those who have had the modern style thrust upon them on all sides. The builders of these old colonial homes did not have the advantage of the monthly publication on interior decoration and artistic furnishings. Being left to their own ingenuity, and the resources of a blacksmith or a carpenter shop, they were obliged to work out their own ideas, and they have certainly produced some beautiful original specimens of their handiwork.

"Kenmore" suffered somewhat from the shelling by Burnside's artillery, there being the scars of five solid shot on the wall facing the Federal army.

The main street of the town is below or under the hill, running parallel with the river. At the upper end of this street, and almost opposite to the Lacey House, is a story-and-a-half log building, sheathed with weather boarding, some ancient-looking dormer windows breaking through a good big roof surface, which is known to the older residents as the Rising Sun Inn, or tavern. Here Washington, Aaron Burr and the early Virginia gentlemen were accustomed to gather to play poker.

Washington was a very methodical man, and kept a record of everything, even to his losses in card playing. One of his private entries reads: "Played cards at Fredericksburg and lost, as I always do at that place."

The Masonic fraternity cherish the old building here as the early home of their lodge. It was in this town that Washington was made a Mason. It was my privilege to have examined the record giving the date and entry, and also to have kissed the Bible upon which he was obligated. Masonic visitors will be courteously shown through the lodge room by their brethren, of whom there are a number. The furniture is hand-made, being brought from

Scotland before the Revolutionary period. Col. Rufus B. Merchant, a gallant Confederate scout who is now proprietor and editor of the *Star*, of Fredericksburg, is, with his Masonic brethren, very much interested in the building of a memorial temple in commemoration of this event in Masonic history.

St. George's Church, the steeple of which our artillerymen used as a target when the Confederate signal officers were inside, looks as natural as ever, except that the three great holes we put through it have been patched over. In the almost heavy stillness of the nights, in these years of peace, when I hear the familiar old bell strike the hour, I think of the nights in years gone by when it tolled, in the same way, the hours to hundreds of thousands of sleeping soldiers, bivouacing on their arms within sound of its tones; and, looking now at the electric lights reflected upon its white surface, its tall spire pointing to the sky, it seems like a spectral reminder of the sure passing of time.

A few days since some workmen, in excavating for a foundation, threw up a twelve-pound solid shot that had buried itself three feet below the surface.

Relics are quite plentiful and genuine here. Perhaps the largest and most interesting collection of war relics to be found anywhere in the country may be seen here in the Museum of the Exchange Hotel. A courteous young gentleman, Mr. W. A. Hill, is the proprietor and owner. The tourist and visitor is referred to my friend Mr. Hill as being a most competent guide, as well as an agreeable young man, whom everybody is glad to have met.

The visitor to Fredericksburg will find listed among the many points of interest, in addition to the battle-fields, some of the residences of distinguished people, among these, modestly claiming a share of attention, is "The Wells House," the home of "Geno," the war heroine of the "Boy Spy" narrative.

Mr. Hill was induced to place this on his published list of attractions because of the number of tourists who stopped off to visit the battle-fields and Mrs. Washington's home and grave inquired of him "if any one by the name of Wells lived here?" The object no doubt being to gratify curiosity as to the truthfulness of this love and war story. Not being familiar with it, himself, he made some inquiries of the older citizens in regard to the Wells family; Mayor Slaughter observing "Oh yes, I knew them very well—they were very sweet girls;" a number of others also knowing them; the interesting family of my friend Colonel Merchant lived neighboring them during the war.

I can only say, briefly, to those who have not been interested in the fortunes of the Boy and his war girl, that she was in the hands of the Rebels in the town, while he was out in the cold on the other side of the river and could only see the roof of the house in which he could imagine they were all having a good time with the Rebel officers.

I am conducting the club around to the Wells House—we will stand together upon the same old porch from which I was so cruelly taken in the summer of 1862, to Old Capitol prison, this by special orders of the Secretary of War, E. M. Stanton; and I insist, for no other offense than that of having fallen in love with this pretty little black-eyed girl. I couldn't help it. She was sixteen and I was twenty; moreover, she was a beautiful girl and wore short skirts, low-necked dresses and in her well-formed bare arms, gracefully held a guitar while she skilfully played the accompaniment and sweetly sang that old Spanish serenade—Juanita—or Wanita.

I invariably ask every pretty girl with whom I become acquainted to sing Juanita.

Though over a quarter of a century has elapsed, I recall every incident as freshly as if it had occurred last week.

The scene on this little porch where I, in the custody of a staff officer, bade Mrs. Wells and Sue good-bye, while Geno, trembling with suppressed emotion, timid and blushing, almost afraid to trust herself to say farewell in the presence of the group, stood by the door. When I turned to her as the last to whom I should give a parting word, the dear little girl broke down completely, covered her face with her handkerchief to hide her tears and embarrassment.

I took the handkerchief from her face and put it in my pocket—and it is in my possession yet—boldly kissed her and said, tremblingly, sincerely and earnestly, "As sure as I live, I will come again Geno." It was the turning point in my life as well as that of Geno's and some others, every one of whose stories from that date would make interesting romances in real life. Their terrible experiences during the shelling—Miss Sue's flirtations with the Confederate officers, Miss Mamie running the blockades to visit her father then a prisoner at Ft. McHenry, Baltimore, the attempts of a handsome staff officer of General Barksdale's Mississippi brigade to capture the affections of Geno, the family's subsequent sufferings and privations, will indeed make a romance in real life that is truly stranger than fiction.

As I have said, I shall never be able to do the subject justice until I write a book about it—and its name will be "Geno."

In looking up the whereabouts of some of the Confederate officers who were courting my girl in my absence, taking an unfair advantage of their military possession, I learned that Mr. Justice Lamar, being a Mississippi Confederate, would be able to give me the desired information.

I wrote him a brief note explaining my wishes and observed that I knew a gentleman of his standing had not much time or inclination to bother with love stories, to which he replied, in his courteous and kindly manner:

"It does not bother me to hear about a love story of the war, provided the *dénouement* is a happy one. I find myself reading them whenever I have an opportunity or the labors and requirements of my duties will permit, and I fear that I sometimes play truant for this purpose. I am very much interested in 'Geno' already," and he told me where I could catch the fellow in Mississippi that made love to Geno.

I have made a good photograph of the house, copies of which I should be glad to supply to any one who may desire them The porch is precisely as it was twenty-seven years ago. On these steps were spent some of the happiest hours of my life, and, by the way, some other fellows, North and South, will say the same thing, and be able to recognize the familiar, hospitable and once happy home of the truly happy Wells family.

The attic dormer window is shown, from which I proposed to conceal myself, under Geno's protection, and by the use of the telegraph code, as applied visually, to signal over the river into the windows of the Lacey house, which is just diagonally opposite, where was located a signal officer with a glass cautiously bearing on me.

For my own gratification and to convince any skeptical parties that the plan was entirely feasible, we might open up a circuit, going myself to the Lacey house, while a signalist companion remains on this side to whom I could communicate by the wig-wag system using simply a wand, a handkerchief or a fan, as fast as I can write this out, in such a way that the casual observer would not suspect that a system of scientific signalling was being conducted before their eyes.

Therefore it is not only possible but practicable to signal from inside an enemy's lines to your own lines without detection—as I have asserted.

As they say in Virginia, I am "tolerably" familiar with Fredericksburg, and "tharfor" able to "carry you all around" and point out the many places of historic interest. I frequently run down "hyar" from Washington with parties of old friends who press me in as a guide to steer them around; besides this good excuse, I love to spend an occasional Sunday on my own account walking around its romantic and historic plains, in the agreeable company of some pretty little girls, that were born and raised here since the war.

There seems to be a singular attraction still lingering about the old Wells house and vicinity aside from its delightful associations.

There are three pretty young ladies living with their parents in the house, not only pretty but accomplished and agreeable. The visitor who may be curious about the truthfulness of its history will be politely received and entertained by them. He will be shown the scars of the great battle, left in its walls. During the terrific shelling of the town by Burnside, while the Wells family lived there and took hasty refuge in the cellar, three cannon balls passed through the house, and one twelve-pound shot lodged inside. This identical twelve-pounder may be seen at the museum.

The sofa on which I had so often sat alongside of Geno, while she charmed me with the guitar, and "them" eyes, was knocked all to pieces by a shell that tore through the parlor.

Unfortunately the handsome Rebel officer was not at that moment sitting there. The battery that fired it was commanded by a Captain Kirby, no relative or friend of mine, however. One of the ladies who is a phenomenal player on the piano and the organist in the church of the town, is always pleased to gratify the visitor by playing or accompanying her younger sisters, who sing charmingly the old songs we used to sing in that parlor long, long years ago. Not only "Juanita," but other old favorites: "My lost Evangeline," "In the Gloaming," "Ever of Thee,"

"Her Bright smile haunts me still," "Annie Laurie," and "Tired, oh yes, so tired, dear," or "Abide With Me." I am very fond of music, and to my old-fashioned taste the new is not so sweet as the old, especially when heard in this Wells house.

There are a number of pretty little female Rebels in Fredericksburg, which is famous for the beauty of its women and the hospitality of its men, and it preserves, to a remarkable degree, its distinctive old-time traditions.

I love to listen to the mild voices and sweet accent of the Southern ladies—even if they have sometimes a mighty decidedly Southern inflection.

I have visited Fredericksburg so often in recent years that I've become a rather familiar figure on the streets, being always pleasantly greeted as "the Majah."

A sweet little girl of thirteen or fourteen years, who had been charmingly entertaining me with her music in her home parlor one evening, was asked the name of the piece she had been playing. Replying in her fast talking way, and in accents sweet and mild, it sounded to me like one word: "Dawncingonthbawnllo." I laughed, and attempted to tease her by commenting on the big name for so pretty a piece of music, when she swung herself around on the piano stool, her black eyes flashing at me, as she stammered out of her puckered lips, to my companion, more deliberately, "The Majah thinks he knows so moch!" Ever since, when my friend feels inclined to differ from me on any subject, he repeats the expression with such effective accentuation that it has become quite familiar among our acquaintances.

But we shall have to tear ourselves away from the attractions of the town, and carry our war club to the battle-fields on the outskirts.

As the "Majah don't know so moch" about the battle of Franklin, on the left, we will take along with us, as a guide, a courteous Confederate, who was, during the battle, a soldier of Stonewall Jackson's line, and can tell, from his point of view, something new on this old story. I suggest that any visitor to the town, who may need a guide, will confer with this gentleman, Capt. Lal Taliaferro, late of the 47th Virginia Infantry, now Post-master for the Republican administration; or his brother, Captain John. The family is well known in the State, having resided in the vicinity almost from time immemorial, and the statement of either of these gentlemen may be relied upon. A rig may be had from Col. Tom Háyden or Mr. Wheeler, for probably one-half that charged for livery at Washington or Gettysburg.

It is some three or four miles to our left, or to the Bernard House or Franklin headquarters where the lower pontoons were laid. Driving down the river road, we cross Hazel Run, well described in official reports of the day. The residence of Mr. Slaughter, on Hazel Hill, known as the Slaughter House, was occupied as the headquarters of Getty and Hawkins.

At this lower field, on the left of our lines, the range of hills on which were entrenched the Confederate forces of Stonewall Jackson, are some distance further back from the river than are the same hills nearest the town.

This is not intended to be a description of the battle

at all. Let it be simply understood that a broad, level plain, used as extensive fields or meadows of the farm, say nearly a mile in width, lay between the river and the range of hills. Over this open plain, the troops of Franklin, with a river in their rear, had to advance, under fire, without any of that protection afforded the right wing in their advance by the shelter of the houses of the town. There was not only a *direct* artillery fire from batteries occupying the hills in their front, but the advancing Federals were enfiladed by Pelham's Confederate artillery located on the plain some distance below.

Running through a little break in the range of hills is a small swampy stream that had cut for itself, in the year of peace and plenty, a little ravine or gully, leading down through the open fields to the river. Along this little swampy depression in the broad level a few trees and some undergrowth had been permitted to grow.

This scene is in the depth of winter: There are no leaves on the trees, or brush to aid in covering that noble division of Pennsylvania reserve troops commanded by Meade, that advanced, almost alone, despite the artillery fire, over this frozen ground, not only to the base of the hills on which were Jackson's troops, *but they went on through the break in the hills.*

They drove before them the enemy and in their advance passed their two lines of stacked muskets. The story is soon told. This division not only broke the "Stonewall," but they advanced six hundred yards beyond it.

Why didn't they stay? Ah, yes, echo answers, why? It is not the purpose of this club to attempt to discuss this question. Gen. W. B. Franklin, one of Gen. McClellan's trusted lieutenants, was in supreme command of the left. He has furnished an official report to the Government of his reason for not supporting their advance, and has given the public, through the Century Magazine, a further explanation of this failure. Those of us who were not of the military rings are apt to wonder why this twin lieutenant of McClellan's was not dealt with as was Fitz-John Porter, who was, perhaps, able to give just as good reasons for his failure to support at Second Bull Run.

That a general movement in support would have been successful is conceded by the Confederates. If this had been accomplished, Lee would have been turned out of his strong position at Marye's Heights, and that terrible slaughter then have been avoided. But this is not an attempt at a military criticism. I offer the testimony simply of reliable Confederates, that each may form his own conclusions.

"When you all advanced thar"—says Capt. Taliferro—"I declaw, Majah, I never saw anything so beautiful in all my life. General Jackson wanted a gun located on that little knoll down thar on the lower side of the railroad just whar that little cut is—wall, sah, I was sent out thar to support it, and I pledge you my word and honor I never was so glad to get a relief from any place in all the wah as I was to get out of that. My regiment was on the hill supporting the artillery, and when you all advanced up that ravine we never thought you all would keep going ahead through that swampy place, but they did go on sure enough, and *every man was taken away from the support of the guns in front to go back thar to drive you out.* Why, I heard one of your officers say, 'Give 'em hell, boys, we've got them on the run—give 'em hell.' If you all had come up to support, you would have found nothing but the artillery in your front. Yes sir, it's a truth that our men in your front, on both sides, were turned back, as it were, in a sort of V shape, and in that way we drove you all out. I was right hyar when you all came back over the railroad, and I never shall forget an officer on a white hoss, I think he wore a black beard, who rode right along here, saying, 'Rally men, rally right here' He road up and down two or three times saying that. It was a brave man who ever he was, and when a gun was pointed at him, some one of our men sang out, 'don't, don't shoot that man'—but it was too late, a volley was fired and his horse plunged, throwing him over. I did'nt know 'till after the battle that the officer had been shot. When you all went back we found him."

Who was that officer, is a question for the club. My belief is that it was Colonel Feger Jackson of the Ninth Pennsylvania Reserves. Can any one of the veteran clubbers give any further information?

In talking on this subject with Rev. Dr. James Power Smith, the popular minister of the Presbyterian church at Fredericksburg, who served as an aid on Stonewall Jackson's staff in this battle, he unhesitatingly stated, "Oh, yes; that came very near being successful too."

Conducting me in the most courteous way into the cosy study of his elegant litle stone chapel or annex, he made a diagram showing the Confederate positions.

"There were three lines. Ewell was on the front, Early next, and I've forgotten who the reserve were. Your forces got through two of these lines, as the swampy point was not sufficiently protected, because it was not thought possible for a successful advance to be made there."

I had heard that Gen. Jackson was at that time absent from the field in conference with Gen. Lee, but Dr. Smith was of the opinion that Jackson was present during the engagement, as he had been sent out by him, and his horse being shot, he delayed while getting a remount from the artillery, and recalled, making this explanation to his General.

"The General," said Dr. Smith, "was very exacting, and required from all his subordinates, as zealous and faithful service as he was willing to give himself. I had been going all day and was anxious to get some rest, but the general ordered me to report to him, and directed that I should convey his instructions to supply ammunition, and orders to relieve or change the line before the moon rose at 2 o'clock. You see," said the doctor, with a laugh, "Jackson consulted the almanac in his military movements.

"After the battle, when your men came over to bury the dead, Gen. Gordon got on a stump here to make a speech of caution to those of our men who were to assist in this work, telling them not to do any talking at all, lest something might be brought out that would react on us.

"I was amused at a big Alabamian singing out from the ranks, 'Well, Gin'ral, can't we tell them we whooped 'em yisterday?'

"Before the laugh had died off entirely, another fellow blurted out, 'Can't we tell 'em, Gin'ral, that we can do it agin?'

"I was present when your burial detail came on the ground, though General Jackson had not instructed me to do so, I knew he was anxious to hear or know something of his brother-in-law, Dr. Junkin, who was serving as a staff officer on your side, and I hoped to find him.

"It was while waiting for this opportunity that one of your staff officers, a handsome young fellow, elegantly dressed, and wearing a pair of fine top boots, rode up to one of our men who had picked up a gun from the field, and ordered him to throw it down—observing to me:

"'This is debatable ground, sir, and your men have no right to take those arms away.'

"The Confederate in the meanwhile eyeing him all over, resting his admiring, if envious, gaze on the fine boots, exclaimed before I could interfere:

"'Say, Mister, I'm going to kill you to-morrow when you come over to fight, and get them thar boots.'

"General Jackson was one of the strictest of disciplinarians in our army, and held every one to a strict accountability, without regard to his rank. General Maxey Gregg, an old man and an officer of distinction, had in some way come under General Jackson's rod, and did not suffer in silence but had protested earnestly to General Lee.

"The night of the battle, Jackson was told that General Gregg was dying. He mounted his horse and rode some distance to the rear to where he was lying.

"The dying officer was overcome at the sight of Jackson, and began at once to offer some explanations, when Jackson interrupted him to say: 'Never mind, never mind; I am told, General, that you have but a short time to live, and I would rather you would give your attention to other matters. May I not pray with you?' and he knelt beside him, and while he offered this benediction: 'Oh God, our Merciful Father, receive into thy hands, this departing soul,' the General's life ebbed out.

"There was of course some friction occasionally between our officers. Ewell, who held the front of our line, commanded what was known and what he was rather proud to have known as the 'Light Brigade.' In conveying Jackson's instructions to old General Jubal Early, it was necessary to mention that Ewell's Light Brigade would be in his front, when old Early turned upon me with an oath and said, 'Tell General Jackson that celebrated "Light Brigade" was too damned light to keep the Yankees from getting in on me, and if he will take his "Light Brigade" out of my way, I will agree to hold this line myself.'"

CHAPTER VII.

THE old veteran of the old Army of the Potomac does not require the services of a guide on these fields. I mean by the *old* army veterans those who followed its earlier leaders: McDowell on the plains of Manassas, McClellan on the Peninsula and at Antietam after the Second Bull Run, Burnside at Fredericksburg, Hooker at Chancellorsville and Meade at Gettysburg. That was an army of American gentlemen, who, without thought of mercenary reward, responded to the first call of Lincoln and gallantly marched to the front, and whose inborn loyalty and patriotism kept them faithfully in the front ranks during all of the dark days in the early years of the war: when the hard knocks of the chivalry and best blood of the South were directed at and received by their bared breasts. We were often whipped, to put it in plain English; that is, our Generals were defeated in four-fifths of the engagements; yet the gallant boys of that *old* army got upon their feet after every knock-down and uncomplainingly wiped the blood from their faces. Every man squared himself for another bout with his adversary. I love the *old* Army of the Potomac—that dear old Army of the Potomac—noble, patient and long-suffering old Army of the Potomac—its greatest battles were fought before Gen. Grant came out from the West to lead its recruited forces to the Wilderness, Cold Harbor and Appomattox. Not one of the old boys who survives will ever forget the frugal Thanksgiving dinner of hard-tack and coffee on those dreary plains, nor the sad Christmas on the Rappahannock—sad not only to them, but to the thousands of homes throughout the country that were placed in mourning, and hearts of mothers made to bleed by the losses sustained here, December 13th.

It is interesting to note the different phases in veteran human nature that are exhibited by those who revisit these fields. They come from all sections, but most numerously from New England and the Middle States, which were principally the homes of the Army of the Potomac, frequently in large excursion parties, their wives and families or friends accompanying them. Sometimes G. A. R. delegations, wearing the old blue uniform, the ladies and children decorated with the badges, headed by a band, will stir the colored inhabitants by a parade from the depot along the streets of the sleepy old town. Those who have come in contact with these visitors as guides or drivers of conveyances, say they can always tell a *genuine* veteran. An old colored driver put it this way:

"Yaas, sah, dem real Yankees what war here in de wah don't want no guide buzzing in dar ears. Dey done tole me to talk to my hosses mor'n onct; and one old man said he'd give me a dollar extra if I'd button up my lips; so I jis keep my mouf shut and open my years, and I hear from them talkin' mongst demselves all bout de wah, dat I can tell to others dat doant know nuffin bout it."

The gentlemen at the hotel say those whose names to their register are familiar are usually the least ostentatious guests.

On the other hand, numerous old-*looking* men, wearing the uniform and badge of the G. A. R., are as aggressive and ready to fight their battles over again; in their casual intercourse with the ex-Confederates who may meet them, they insist upon injecting their political sentiments, mixed with war opinions.

If this class are sometimes cornered as to their service, it usually proves to have been during the last year of the war as a reserve or home guard; and if the regiment is asked, probably the answer may be as uncertain as that of the Irish recruit, who belonged to the "bloody 99th Ireland, be jabers."

The old veteran who goes off alone, or accompanied, perhaps, by one or two old comrades, makes a bee-line for his old camp on Stafford Heights; but the chances are that he can not find the location. But few can realize what changes may be wrought in the surface or surroundings of a once-familiar spot by the growth of twenty-five years. The obliteration of the numerous military roads and fencing-in of the country entirely alters the topography of the old camp.

The old fellows go about in a dazed manner, as if they had lost something they were trying to find.

They are all sure, however, of the railroad tracks and embankments, the ruins of the Phillips House and the Lacey House. The church steeples of the town, the old mill and the contour of the hills back of the town, once burned into their minds and hearts by a brand of fire and iron, as Marye's Heights, is sadly familiar. The old boys gaze long at this scene; perhaps their visions are not now so clear as when they were younger, and maybe their sight is dimmed by a tear-drop, as with a sigh they walk meditatively to the upper pontoon anchorage at the Lacey House.

No one ever forgets a pontoon bridge.

To how many thousands of brave hearts does it remain in memory as a bridge of sighs, a home on one side, and a prison or death on the other. Truly, it was the crossing of the river of death to the many who never returned, and, I may add, even a river of oblivion.

Fredericksburg is, I believe, the only place in which pontoons were extensively used during the war. I do not recall any other place where the armies were obliged to cross a navigable river under heavy fire to fight an enemy entrenched on the opposite shore, as was the case here.

I am not attempting a description of this battle—only trying to tell what I saw. I may be permitted to record my opinion, therefore, based from actual observation, that more heroic service *was never exhibited anywhere* than that of the launching and building of these pontoons by the brave men of the regular and volunteer engineer corps of the Army of the Potomac.

I often wonder why some of the accomplished engineer officers do not, in these days of prolific war literature, put in form the heroic work of their corps at this place.

When it is remembered that the heavy lumbering boats were hauled to the water's edge, launched and anchored by men working *en masse,* without arms, all the time exposed to a deadly fire of the enemy's sharpshooters on the opposite shore of a narrow river, wonder grows to amazement that *anything* at all could be accomplished.

Yet these noble boys of the neglected engineers kept to their work bravely, the deadly fire from the Rebels not being at all silenced by the terrific shelling of the town.

Right here I will record another remarkable fact: Fredericksburg was the only town of importance bombarded at close range. Burnside's entire artillery shelled the old place for hours, yet *not a single death resulted from this* hail of fire and shell.

When it became apparent that the pontoons could not be laid in the face of the incessant fire from the houses along the river bank, *the engineers volunteered to row their boats to the opposite shore* and assist in charging upon this Mississippi brigade.

Volunteers were not called forth first as the official reports indicate, though as a reinforcement to those who had originally proposed it, others were called out. These brave boys—some of them had but recently left their college at Easton, Pennsylvania—were ferried over, and gallantly charged upon the hornet's nest and drove the Rebels out.

Then the pontoons were laid and the army started to cross on a bridge, every plank of which represented a dead hero.

There is no monument to mark this spot at Fredericksburg, except the tree to which one side was anchored, where as much daring heroism was shown as at any of the many marked places at Gettysburg. But the boys will *never* forget that place. I can hardly keep it out of my mind. I made a good sketch of the location, showing both shores, that I should like to show to the club in a magic lantern or stereopticon view, as well as some other deeply interesting places which I shot from my camera. I'm an amateur photograph crank, and on this trip had this box instead of the gun I used to carry.

Fredericksburg is debatable ground. Realizing that I may be treading on somebody's toes in attempting a description of the battle, I will shift the responsibility on to the broad shoulders of my friend, Col. Carswell McClellan, who, as an officer in Humphreys' staff, is thoroughly competent to tell the truth about the last great onslaught on Marye's Heights. If any one desires to fire back on this question, let him point his missiles at the Colonel, addressed to St. Paul, and not at my head.

There was not only one charge at this battle of Fredericksburg, but *a series* of charges, during all of that fatal day, any one of which equalled in heroism that of Pickett at Gettysburg.

The Irish Brigade have had their story well told, though Couch's and Hancock's are known only by the official reports and the *Century* papers. Colonel McClellan says of the last charge:

"On the morning of the 13th, General Humphreys' 3d Division of the 5th Corps was massed near the Phillips House, where General Burnside had his headquarters. At half-past two P. M., General Humphrey, who had been in consultation with Burnside, came out, with an expression of intense satisfaction. He told me that Burnside had informed him that our division was to go over the river at once to act as the reserve of the assaulting force, and he concluded his statement with the emphatic assertion that when we were sent to the assault we *must* gain the crest.

He directed the order for crossing to be given, with a request that the Brigade Commanders should give brief words of encouragement to their men, and as most of the troops were now entering upon their first engagement, he was anxious lest their spirits should be depressed by the sight of the wounded who were being brought to the rear, and that he should have that terrible stream turned aside while his command was advancing.

"After reaching the town the troops moved along the elongation of the telegraph road to Hanover street, reached the intersection, when Gen. Humphreys riding forward along his column found Gen. Hancock alone, apparently waiting there for some one. Just then Gen. Couch, almost, if not entirely, unattended, rode up, inquiring for Griffin's Division. It was evident that Gen. Couch's sympathetic nature was thoroughly aroused by what his troops had been through during the day. He stated that they had '*gained the Heights*,' but were out of ammunition and needed support. It became manifest later that 'the Heights' he referred to was the slight rise of ground below Marye's Heights, where Gen. Couch's troops lay. Couch not finding the support he expected, was exceedingly solicitous, when Gen. Humphreys said to him, 'I am ordered into position here, as you see, but you are the ranking officer; and if you will give me an order to do so, I will support you at once.' The order was given, as suggested, and guided by Capt. Mitchell of Hancock's staff. Humphrey rode out to the front, closely followed by Gen. P. H. Allabach's Brigade. At the foot of the hill General Hooker was met, who confirmed Couch's order. General Humphreys was then informed by Hooker that Gen. Burnside desired the Heights carried before sundown, and that he, Hooker, expected Humphrey to accomplish it. Allabach being ordered to form his brigade in two lines, Gen. Humphreys rode out into the field to observe the ground more closely—returning to his troops he said: 'The bayonet is the only thing that will do any good here—tell Allabach so and direct him to see that all muskets *are unloaded.*' Col. Allabach, a sturdy graduate from the 'Bloody Third' U. S. Infantry of the Mexican war, rode through his command as the formation was being completed, and had the muskets 'rung' to prove them unloaded."

Put a pin in that point—they were ordered to charge and *unload* their guns, and to prove it, they were "rung" while forming under fire. "With his brigade formed, the front line at charge bayonets and the second line at right shoulder arms, Allabach reported his command, ready to move forward. As the bugle sounded the 'charge,' General Humphrey turned to his staff, and bowing with uncovered head, remarked as quietly and as pleasantly as if inviting them to be seated around his table, 'Gentlemen, I shall lead this charge. I presume, of course, you will wish to ride with me.'"

Now compare *that* to *Pickett*, who was not within a mile of his column when they charged at Gettysburg—Pettigrew and Armistead, *led* Pickett's Division there. Of this grand assault of Humphreys', I can do no better than quote Gen. Hooker's report:

"This attack was made with a spirit and determination seldom, if ever, equalled in war. Seven of General

Humphreys' staff officers started with the charge, five were dismounted before reaching the line where Gen. Couch's troops were lying, and four more wounded before the assault ceased."

Gen. Humphreys said of his experience: "The troops I was to support were sheltering themselves by lying on the ground. This example Col. Allabach's Brigade followed, in spite of an effort to prevent it. The men who were lying, shouting to the others, 'get down, don't get up there,' etc. Only a part of his men were able to reach the front rank, owing to the numbers already occupying the ground. I cannot refrain from expressing the opinion, that the greatest obstacle to my success was the troops that had previously charged and been repulsed, but had not been withdrawn, though they were reported out of ammunition—this should have been done and thus left me a clean field—they would not advance with us, and the men of Allabach's Brigade, who had never before been in battle, instinctively followed their example and lay down. The troops on the right and left of us would have prevented the enemy from advancing. Had the enemy come out from behind the stone wall, we should have carried the positions."

Here it must be observed, in comparison with Pickett's charge, that at Gettysburg all things were equal; there were no hills and heavy stone walls and sunken roads, their troops advanced and were met bravely by our own, standing up like men, and repulsed disastrously, at a hand-to-hand combat; while at Fredericksburg *we never saw a Confederate* from behind their four lines of muskets concealed by stone walls and embankments. We saw nothing but the white smoke from their guns.

Our troops advanced to within eighty yards of them and *remained there* till night. No prisoners were taken at Fredericksburg. The writer, during a lull in the firing from the stone-wall ridge, could see Gen. Humphreys, sitting quietly and alone, viewing the ground after the repulse. As I neared him a peculiar sound was heard coming clearly and distinctly through the noise of the intermitting battle, and as I approached closer the notes of the song so familiar in those days—"Gay and Happy"—died from his lips. That air has been fixed indelibly in my mind.

"Returning on this road," says Col. McClellan, "I met Gen. Hooker with Gen. Butterfield. His greeting was, 'Give my compliments to Gen. Humphreys, and tell him he is doing nobly—nobly.'"

Gen. Humphreys was at the front to personally expedite the formation of the *first* brigade for another charge. Gen. Butterfield had given the order that the Heights *must* be carried before dark.

Again Humphreys rode at the head of his troops, joining with the movement on foot until the charge had *passed the brick house,* and the column was being crowded over to the right. As the brigade reached the mass of men lying there, every effort was made by the latter to prevent our advance. They called to our men not to go forward, and some attempted by force to prevent their doing so. The effect on Humphreys' line was to disorder them; but they were reformed into a column and again advanced.

The moral of this rather old story under new light is

this. Humphreys' Division would have gone right on to the stone wall, though all might have been slaughtered, but for the impediment of our own line lying on the ground.

As it was, Humphreys' Division of the 5th Corps must be accorded the honor of having gotten *nearest* the stone wall.

These statements are submitted not with any view of detracting from the glory and honor of the others, but simply as truths that may be recorded by living witnesses for the benefit of those who may come after us.

Perhaps in the future ages one stone may be erected on this historic ground to mark the point of the farthest advance of the Union line. It ought to be an equestrian statue to *Andrew Atkinson Humphreys*.

It was written of General Humphreys at the time that Fredericksburg had "developed a quiet, courteous and accomplished man of science into a splendid field-general of the most vigorous mien and distinguished bravery." And yet there was far more of demonstration than development in the magnificent effort of that man of science. The duty laid upon him there brought clearly to the light the magnetic leadership which was as natural to him as his breath and subsequently proved that he could serve as well, or as loyally, as he could lead. It is not to be supposed that General Humphreys was blind to the fearful errors of that fatal field. He "knew his duty and obeyed his orders" with an imperturbable courage and consummate ability and zeal that would, if possible, wrest success from the most hopeless task.

Does any one ever think that the charge of Pickett

was the only one ever made by the Confederates? Of course they have made advances, but this final-charge of Pickett, preceded and attended, as it was, by peculiarly dramatic surroundings, was their only grand charge of all the war, and probably for this reason it has furnished a subject for more speeches, historical essays, paintings and poems than any other event which ever occurred in America. Yet either one of the gallant charges made on an impregnable position, where everything was against us, as at Marye's Heights, excels, in every particular, this much vaunted fire-works exhibition at the close of the great battle of Gettysburg. I am not personally fond of talking on war subjects—in fact, at the close of the war I was so sick of it that I made a vow never to refer to that experience, and I have kept my word—except at long intervals—ever since. I considered it a most gratifying compliment to have an old friend say of my war story:

"Oh, that's all imagination—he was not in the war at all—I've known him for years, almost intimately, and his best friends say they never heard him talk about the war at all."

Though I'm a Pennsylvanian and proud of Gettysburg, yet this Virginia "burg" has a greater fascination for me than our Pennsylvania "burg." I am glad to be able to record the fact here that the Pennsylvania Reserves made the *first* charge and broke "Stonewall" Jackson's line, but the Pennsylvania general, Franklin, failed to support them, and it was lost. It was a division of Pennsylvanians under Humphreys who made this *last* final onslaught, and it was Pennsylvanians and Pennsylvania generals,

Hancock and Meade, who received Pickett's charge in the Pennsylvania town of Gettysburg.

To properly fortify the statements regarding this debated ground, I here have attempted to outline what may be termed an official report in giving the views of the officers. Permit a newspaper scout to record some personal impressions of the scene. I have some splendid views showing the Rebel position, that I should like to throw upon the scene before the eyes of the club while I deliver this lecture.

The Confederate artillery was stationed along the crest of the hill; below them to the front were four lines of their infantry, securely entrenched behind stone walls on each side of the sunken road, forming a glacis, along which our troops had to charge, against guns four-ranks deep levelled at them.

Against this naturally magnificently defensible position, strong as Sebastopol and more dangerous to an attacking force, on account of the river in the rear, our troops were hurled, not once, but time and again, during all that dreadful day. French's and Sturgis' Divisions led, and held their ground right under the muzzles of the heavy Confederate batteries; then Hancock's, and then Howard's Divisions each charged more savagely than its predecessor, all holding their ground in front as long as their ammunition lasted.

The sun had set behind the Rebels' position, the crimson-edged clouds of a winter's sunset gleamed luridly through masses of smoke which at times almost obscured the placid sky, so peaceful in its quiet evening tints and so suggestive of the cessation of the day's labors. Not for the long-suffering Army of the Potomac did it indicate repose.

The Rebel fire breaks out with more ferocity than ever, sweeping across the field at the advancing divisions of General Humphreys. Onward, with a forlorn hope, they advance, the ground encumbered by the countless bodies of the fallen comrades; knapsacks, blankets, guns, haversacks, canteens, cartridge boxes, etc., strewed all over the plain; shot, shell and canister, shrapnell and grape are hurled as they approach by columns of regiments led by their officers, and without firing a shot the noble band continues on. General Humphreys dashing ahead to a swell rise in the ground, takes off his hat to cheer on his men; with reckless ardor his men, rapidly closing in on their gallant leader on the double-quick, answer cheer with cheers, Humphreys having two horses shot under him and his staff nearly all dismounted. Here were encountered the troops lying on the ground who had been holding their positions with the bayonet, being out of ammunition. They oppose the advance of their comrades, and use force to prevent the passage of the Division over their prostrate lines, thereby throwing the advancing column into confusion—a confusion which may have prevented this last effort of the army from being successful; for through the smoke the Rebels were seen to be in great confusion.

Humphreys' Division had never been under fire, and would, undoubtedly, have gone to the wall but for this impediment. Military history teems with instances proving that, when receiving its battle baptism, a command composed of such material as this seldom fails to deliver home a charge that is properly led, provided no obstacle other than the fire encountered distracts its attention from its objective and from its leader. But before that awful sheet of flame from the stone wall were enveloped the heads and flanks of the column. In front of that terrific hurricane of bullets no heroism could avail. The very hillside appeared to vomit forth fire, which, with its glare flashing through the fast thickening obscurity, pours upon the storming columns till, being unable to stand against it longer, though within *eighty yards of the wall,* the brave remnant *singing* in the abandonment of its courage, falls back in good order, leaving seven hundred of their comrades lying helpless upon the field.

The people of the South generally, and especially the ladies of the present *new* South, as well as the mothers of the old, do the Northern people and their own children great injustice in clinging to their prejudices against the personnel of the Federal army, and by persistently teaching their children that the motive of the Northern soldier was not inspired by patriotism, but was prompted by the wish to devastate their homes and rob them for mercenary gain. Only a few days ago, in the presence of some Fredericksburg ladies, my face was blanched by one of the company observing flippantly, "The Yankees were simply hirelings and foreigners sent here for pay. They were not *brave* men like our Southern boys. Why," said she, turning to me, "if a few of our men were to pick up guns I reckon you all would run again."

I could only remind her that the "poor white trash" of the South were merely slaves or their white serfs, who were conscripted into their army and heartlessly driven to their deaths by their leaders, who, if they had been successful, would have continued to fight amongst themselves, and treat their masses as "mud sills," of which she might have been one but for the "hirelings."

Some of the purest and noblest blood of the Anglo-Saxon was spilled upon the plains before Marye's Heights as a free sacrifice upon the altar of liberty. At last night came and ended the struggle; the great God of Battles and Commander-in-Chief of all gave the signal to cease firing by covering the Earth with darkness. The mantle of twilight, pinned by the evening star, was dropped upon the terrible scenes. An *aurora borealis* in the Northern sky soon lighted up the scene with its lurid gleams in a manner never to be forgotten. The horrors of that night, the scenes of despair and gradual death upon that bloody ground, in the bitter cold darkness, can not be described. There was no help for the dying. Oh, women of the South, reflect! There were brave men lying on your soil dying unattended, with little children dependent upon them, who, perhaps, were kneeling besides a mother's knee, saying their good-night prayers with a "God bless papa." There were men there whose wives trembled for them: men who had been little children, and whose mothers would have feared to have a cold wind blow upon them. There, they lay on the frozen ground; affection of no avail; not for them the soothing touch, the warm chamber, and the thousand nameless attentions of loving hands.

Wearily, and with faint hope for the morrow, dying, they must stay; their noble efforts idly wasted in a fruitless struggle; but they did not die in vain—in the end they were successful. Some of their bones rest in unknown graves to-day upon the crest of Marye's Heights they charged upon in vain, and they now sleep under the protecting folds of the flag that floats over the National cemetery there.

As illustrating the types of American manhood of which the soldiers who bravely charged upon that fatal day were, I mention a group of half a dozen who recently revisited this ground, along with whom I had the pleasure of spending a couple of delightful days: Senator M. S. Quay was in the line of battle; Captain Wm. R. Jones, well known as the general manager of the extensive Edgar Thompson Steel Company, whose abilities may be expressed most forcibly by his salary of $40,000 per year, was "only a private" in the 133d Pennsylvania Volunteers—Humphreys' Division of this charge; Col. Gray, ex-sheriff of Allegheny county, Pennsylvania; Judge E. A. Monbooth, of Pittsburg, a probable governor for the State, was an adjutant here; Mr. McKenna, of Pittsburg, a well known attorney; Col. Edward Jay Allen, who commanded the 155th Pennsylvania in the charge; Gen. P. H. Allabaugh, our handsome veteran, who may be seen any day at the rotunda of the Capitol in Washington; Capt. H. H. Humphreys, 15th Infantry, U. S. A., a son of the General.

I might add a great many names of men now prominent in the professions and successful in business circles or managing great corporations, who were of the "private hirelings" that survived this battle, and whose best efforts since the war have been devoted to the development of the entire country, North and South.

Captain Jones, a jolly, companionable man, made the trip quite enjoyable through his quaint and original stories of the battle.

I walked at his side over the entire field, and, as he is now dead, I will try to put on record his observations, in his own words or as nearly as may be.

Captain Jones was one of those who find something humorous in even sad scenes. Pointing to a fence along side the road, he remarked:

"You see that panel of fence? That's where I lay down that evening after the charge was over. I saw a couple of other fellers lying there who didn't seem to be at all disturbed by the infernal racket that was going on, so I turned in alongside, thinking it a safe place. I didn't know they were dead men until a posse of ambulance men took hold of me roughly, thinking that I was one of the dead fellers they were ordered to pick up, and were scared half to death when I jumped on them for disturbing my sleep."

Any person who ever met Captain Jones will understand that it would be very funny indeed to undertake to pick him up as a dead man. He would make a very lively corpse under such conditions.

His regiment was on the left of the line, and as we stood together in the little depression which sheltered them while forming, he related some curious expressions and antics of the boys, showing that even in the face of almost sure death, the funny fellows have their last say. One big fellow, with mock heroism, stepped out from the line saying, "Who's afeard! Come on, boys; I'll lead you!" strutted up the little rise where he looked over the top, turned around quickly, and marched back again saying, "I guess not."

Jones says:

"We went along here at a hell-bending trot, and when we came to that fence, the first impulse was to climb over, but it looked as if every fellow that got up on top was knocked off, as if some one had been throwing rocks at a lot of blackbirds—all disappeared at once from the fence—and then every fellow made a rush for the gate. Not one of us had sense enough to knock the fence down; and, of course, the mass of men crowding at the gate gave the Rebels a dead sure chance, and we got hell right there."

He then pointed out the location of the fence that had been there, even to the gate, and in order to fortify his memory, the party accompanied him inside the yard surrounding the little frame cottage, known now as the Stevens house, which stands there yet, precisely as it did during the battle—its weather-board walls literally riddled with bullet-holes.

The owner, Mrs. Martha Stevens, who lived there during the battle, has steadily refused to have any alterations made to her home. Thousands visit it annually, and, perhaps, she reaps a richer harvest from the tourists who usually contribute something by way of compensation for the damage, and for her trouble in explaining it all.

I regret to say that Mrs. Stevens has also passed to the other shore, and as we may all unexpectedly be called there to join that army, I desire to record now for the benefit of others, in a wholly disinterested and truthful way, the *fact*, attested also by visitors of this group, that Mrs. Stevens on this, as well as on every other occasion, asserted positively that the men who made the *last* charge, just before night got the *nearest to the wall.*

As many as *forty dead men were taken from her yard,* which was *beyond* the line of prostrate troops, and within forty yards of the wall.

Mrs. Stevens and others, who were cognizant of the affair at the time, have not hesitated to volunteer this information to any who have called it out. She is not at all boastful, and in no way interested in the matter, being a most uncompromising female Rebel—one of the bitterest in her expressions of hatred to the Yankees to the day of her death. So that the statement comes from her rather as a reluctant confession. She asserts that "the Yankees did get in her yard—piles of the dirty brutes. Of course I couldn't do anything but hide, and the Confederates never came out from the road, so your old miserable Yankees skulked behind the house and hid in the corner. Oh," she added, by way of amendment, "thar warn't nothing to brag about in sneaking into a poor woman's back yard; but they dassent go any farther, and was afraid to show themselves by running back."

In this connection Jones told a funny story at the expense of his own color-bearer. "You know men under fire are like drowning men—they will catch at a straw. Why, we know brave men to stand behind a cornstalk, forgetting, in their excitement, that any such object merely serves as a mark and is no defense. Well, that's why our fellows stayed in this yard. It was, in a sense, untenable, yet these poor devils, no doubt, imagined a board fence a protection from those four lines of muskets right in front.

"Our color-bearer was as brave a man as ever walked. In the charge he got into the yard, and, in order to protect himself and his flag, he and a couple of others shut themselves up in the little outhouse. They were afraid to come out or even to peep out of the door facing toward the Rebels, and they knew nothing of what was going on around them, staying in there in fancied security long after the regiment had been called off the field. Inquiries were, of course, made about the colors, and, as no one could answer, it was supposed that they had been left upon the field. Along in the night, under cover of the darkness, and during the quiet that followed, the boys crawled out and brought their colors safely back.

"The story leaked out, however, and after we got back to our camp over the river, in the days following, at every dress parade, when the colors were ordered to the front, the boys could be seen holding their noses in their fingers, as if the scent of the battle hung around it still."

The Confederates occupying the Heights were of Longstreet's Corps, the troops principally from the extreme South, so that it is difficult to find an old residenter who was in the lines then.

Capt. S. J. Quinn, who is now superintendent of the city water works, was, I believe, a member of Barksdale's Mississippi Brigade, that assisted in preventing the building of the pontoons.

Col. Rufus B. Merchant, the editor and proprietor of the bright little Fredericksburg *Star*, though a native of this part of Virginia, was so eager to get into the war that he enlisted in Cobb's Georgia Legion before his State seceded. Being thoroughly familiar with the country, he was detailed as a scout, and as such served inside our lines during the greater part of the war. He was known as a fearless, daring little man, on whom Longstreet depended largely for reliable information.

Probably there is not now a more popular resident of this old town than Mr. Merchant, and numerous Federal visitors in recent years have testified to his many courtesies and kindnesses. Through the columns of his *Star*, many of the families of Federal soldiers have been able to look up matter of personal war history. The Rebel scout and the Yankee scout, though opposite in politics as well as in temperament, each holding tenaciously to the belief that he was right, are to-day the best of friends. Indeed, I do not know of any one whose friendship I more esteem than that of my little Rebel.

There is generally the best of feeling exhibited between the men of the Northern and Southern armies when they chance to meet. Indeed, it may be safely asserted that the genuine old soldiers of both sides are always friendly in their intercourse. The men who carried guns and used them have now no enmity towards those that, in turn, fired back at them to kill. It is only the latter-day warriors or those who stayed at home that now shoot their mouths off. As there was, comparatively speaking, no stay-at-home in the South, the old ladies do their talking. We can, therefore, allow our old-women soldiers to fight it out with those of the South.

As illustrating this feeling, I tell this true story of a recent experience:

I happened to be in Fredericksburg on Memorial day of 1888, doing some newspaper scouting, of which more anon. One evening, while seated on the hotel pavement, enjoying the delightful weather and eyeing the pretty Virginia girls that do their shopping in town on horseback, I was accosted by two gentlemen wearing the familiar old butternut gray, who quietly intimated that they had been sent to escort me up to their "camp." They declined to give any further information and looked as if they meant business. I saw that it was useless to resist, so nervously accompanied them up a back street with dire apprehensions of a ku-kluxing that the Northern newspaper man was to be subjected to. Into a large room of the town hall we were ushered, introduced to the High Mucky Muck who was sitting on a dais, wearing a Confederate officer's uniform from which dangled the Rebel battle-flag badge.

This gentleman's courteous manner, genial face and warm greeting rather assured me that I was in safe hands, as long as he held the baton. It was Captain Dan Lee, a brother of Governor Fitz-Hugh Lee and a nephew of Gen. R. E. Lee. In a neat little talk, he explained that the members of the M. F. Maury Camp of Confederate Veterans, learning that four Federal soldiers were in town, of which I was one, desired to learn their wishes in the matter of the Confederate camp, offering their united services in assisting the four Federals in decorating the graves of the Federals in the National cemetery on Marye's Heights, and adding that their services were tendered gladly to this end; though they preferred not to be associated with the mob of colored people, who had been in the habit of making a picnic out of the day.

As I had no authority to act for the G. A. R., except in an individual capacity as a comrade of the Kit Carson Post of Washington, I could only express personal gratitude to the camp for their generous offer, which I knew was prompted by the noblest of motives of friendship, loyalty and charity.

Major Birdsall, an ex-Union soldier and the efficient superintendent of the cemetery, being present, accepted the services tendered.

On the morning of that Memorial day—one never to be forgotten, and I would that my poor pen could record it, so that every G. A. R. comrade in the land might become interested—the Fredericksburg Grays, a crack military organization composed of the young men of the town, fitly representing the New South, headed by the brass band of the town, escorted the four solitary Federals to the rendezvous of the Confederates. Here we found eighty-one old Rebels in line to receive us; instead of the guns they used to carry, each had a boquet of beautiful flowers in his hand. We were placed at the head of the little column; Captain Dan Lee, on behalf of some ladies, then presented each Federal with a beautiful boquet of flowers, stating that the ladies of the town had, on this occasion, divided their offerings between the Confederate and Federal cemeteries.

Under command of Captain Lee, we marched out the same old Hanover street, or telegraph road, the band playing patriotic airs, followed by the eighty-one Confederates in gray clothes, armed with bouquets. We followed precisely the same paths our army trod on their way to that terrible battle on that dreadful December day, twenty-five years ago. Reaching the elevation known as Federal Hill, we pass the house Hooker occupied as his headquarters; at this point our troops came in sight of the Confederates and received their baptism of fire; moving slowly down the little declivity, I point out to my companion the spot where Hancock, Humphreys and Couch held their brief consultation before the final charge. We cross the mill-race running through the low ground and go on beyond the depression under which our lines were formed. Passing the point usually designated as "the farthest advance of the Union line," we turn into the "sunken road," marching along it, behind and between the remains of the stone wall, past Mrs. Stevens' house. Right here is erected a solitary stone, the only monument at Fredericksburg which marks the place where General Cobb, of Georgia, was killed. Almost involuntarily, we four Federals follow the example of Captain Lee and lift our caps as we pass it.

Reaching the gate of the Federal cemetery, which is located on the point farthest south or nearest the railroad cut, the band files to one side and plays a solemn dirge as we enter the sacred precincts of the dead. Every Confederate, as he moves in, reverently takes off his hat, uncovering to the light of a bright May sun eighty-one gray-headed and gray-coated noblemen. Great God! what a scene was this. When I look back upon this picture and listen to the war talk of the croaker or politician, who, to get soldiers' votes, may appeal to his former prejudices, I recall this day and regret that all may not have witnessed it as I did; that it was wholly a sincere and disinterested exhibition of genuine good comradeship, goes without saying. There was no other motive, there could be none other than that prompted by genuine good feeling, as nothing was to be gained. Inside the cemetery were assembled a number of ladies of the town. Addresses were made by both Federals and Confederates, and at the conclusion of the services at the rostrum, every grave was decorated — the Confederates and Federals—ladies and children assisting in this pleasant and beautiful task. This cemetery is one of the most beautifully located in the country. From this ground, once occupied as Lee's headquarters, and bristling with Confederate glory, may be had a magnificent panoramic view of the section of country occupied by both armies. Across the river are the Stafford Heights, the ruins of the Phillips House being barely outlined among the trees that have, in late years, grown around its crumbling walls. The Lacey House, freshened up as the residence of a wealthy Northern gentleman, nestles quietly on top of its beautiful green terraces. The "Slaughter-house," now the residence of Judge Souther, of Pennsylvania, on this side the river, while right below it on the bank, may be seen the walls of the Bernard House, where Franklin crossed. Immediately below the cemetery is the railroad cut where so many brave men lost their lives, and directly in front the Irish Brigade charged. It is a singular fact that this very ground on which the Irish charged, was once a corn-field, and during the Irish famine the crop from this identical spot was gathered and loaded aboard a vessel then in the river receiving supplies to be sent to Ireland.

Through the good management of Major Birdsall, this Marye's cemetery is each year becoming more attractive. It is largely patronized by the town people as an attractive resort, and many walk out to its agreeable shades in pleasant weather.

I have previously stated that the number of interments almost equals Arlington. There are buried here 15,273 Union soldiers; of this *number 12,243 are unknown.* In every other respect it excels Arlington—it ought to excel Arlington in general interest to the old soldier of the Army of the Potomac. Those who sleep in this Marye's bivouac *died at the front;* a number of them in battle, or from wounds resulting therefrom, *and are buried on the battle-fields.*

After the war the bones of a number were gathered from the surrounding fields and reinterred at this place. A great many could not be identified, and these sleep sometimes as many as six in one grave, being simply marked "unknown."

Probably every State in the Union is represented in this "unknown army." In a majority of cases, no doubt, they are the remains of young men who were so far from home and their parents and friends were too poor to have their bodies, when identified, lifted and taken to their homes, as was the custom with the more favored. Yet, practically and bluntly speaking, this cemetery is *neglected* by the G. A. R. as an organization. Being in the Department of Virginia, which in the very nature of things is weak in G. A. R. Posts, is no valid excuse for this shameful oversight of years. Undoubtedly the comrades of the Virginia department would gladly accept the tender of assistance from Washington. The three thousand comrades in that district, who, with their families and friends, crowd to Arlington each recurring year to listen to proper tributes from popular orators, and employ bands to play dirges, hire glee clubs to sing requiems, and endure poets, might at least induce their overflow to come to Marye's Heights and put a few flowers on the neglected graves there. It is but an hour and a half ride from Washington and is on this account practically as accessible as is Arlington, as trains will comfortably carry the tourist directly to the field where an afternoon may be most profitably spent in a battle-field.

Through some personal effort in the year following this event, the members of the G. A. R. were stirred up by this correspondent, contributions were solicited by the Richmond Posts to enable them to decorate Marye's Heights; a special train was engaged for the Richmond Posts and comrades, who were met by a number of Washington persons who volunteered their assistance and paid their own expenses. The Commander of Virginia, in making his address said: "The little band under whose auspices these ceremonies are held, these graves garnished with flowers, are only messengers to bring garlands furnished by mothers, sisters and daughters of those friends. All over the country from Maine to California came pouring into our treasury the means necessary for this demonstration of devotion." Though only a year following the voluntary offer of services by the Confederates and the offerings of flowers by the ladies of the town they were forgotten. It is but just to say, however impolitic it may be, as comrades of the G. A. R. who contributed to that end should know it, that the offer of the same Confederates to again assist in this service, was tendered, but for some unexplained reason it was declined. Was this gracious or manly on the part of the Virginia comrades who had previously overlooked Fredericksburg for years? There is no politics in the G. A. R., of course not, but I sometimes imagine that the ungenerous refusal to permit the Confederates to again co-operate in this service, emanated from the fact that there was probably some personal politics underlying it. I am personally a Republican from away back, one who votes with three generations of the family consistently—my father being one of those who voted for the elder Harrison twice, both when defeated and elected—so it will be remembered that I write as a Republican and Union soldier.

CHAPTER VIII.

RELUCTANTLY we are leaving Fredericksburg, the scene of so many bitter and sweet memories. To the old soldier there is a peculiar magnetism about the old town that attracts and holds him here like a loadstone. To the student or the tourist from any country it presents many very interesting features. The invalid also may here enjoy in quiet and comfort the agreeable and exhilarating climate, on what may be termed the foot-hills of the Blue Ridge, far enough in the interior or from the tide-water to avoid the dampness and malaria, but yet, happily convenient enough to the waters to obtain the abundant oysters and fish fresh from the Chesapeake, and to the rich soil to get its products. The manufacturer here will find unequalled water-power supplied from the falls above town, as well as water navigation, enabling the largest vessels to come up to its wharves to bring fuel and carry away the products.

There are a number of mineral springs inside the corporate limits, the most remarkable being that known as "The Gunnery spring," which is located on the battle-ground. A stream of pure cold water, sufficient to supply the entire town, bursts from the rocky hillside and flows in a never-diminishing volume into the neighboring Hazel Run. There are any number of traditions and legends and true stories associated with the numerous glens and romantic nooks hereabouts. It is said of Gunnery spring that any one who ever partakes of its water is fated to return again to the fountain head. A very sweet little girl, with whom I walked down there one moonlight evening, was the Eve who tempted me by proffering the cup, from which I innocently accepted the fatal draught. She is now fully convinced of the truthfulness of the legend and the efficacy of this water.

Perhaps the time may come when this old town, so close to the Capital, may become a Mecca; such as has been made of Gettysburg, and maybe the blood-stained soil may yet produce a crop of monuments that will equal Gettysburg. If each separate deed of heroism done here were marked by a stone, the ground would be a forest of monuments. Who knows—perhaps the Government will, in time, reserve more of this battle-ground as a National park; hotels may spring up around its numerous springs. Here might appropriately be commemorated alike in a commingling of monuments the heroism of both sides.

We linger around the outskirts a little while, driving out to Chancellorsville, about eight miles distant. It was one of my privileges, while in Fredericksburg, to have accompanied Rev. Dr. Smith and Mr. Vess. Chancellor, who were a committee to select the location for a monument to mark the spot on which General "Stonewall" Jackson received his mortal wound. Dr. Smith, who is the popular minister of the Presbyterian Church, is one of the historic characters of this historic place. It was he who contributed the *Century* article on "Jackson's Last Battle," that attracted so much attention. He was the aide on General Jackson's staff, who so gallantly dashed to the front on learning that his General was wounded, finding him on the road near the spot that he pointed out to me, which they decided upon as a proper site for the monument. Though it was a dark night, he recalled the location, because of a slight depression or cut in the road; he remembers having to step up to get off the road. It is the only place in the neighborhood with that distinctive feature. When the terrific shelling from the Union artillery struck down the litter-bearers who were carrying Jackson off the field, the young aide-de-camp threw himself over the prostrate form of his General, with the noble, self-sacrificing intention of shielding him by the interposition of his own person. Our "Major Pastor," as his friends sometimes call him, is a rather quiet, modest little gentleman, whose happy manners, light steps and smooth face rather remind one of a theological student who is at home, glad that school is over. The Doctor is a Northern man by birth and education, his father being one of the early pastors of a large congregation in Greensburg, Pa. He attended school in Pittsburgh, and was graduated at Jefferson College, in Washington, Pa., in the same class with that other Presbyterian soldier, Governor Beaver. He spent most of his time in the South, however, and married an estimable Virginia lady, Agnes, the daughter of Major Lacey, of the well-known Lacey House, opposite Fredericksburg, now the lady president of the Martha Washington Association—Mrs. James Powers Smith.

It will be remembered that in the battle following the one previously described, the Federals crossed in force at United States Ford, above town some miles. The 6th Corps, under Sedgwick, crossed in front of the town in the same manner as before, advanced over the same ground, and, on an early Sunday morning in May, 1863, this Corps *assaulted and captured* Marye's Heights, putting the Confederates to flight. They were pursued out this same road we are driving, making a brave stand at Salem Church, about three miles from town, which bears the marks of the Federal bullets. It is conceded that Lee was surprised and turned out of his position by Hooker's admirable manœuvre. At this time the Confederate army was literally confronted by Hooker's superior force at Chancellorsville, while Sedgwick's magnificent 6th Corps was in his rear. Up to a certain point here Hooker was successful; but then came a most disastrous halt, or hesitancy, of some hours, if not an entire day, which enabled Lee to gather himself up, who then hurled Jackson on the rear of the 11th Corps and demoralized the army, and then turned around and drove Sedgwick's isolated 6th Corps back.

The "explanations" for the disaster would fill a good-sized library, not alone one book, and can not even be outlined in this chapter. Hooker was so confident of success that he telegraphed Mr. Lincoln "I've got Lee in such a tight place that God Almighty can't get him out;" and, by the way, that is the only recognition of God there ever was in his dispatches. Yet within an hour from this time Hooker's magnificent army was defeated. What caused it? Why did Hooker stop when he should have been most energetic? Some say the explosion of a shell incapacitated him. I do not give it as my opinion, but we have heard it whispered that in the headquarters a bottle of whiskey caused the inaction. I make public this report that it may be controverted by those who should know. I would not like to furnish the temperance cranks with such a text for their lectures, but it does seem as if whiskey is responsible for the deaths of a good many of those who touch not, taste not and handle not.

About half a mile beyond the Chancellor House, which is about all there is of Chancellorsville, we found a large quartz rock which Mr. Chancellor and Major Lacey had placed there some years since, as a rough mark to indicate the spot where Jackson fell. This will be recalled by those who have visited the ground since the war. The completed monument stands near where this stone lay. As a matter of fact, however, neither of these stones properly mark the spot where Jackson received his wounds. It is conceded that he received the three balls while riding in the woods, over a quarter of a mile from the place indicated by the monument. He was subsequently carried out in the road and laid on some stone. The object in placing the monument in this location is plainly stated to be:—because it is more convenient to tourists on the roadside than if it were placed in the rather dense wood where Jackson actually received his wound. It approximately marks the spot, the inscription reading: "*Near this spot* General Jackson received his mortal wound." Dr. Smith told me he found Gen. Jackson in the woods shortly after he was wounded, lying upon the ground with his head in Gen. A. P. Hill's lap. At this time it was but a short distance outside of the Confederate lines and if an advance had been made by Federal skirmishers, both Generals, Jackson and Hill, would have become prisoners of the

Federals, probably with numerous others who were attracted to the wounded General.

Major Lacey, who was on the ground as one of the Confederate committee with the Smiths and Mr. Chancellor, the owner of the farm, surprised me by expressing his opinion in a decided manner. "This will do as well as any place near here to put our monument. No one can give us anything at all definite about the exact spot where he was wounded." My interest and curiosity becoming aroused by the observation, and the quiet and tacit manner in which it was received by the other gentlemen of the committee, I availed myself of the first opportunity to interview Major Lacey on the interesting question of the manner of General Jackson's death. Major Lacey is well known as the companion of General Lee during the war. In earlier days he was the proprietor of Chatham, where he lived, which subsequently became universally known in official correspondence as the Lacey House. He was the owner of this vast estate, comprising some 600 acres and 300 slaves; and it is said General Lee courted his wife there. Major Lacey is yet a vigorous man, erect in carriage, and retaining his old-time courteous, but dignified bearing. He now lives at the Wilderness. In his positive manner he continued: "Why, Jackson was shot nearly a half-mile from here, over in the woods there. It was a dark night and he evidently made a miscalculation, both as to his own and the enemy's lines, which was fatal to him and might have been to our army." In reply to the query that naturally comes to every old soldier, "Why should the Lieutenant-General of all that army go, personally, outside his own lines to reconnoiter or locate an enemy's picket-line, in the darkness of a wood at night?" It was not a necessity at all; and, if it had been, we all know from a terrible experience that it is the "common soldier" that is so frequently sacrificed to "feel" an enemy by being pushed forward to "draw his fire." Major Lacey looked at me curiously as he said more hesitatingly: "Of course it was a mistake for Jackson to put his own life in jeopardy and thus imperil his Army." While Dr. Smith and Mr. Chancellor were busy using a tape-line and driving pegs to mark the half-acre selected for the monument site, I endeavored to keep Major Lacey's attention to the question. He is a brilliant conversationalist as well as a writer, who also contributed to the *Century* war papers. Among many other interesting incidents he then related, I repeat in substance his words:

"I never believed Jackson was killed by his own men." This was something entirely new, as I had always supposed, from the general accounts furnished by the Confederates, which no one seemed or cared to dispute, and for that reason generally accepted as true, perhaps, that Jackson was accidentally killed by a volley from his own command.

Pressing Major Lacey for his further opinion, he continued in the same unguarded way, without being corrected by the others: "Well, in the first place, no one can know positively anything about it, as those who were beside Jackson at the time were either killed or died soon after without leaving any testimony on this point. He was taken from his horse and carried over on to this road here; after that, we have only the evidence of those who attended him."

"It is not stated that Jackson himself left any positive evidence of the fire having come from his line?"

"No, I believe not; probably he never once referred to it; though it may be in reply to some suggestion, when in a semi-conscious condition, his answers may have justified such an inference on the part of those who preferred to put such an interpretation upon it. We know the point at which he passed *out* of our lines; and the instructions he left to fire on any noise coming from the direction he was then going is explained on the hypothesis that he intended to return to his lines from another direction."

"But, Major Lacey, wasn't that rather reckless in a general to cut down the bridge he passed over, expecting to be able to pass inside of *his own lines* in safety in the darkness of a night in a dense wood? His own troops would naturally be looking for only enemies coming from that direction, and as our lines were so close that the picket-firing was constant, it was dangerous on all sides and utterly useless."

"Yes, that is all true enough, and the reports say that he had scarcely gotten beyond his lines when firing began in his front. This was probably replied to by some of the Confederate pickets, but the fact is entirely lost sight of, that without exception the Confederate troops who were in front of where Jackson fell, deny most strenuously having fired to the front at that time. In this they were fully substantiated by their officers, in an official investigation." He concluded in an emphatic tone: "There has never been any evidence yet produced to prove that Jackson was shot by his own men, though every effort was made to establish this point."

In mentioning this matter to Dr. Smith at the time, he expressed his dissent from Major Lacey's conclusions and says he is satisfied that Jackson was killed by his own men. In subsequently looking up this question during some time spent in the neighborhood in which I took every occasion to question ex-Confederates, I found that very many prominent Confederates were of the opinion that the shots that wounded their favorite general came from the Union advance, or skirmishers that were in the woods in Jackson's front at that time. I regret that I am prohibited from giving the names of some of the Confederates who entertain this opinion. They naturally dislike to be quoted publicly as antagonizing a popular delusion, that so many of their people innocently cherish. A member of Mumford's Ninth Virginia Cavalry who was on duty on the advance of the Confederate line and saw Jackson go out near his post, voluntarily observed: "Jackson was shot by a fire from the woods in my front, and not from our own line. We were on advance picket post *in front* of North Carolina troops and if the fire had come from them, we should have received it." This is from a well-to-do farmer and a reliable gentleman living in Stafford county, Va. This universal testimony from *Confederates only*, and all of a prominent character, is offered in these War-path papers as serving to correct another historical error. It may be established by this agitation from what regiment or what detail of skirmishers of the Federal troops these shots were fired. It is clearly shown that the Union troops farthest in advance in the woods, a quarter of a mile directly in front of the Chancellor House, and on the same side of the road but back in the woods some distance, fired the volley that deprived the Confederate Army of their greatest chieftain. It may be termed the *fatal shot* or death-wound of the Rebellion. After Jackson's death, the Army of Northern Virginia *never* again won a battle. General Lee took them to Gettysburg and Grant subsequently fought them on nearly this same ground, at the Wilderness and where Sedgwick was killed, and a companion monument to this glorious Union General rests in the shadows of those solemn woods.

Dr. Smith kindly piloted me over the ground occupied by the Confederates during the battle of Chancellorsville. from Salem Church to the forks of the road, where Generals Lee and Jackson held their last counsel, in which was arranged the hazardous flank movement of Jackson's, which resulted in successfully routing the 11th Corps. A question arising amongst the gentlemen of the Confederate Monument committee then present as to the distance Jackson's troops were compelled to march to get around Hooker, Dr. Smith thought it less than ten miles, but he was an aide and had a good horse to do his marching for him; while Captain Lal Taliaferro, then a Lieutenant of the Forty-seventh Infantry of Jackson's Corps, tramped the ground and is positive they marched fully fifteen miles. Dr. Smith's story of this last bivouac of Generals Lee and Jackson, as related to me while we were together on the very ground they occupied, was very interesting. "I was acting as chief of couriers at the time," the Doctor said, as he jumped out of his buggy, "and if you will step over this way we will stand under the identical trees where I found Generals Lee and Jackson sitting on the two boxes, talking earnestly to each other, the light of the little fire beside them weirdly illumining their faces so that none of those who witnessed that scene can ever forget it."

"Doctor, did General Lee originate the flank movement?"

Looking significantly and smilingly at Captain Chancellor and the other gentlemen present, he replied: "That is a disputed question, and I do not care to give my opinion; but it is thought the evidence bears strongest in favor of Jackson, as you will remember General Lee, in his note to Jackson, received after his wound, gave him the credit for the victory."

The Doctor, walking toward the road, pointing to a woods on the right, continued: "There was a battery of yours down there some place that kept up a desultory shelling all day. It annoyed General Jackson strangely; for some reason he kept sending his aides out, as fast as they reported to him, to locate it. It fell to my lot to ride over into the thicket to try to find out where those shells came from; but on account of the density of the growth I could not get through there, so I rode around to the other road, and it so happened that I did not get back until late that night. It was then that I found the two Generals under the trees there in private consultation; I did not intrude myself; being very tired, I lay down for a little rest, intending to report to Jackson when he had separated from Lee. I soon fell asleep, and when I awoke the apparition of the two Generals had disappeared, as if I had dreamed it as I slept there.

"I roused myself, looked about me, but could not see Jackson; finding upon inquiry that he was lying down near by, I quietly crept up to him, not desiring to disturb him if asleep. I found him lying on a blanket, his head resting on a saddle. My approach seemed to rouse him, and, noticing him move, I spoke gently, simply announcing my return. Calling me up to him," and here the Doctor's eyes filled with tears, his voice tremulous with emotion as he continued: "the General bade me sit down by him, putting his arms about me, and drawing me to him, as if I were his own boy, he said, kindly: 'It's too bad that all you boys allowed that battery to annoy your old General so much.' He asked a few questions as to my work during the evening, and in a most feeling manner, bade me good-night, without saying a word of to-morrow. I left him and lay down myself near by, sleeping soundly until awakened late in the morning by the clinking and clattering of canteens and arms, and the hushed voices of the troops of Jackson's Corps, who were filing down this furnace road to the left, on their way to the great flank attack that was soon to be delivered on the rear of the 11th Corps. General Jackson had disappeared, and when I next saw him it was after he was wounded."

I could not help thinking to myself that the services of one good scout, that Hooker so indifferently regarded, could easily have discovered and reported that stragetic movement in time to have prevented the disaster that followed. I do not mention it egotistically, but it has *often* occurred to me that the *neglected* scout *has* done service alone equal to that of an army corps, the generals appropriating all the credit, as due to their "strategy." This re-opening of the wounds, in discussing the manner of Jackson's death is not agreeable; it is prompted by a very general interest in that distinguished Confederate chieftain, whom General Grant has referred to as the "Havelock of the Confederacy." Perhaps a better comparison may be made with the late English General Gordon. For some unaccountable reason the Southern people generally, and of course their historians, prefer to have the statement remain undisputed that Jackson was killed by accidental fire from his own troops. The significant feature about any attempted discussion of Jackson's death, is that, with singular unanimity, the intelligent Confederates desire to avoid any agitation of this matter. This over-cautious manner impressed itself so strikingly on my mind, that it served to arouse my curiosity, and I began to wonder if there might be anything to conceal on the part of Confederates about the death of their great chieftain.

During a stay of some six weeks in Fredericksburg, I came in pleasant contact with a number of ex-Confederates, and I took every occasion to broach the subject, and nearly all conversation tended to corroborate the statement of the fatal shot having come from the Federals. In a word, the testimony of Confederates may be summed up as follows: "I wouldn't for the world have any one know that I said so, but, confidentially, I always believed that Jackson was killed by your men." There are many Virginians, of course, who doggedly insist that the North Carolinians killed their general because he had ordered them to fire on *any one coming to their front.* My breath was almost taken by the surprise occasioned upon receiving instructions as a newspaper scout to investigate some rumors that "*Stonewall*" *Jackson committed* suicide by deliberately placing himself between the two fires, in the manner already described. This was a new idea. The question is an important one in some respects. It will be seen that historians have been in error as to the manner of Jackson's death. There seems, therefore, a possibility for the suspicion that the cause of his death may not yet have been properly explained. I wish it distinctly understood that, in recording this matter, I am in no sense ventilating my own personal opinions, nor flying any decisions. As a matter of fact, I am strongly prejudiced against the theory of Jackson having wilfully and deliberately courted death. All know that Jackson was a conscientious and devout Christian believer, yea, almost a religious fanatic, and no one will for a moment believe that he would, with his own hand, have committed such an act. I desire to present some facts wholly from Confederate sources of a most reliable character, so that each may form his own conclusions. The first question that naturally arises in the mind of everyone will be as to the motive that would induce a popular and successful general to commit such an act.

There is a great deal of the inside history of the Confederate States that has not been permitted to come to light. They were not a band of brothers fighting for their homes during the war—though they are "solid" for each other since—but had pretty much of the same sort of bickerings, intrigues and jealousies amongst themselves that were popularly supposed to exist only in our armies, or between the army and the War Department. Jefferson Davis and his Jewish Secretary of War were probably as severe in some directions as was Mr. Stanton. It is pretty well known that there was a great deal of friction and bitter personal feeling between the extreme Southern soldiers and Virginia "Yankees," as they termed Virginia Confederates. This was intensified among the higher army officers. There was great jealousy on the part of some distinguished Georgia generals regarding the Virginia generals, and especially "Stonewall" Jackson. When in Richmond I saw an autograph letter from "Stonewall" Jackson, addressed to Governor Letcher, of Virginia, asking—yes, demanding—to be relieved of his command and returned to the Virginia Military Institute.

A satisfactory explanation of Jackson's putting himself deliberately between two fires on a dark night has not yet been given, except upon the impossible hypothesis that he did not know what he was about. It may be asked if he courted death, why did he not satisfy himself at the head of his troops leading a charge? The answer would be that he would shrink from such an attempt to dramatically end his military career, besides his conscientious scruples would not permit him to slaughter any of his own men in such a vain attempt at seeking glory for himself.

Another feature not fairly understood is that Jackson's wounds were not necessarily fatal. He received two shots on one arm and a slight flesh wound on the hand of the other arm. That was all. *He did not die from the effects of his wounds*, but against the well-known advice of his surgeon; and in the absence of the latter, he again deliberately exposed himself to almost certain death, aggravating his condition by compelling a negro servant to wet a blanket in cold water and lay it over him. This deliberate act was more fatal than the wounds received by his former exposure, and caused his death from pleurisy. It is said he was semi-conscious shortly before his death; Dr. Smith, who was with him, reports his last words: "Let us cross over the river and rest under those trees."

As indicating some of Gen. Jackson's movements immediately preceding his death, I will quote only the observations of distinguished Confederates. Perhaps one of the most popular citizens of Spottsylvania Co., Va., is Mr. John Hayden, familiarly known in that county as "Uncle Jack." He is a well-to-do old Virginia farmer, whose jolly greeting and hearty welcome to Federal visitors to Fredericksburg has endeared him to many of the Yankees, as he still calls everybody who hails from north of Mason and Dixon's line. He is one of the most interesting war relics and valuable witnesses in the discussion of war matters occurring in this vicinity. It was on his farm, located on the south side of United States ford, that our army bivouaced, after crossing the Rappahannock. His name has not heretofore appeared in any of the histories of the war, but it is doubtful if any one person, outside of Lee and Jackson themselves, bore so important a part in the movement that brought about our defeat at Chancellorsville, as did Uncle Jack. He was Jackson's guide, as well as the trusted pilot of General Lee. He was born and raised on the farm adjoining Chancellorsville, and as he says in reply to a question as to his familiarity with the country: "Yes, sah, when I was a boy I hunted deer in them woods, and I know every hog path in the country." He is one of those old-fashioned, honest-speaking men whose blunt, straight-forward words would tell before a jury. When I jokingly observed before a crowd of Federal visitors that it was his fault that we were whipped at Chancellorsville, because he showed Jackson around the back way and caught the 11th Corps napping, and suggested to some of the boys that he ought to be hung yet for it, he thumped me on the shoulders, spread his legs, and protruded his bay-window belly: "I have done the very best I could, sah, agin you all, but we didn't catch you all napping; they was cooking dinner; they had their guns all pointed the other way, so we went in the back gate, sah." When I threatened to put his photograph in a book with an account of his being the man who stampeded the 11th Corps and was responsible for killing so many Yankees, he retorted with emphasis: "I never killed nary a one, they all run away, but I will kill *one* if you tell any Yankee lies on me in a book; now, sah, jist you mind that." Uncle Jack says of Jackson the day preceding the battle:

"General Jackson sent for me that mawning and when I got to his tent he was off some place but had left orders for me to wait. The little man never forgot his engagements."

"Was Jackson little? Why, I always thought him a big, lank man."

"Well, you Yankees all thought him a giant, I reckon, but he was no bigger than you are, and you are a mighty trifling-looking Yankee too. Well, when the General came back I was surprised to see him all dressed up in his full uniform. I had seen Jackson often, but this is the only time that I ever saw him wearing his full uniform, and I thought it mighty queer, and some of the rest of them was talking about something going to happen. He told me he wanted me to watch that ford by the road, and to be sure and report to him if the enemy made an appearance at a certain point. He then asked me how many cavalrymen I wanted to carry the news. I told him two would do. 'No,' he says, 'I want you to send two couriers,' as he called them, 'every hour to report direct to me. I will give you twelve men subject to your orders,' and he did. After the General had finished his talking to me I turned to come away, but I began to think it so queer about his being all dressed up that way that I turned back and said to him in a familiar plain way—something I would never have thought of doing if I had not been sort of impressed by his appearance: 'General Jackson, you have given me my orders and now I am going to give you yours.' He was just getting on his horse and had one boot in the stirrup. He looked sort of funny at me as he put his foot down and turned to me, expecting, I reckon, that I had something important to say. I was scared, but bound to go ahead, and said simply, but I reckon he saw I meant it kindly: 'General, you must take care of yourself to-day.' He reached out his hand and thanked me without saying another word, and in a moment more was on his horse and rode off, and I never saw him again. I always thought he knew he was going to die then." Mr. Hayden is a man of unimpeachable character, who is easily accessible to the visitors to Fredericksburg, and will confirm this statement and perhaps give further interesting information about Jackson's last battle. I may be permitted, as a Union scout, to observe here, that to the Confederate scouts and guides—and they were numerous and zealous—is due much of the glory achieved by Lee and Jackson on Virginia soil. This one man was as valuable as an army corps of observation. All their natives became guides and scouts and worked in comparative security in their own country. As a Union scout, I, for one, worked *alone* among strangers in a strange land and among enemies.

I can not close this lecture on "Stonewall" Jackson, without submitting the testimony of another distinguished ex-Confederate, bearing on Jackson's earlier views of his own end and that of the war. Professor R. S. Dabney, of the University of Texas at Austin, says: "During the Valley campaign and that around Richmond in 1862 I was General Jackson's Chief-of-staff. His prudent reserve was noted; it was such that he never disclosed anything of his own military designs except the necessary orders to his Chief-of-staff, or even to his Major-General next in command, and he was chary of expressing to them his thoughts on the general conduct of the war. I was selected, not by myself—not having taken up the faintest idea of such an attempt—but by General Jackson's family, to write his biography. I sought the help of all suitable documents which the family possessed. All help which was allowed me I employed diligently and faithfully. It scarcely need be said that I am not responsible *for such as were withheld.* On the 18th day of May, 1862, I was riding alone with the General along the valley of Mossy Creek in Augusta county, to visit the bivouac of the famous Twelfth Georgia regiment in our front. He was, what was rare with him, in the mood to converse with me. Our thoughts traveled naturally upon the prospect of our struggle. Encouraged by him, I expressed my own conclusions with the unreserve perhaps of indiscretion of one of those citizen soldiers whom Jackson thought so well of; I said that the manner adopted by the Confederate government for conducting the war, filled me with apprehension. The Government, dominated by the technicalities of West Point and of professional soldiering, seemed to forget what was needed in a revolutionary war such as ours. They were relying upon routine methods good for standing mercenary armies, but inappropriate to our circumstances. In this species of tactics the enemy's superior numbers and riches, backed by Europe, would in the end beat us. The longer the catastrophe of war was delayed the more we should lose of the martial spirit of our gentry and yeomanry; mere drill carried to completeness would replace their *élan;* that a defensive war would be sure to wear us out and crush us in the end. He replied by reminding me of how much had been done by the Confederate government in the first year in creating resources and armies, spoke of the victories already gained, hopefully, and of the kindness of the good Providence in which he believed. I proceeded to further argue my apprehensions, when he turned himself toward me in the saddle and said with a smile, more sad than cheerful: 'Stop, Major Dabney, you make me low spirited.' I of course ceased, with an apology for my insistance. After riding in silence for twenty paces he said with an air and a tone of profound seriousness: 'Well, I do not profess any romantic sentiments as to the vanity of life. Certainly no man has more that should make life dear to him than I have in the relations and affection of my home, *but I do not desire* to survive the independence of my country.'"

CHAPTER IX.

WE will drive into Washington via Manassas. The trains coming up from the South several times a day would take us direct from Fredericksburg to Washington in less than two hours, but we shall be all day on the road. It will be remembered that during the war, and for some years subsequent, the railroad only extended to the Potomac ten or twelve miles beyond, where transfers were made to the boats, at Aquia creek.

Now, the abandoned roadbed from Brooks Station to Aquia is used as a wagon road. Nearly all the soldiers were camped convenient to this line of road, upon which we depended for supplies; and, by the way, in all the voluminous war literature, scarcely any mention is made of the military railroaders, one of the most important auxiliaries to the armies. The value of their services in connection with our military movements is indisputable. But there is no record in the archives of the country of their indispensable aid, except, perhaps, such as may be found occasionally in the beggarly mention in the official reports of the generals who profited by the hard-working and ever-faithful civilian railroader.

These gentlemen do not even have the satisfaction of having their names on record with those who served their country in time of need.

As a rule, the survivors of the military railroaders and

telegraphers have become gentlemen of prominence since the war, and, in a large manner, represent the officials of the two great interests, *i. e.*, railroads and telegraphs. Indeed, to attempt to name them would be like reproducing an official railway and telegraph directory.

There is probably not a railroad or telegraph company that does not contain on its roll of employés some of these war workers. If an engineer, conductor, brakeman or bridge-builder is occasionally met whose head is silvered with gray, it is pretty safe to assume that he served on some of the military railways during the war.

If you question such an "old man," it is probable that he can tell you more correctly about the movements in the field of certain troops than the soldiers who served in the ranks.

He will tell you that they rebuilt the roads as fast as the enemy destroyed them.

It is a truth well known to soldiers in the field that the whistle of a locomotive was one of the most agreeable "sounds from home"—it either brought us more reinforcements, letters, s. o. b., or perhaps carried off the dead.

It should be remembered that the very first persons to respond to the call of Mr. Lincoln was not the Massachusetts regiment, as is stated in history, but Col. Thomas A. Scott, of the Pennsylvania railroad, with his corps of railroaders, who *rebuilt* the Baltimore and Ohio railroad, which had been destroyed by the Rebels, and *operated it*, as a government institution, upon which were carried, not only the first, but all the troops that came to Washington. *These* gentlemen are not eligible to comradeship in the G. A. R., they are not accorded even associate or honory membership in that organization as are Women's Relief Corps, etc.; while mule-whackers, hospital pimps, servants, etc., who happened to be sworn in some place, so they would be entitled to bounty or substitute money, may become leaders in the G. A. R. But my purpose is not to discuss the question here, simply desiring to call attention to the neglect. Wonder grows into amazement that such continuous service during all the trying times of the war, night and day, cold or wet, of these men, often working in the front and under fire, should have been so long unrecognized. "Are Republics ungrateful?"

Our route takes us through Falmouth, which, by the way, looks precisely as old and dilapidated as during the war. This is one of the earliest Virginia settlements, was at one time a port of entry at the head of navigation, just below the falls of the Rappahannock. Vessels of considerable draught were here loaded with tobacco which was the staple crop of this section.

Every one who has traveled this road will remember the hill just back of Falmouth, from which the first view is had of the distant steeples of Fredericksburg, and the Marye's Heights in the background.

Certainly none of the survivors of the army who marched along this road with Burnside on that dreary November morning of 1862 will forget the scene.

I will not attempt a pen description of it. On this buggy ride, I was accompanied by an accomplished young artist, Mr. Willie Hazard, of Fredericksburg, who "sketched" points as I desired, with pencil, while I "sketched" others by taking observations through the lens of my camera. I believe that I have already confessed to being an amature photo crank.

From this point we obtained several fine views that almost any soldier who has been there will recognize. It was the original purpose to include these sketches as illustrations; but, finding it impracticable, from their great number and variety, I have collected them into a portfolio or sketch-book of War-path views. If any member of the club should desire any of these, they can be supplied separately.

The morning of our departure for Gettysburg happened to occur on the same date on which the Headquarters Army of the Potomac started, when this country was a quarter of a century younger. I rode on that occasion with the staff, and in this drive endeavored to follow, if possible, precisely the same path we traveled then over which I am now attempting to act as your guide.

As long as we kept to the public highway it was plain sailing; but in attempting to find short cuts to Germania, United States, Beverly, and other once-familiar fords on the Upper Rappahannock, we invariably got lost and became tangled up, under our feet as well as in our recollection, by the new and almost dense growth of young pines and scrub oak which has sprung up to replace that which our troops cut down for corduroy roads, fuel, or, perhaps, as a clearing for artillery. The oldest inhabitant of Prince William and Stafford, which are the counties we are now traversing, account for the general poverty of the soil as well as that of the very few farmers that occupy it, by the explanation that the early cultivation of tobacco in this section robbed it of its strength. The weed was extensively raised in all this region as long ago as fifty years to the exclusion of most everything else.

Slaves were, of course, the only labor employed, and it is said that the vessels that ascended the Rappahannock to Falmouth, or the Potomac to Dunfries and Alexandria, brought *all* the supplies for these plantations and took off the entire product. Nothing being done to fertilize or feed the soil, it was, when exhausted, abandoned and new fields opened up, which, by the way, is "looking backward" to the days of free trade.

Wherever pine or cedar trees are growing now is said to indicate that the ground so covered was at one time a tobacco plantation. So that it will be seen that the cavaliers themselves first outraged the virgin soil of fair Virginia that has since been devastated by the tread of the armies.

Slavery and tobacco were the greater curse. An old soldier whom I met walking disconsolately over the Stafford hills, looking around as if he were hunting some landmarks or stakes, pointed to what looked as if it might have once been a cellar under a log house, told this story about it: "No, it's not a cellar, but it was once intended as a powder magazine or a storehouse for ammunition for the reserve artillery packed down there.

"It was a sort of dug-out on the hillside, lined with logs and roofed with the same; over this was thrown about a foot of dirt, then sodded; a little box pipe about four by six, looking like a chimney, was run through as a ventilator. At one gable was the entrance, protected by *two* heavy doors, allowing a sort of vestibule between them. These were, of course, strongly barred and locked. The whole affair was as strong as logs and earthwork could make it, not only fire-proof, but bomb-proof, and supposed to be burglar-proof and soldier-proof, yet I can prove to you that a couple of us got a barrel of whisky out of it one night without opening the doors at all." This looks like an interesting puzzle that I'd like the club to propound to any old soldier who ever saw a bomb-proof. "Well," he continued, "they found it was too damp for the storage of ammunition, so permission was given to the head sutler to use it as a storehouse for his supplies. You know the boys *would* steal from the sutlers; in fact, they would openly *raid* them for whisky, and it was thought this bomb-proof would be an absolute protection, with its long roofs and double doors and locks and bolts. Well, one day a couple of us were helping the sutler to store his goods in here; among the rest was a barrel of whisky, branded 'vinegar.' We were *wild* for a chance at that 'vinegar' barrel; but, of course, it seemed like barring us out forever to have it rolled in to this cave; we knew the officers would soon use it up. There being no light at all, except from the open door, the little hole through the ventilator significantly cast a ray of light, and at the same time of hope, by its little reflection on the ground below. It gave me an idea. Without even telling my chums that I had been struck by an idea, I managed in the general handling of the stuff to have that barrel of vinegar set on end over the spot where the light was shown and directly under the little ventilator. When we finished our work, the doors were both closed, locked and bolted, and the boss sutler put the key in his pocket, went off with a feeling of perfect confidence in the safety of his goods.

"The 'idea,' however, began to work on me; and, at the first opportunity, I explained my plan of attack to two or three comrades. We got a piece of light rope, and stole an elongated rifled eight-pound shell from the ammunition chest. The rope was tied to it like a sinker, so that the percussion cap faced up.

"After dark one of the boys was put on guard to prevent a surprise, another climbed to the apex of the little mound of a roof, knocked off the broad cap over the ventilator, let down his shell as a feeler for the barrel and being satisfied that it was plumb under him, it was drawn to the top again and *dropped onto the head of the barrel of vinegar*."

"Great Scott," said I, "What if the percussion end had gone down first?"

"Why, it was a bomb-proof, wasn't it?"

That was so.

"Well, we let that thing pound away till finally she went through the head, into the *vinegar* Then the *shell* was withdrawn and in its place we substituted a big horse sponge; to the bottom of this we loaded some small shot, as sinkers; this was let down into the *vinegar*, drawn up and squeezed out into a bucket, and so on till we got so drunk that it was given away, and others got onto it; so the whisky was extracted from that barrel without opening the door. If the boys had not become so hilarious, they never would have found out how it was done, either."

It would be difficult to find in Virginia a more uninteresting and tiresome drive than that which we are following, over what is termed the "hill-road," between Falmouth and Manassas. The country is poor in every respect, sparsely populated by a class of small farmers that the traveler might imagine to be the remnants of what we have heard the Southern people call, "Poor Whites." The few fences and buildings show a neglected, almost abandoned, appearance; no attempt is made to keep the roads in repair, as there is but little use of it, the people seldom going away from their homes, as we judged by their general ignorance as to where the roads that passed their doors led. No correct idea of distance could be gained by inquiries, as we soon learned by the contradictory answers we received. We amused ourselves, however, by interviewing every person we came across as to the distance to Manassas, merely as a study of the effects such isolation might show on the minds of the different types of character we encountered. In not a single instance did any two of a large number we questioned, agree, the differences in most instances being so great as to stagger a stranger not familiar with their primitive methods of computing distances from other worlds they have heard of.

In bad weather the roads become almost impassable, so that, in one sense, the length of a journey depended on the time of the year it was begun.

The old soldiers who footed it along here during all seasons and sleeping in pup-tents at night, and for days carrying in their haversacks an assortment of family groceries in the shape of four days' rations, and on their shoulders a gun that would get as heavy as a cannon, retain a lively recollection of the cohesive tendency of this sacred soil. Those were times that tried men's "soles."

The Virginia mud was as great a factor in the favor of the Confederates as an army corps, they being on the defensive remained comparatively passive, while we were obliged to make all the movements. It is well-known that many golden opportunities were lost because of the mud that held us fast in its miry grip, or made the attempted movement so difficult that they were easily in position to check-mate it.

Not even the "Army of Observation" of Lee, comprising the numerous men, women and children, amongst whom we lived and moved and had our being, were more beneficial to the Confederates than the tenacious Virginia mud. Burnside's stick-in-the-mud campaign is only one instance of its efficiency.

My artist companion succeeded in "catching" on his sketch-book several "types," but these represent your guide as interlocutor in such ludicrous poses that they are not offered for exhibition, though very funny.

Like most artists, Mr. Hazard sang well; after I discovered this accomplishment, the remainder of the tiresome journey was made pleasant. We sang not only "the songs we used to sing," but I believe we tried everything that we had ever heard.

Our repertoire was quite extensive; the free matinee the country people along the road had that day no doubt astonished them. We made Rome howl sure enough, our only audience the lonely trees and the old hills which indeed applauded us to the very echo.

Probably there is nothing that will so quickly awaken the bitter sweet memories of old soldiers, that now slumber, as to hear some of the old songs at such a place. I wish I might put the scene before you while the ladies sing

> "How cruelly sweet are the echoes that start
> When memory plays an old tune on the heart."

In these latter days an immense deal of "war music" is thrust upon an undiscriminating public at the G. A. R. gatherings and reunions, as "patriotic army songs" that we used to sing. No person can appreciate music of all kinds more than myself; but the insufferable "rot" dealt out to veterans in the shape of war poetry set to music, is calculated to spoil even an appetite for the "army bean" song. There are any number of so-called battle hymns, and the "flag" is smeared all over with doggerel. I would like to ask any genuine soldier if he ever heard a battle song at the front. I am sure that I never did, though we listened to a great deal of really fine music from gifted comrades in camp or on the march. .

The recollected music of those unforgotten days was not generally of the patriotic character one would imagine from the slush we hear now-a-days. It was rather comic than sad, and of a sentimental character not at all patriotic. The music most familiar to the old soldier was the love songs of that day.

"We sang of love, and not of fame,
Forgot our country's glory;
Each heart recalled a different name,
But we all sang 'Annie Laurie.'

"Voice after voice took up the strain,
Until its tender passion
Rolled like an anthem o'er the plain
Our battle-eve confession."

"Mother, is the Battle Over?" seems like a parody to me, and I am sure the person who wrote "Let me Kiss Him for his Mother" never saw a dead soldier, or he would never have expressed any such desire in poetry and music.

"When this Cruel War is Over" was a popular song in camp; while "John Brown's Body" was sung by the Zoo Zoo regiments, as we used to call zouaves on their fancy parade, when they first came out.

In camp, lying upon the frozen ground or snow, wrapped in a blanket, looking through the leafless trees at a clear sky and a Southern moon, knowing that an army of Rebels were our bed-fellows, and not knowing what to-morrow would bring forth, is a realistic as well as an effective scene for a stage setting; a manly voice ringing out from a blanket the air and words of that beautiful old song, "Ever of thee fondly I'm dreaming." Many that listened to it dreamed, perhaps, for the last time, of the "gentle voice." The tones had scarcely died away, when the bass voice of a soldier who, though some distance off, had heard the other song broke the heavy stillness that followed by responding with that other pretty old war song, "No one to love, none to caress," another song, "Mary of Argyle," and so on through the list of the old songs, that are yet more sweet to the veteran than the new ones.

I knew a staff officer to be shot from his horse by guerillas, which infested this country during the war, while riding along leisurely and in supposed security singing "Happy, O happy be thy dreams."

We became so much infatuated with our own music that we let the old horse have his own way, and followed the "main road" until we "found" ourselves "lost" in a pine woods. Because of our unsatisfactory experience with the natives in getting directions, we had determined not to ask another question, but, hoping we were right, we would go ahead and trust to luck and the horse's legs to get us "some place" before night. We had serenaded several houses as we passed along, without halting for the usual quizzing. It was getting late in the afternoon when, coming up to a house where I had espied a young lady, I thought it advisable to jump out and make some inquiries as to the road. Saying to my companion, "I'll bet a dollar they send us off our road," I lifted my hat in the most approved dudish style, smiled a seductive smile, and, in a voice full of tenderness and beer, asked the distance to Manassas. "It's about twenty miles from here, sah," said she. It was but twenty-seven when we started, and we had been going steadily nearly all day, but I thought the Virginia miles awfully long, and made some observation to this effect; but, my companion being a famous lady's man, discovering me in conversation with a lady, at once jumped from the buggy to get a drink of water, as he said. His black hair and pretty brown eyes so attracted the attention of the lady, no reply was made to me. Just then we were further embarrassed by the old horse walking off, and as it was Hazard's fault and his legs were the longest, he had the race, while we laughed.

The fun was spoiled, however, by the intelligence subsequently gained that we had been singing along the wrong road all afternoon, and were at that time nearer to Mount Vernon on the Potomac than we were to Manassas. Instead of keeping almost due north, we had veered over to the right and left the Manassas road.

Hazard wanted to stop right there all night, but I was determined to get to the battle-field. After some confusing directions, we started back on a short-cut road through pine woods, that had been made by men hauling ties out. It was not intended for a top-buggy at all, and we were in such a hurry to get on to the battle-field that we could not prevent the overhanging limbs from tearing the top of the buggy.

About sundown we came to an opening that gave us a beautiful view in the distance of the Bull Run Mountains, outlining Thoroughfare Gap, that I at once recognized. Driving along rapidly we reached Catlitt's Station, which will be remembered by the old soldiers; this was not the point we intended to reach, we were yet quite a ways from Manassas, but we felt, in getting near a railroad track once more, we were at least within the bounds of civilization.

We got a view of Catlitt's precisely as it looked during the war, as also a sketch of the point where "Jeb" Stuart captured John Pope's headquarters camp. It will be remembered his headquarters were supposed to be in the saddle, yet the Rebs, soon after he issued this order, came into posession of his real headquarters, tents, camp and garrison equipage, as well as some important papers.

Through this neighborhood there are some fairly good farming lands and our ears were made glad by the busy hum of the mowing machines and the occasional whistle of the locomotive.

General Grant advanced along this line to the Rapidan, and here again the services of the railroaders were brought into requisition, the railroads being operated by them from Alexandria, along which were transported all the supplies for Grant's immense army.

When it is remembered that this is the region infested by Mosby's guerillas, the services will be more highly appreciated. Of course military protection was offered, but one who has gone into a country through which an army has passed, will understand that this rear with its light protection was more dangerous than the front, guerillas being so very uncertain, both as to their first movements and their subsequent methods.

We hugged the railroad tracks as closely in this drive as we would have done when Mosby was around, passing over much historic ground after dark, reaching the hotel at Manassas about midnight.

When we had explained our route to the landlord, he observed that we had traveled about 60 miles since morning and he thought the horse needed a rest; he didn't express any sympathy for the two tired travelers. We went to bed supperless and very hungry.

There is much of interest about this part of the country. The railroad leading from Alexandria through Manassas, on to the valley of Virginia, over the Rapidan, Brandy Station, etc., is, in a way, another and a distinct war-track that crosses our war-path at right angles.

I should love to take the club along its historic route to Brandy Station—the great cavalry battle-field of the war—or guide you over Stoneman's great cavalry raid to the very gates of Richmond. Perhaps at another time we may be able to make such a trip, following Grant's path into Richmond, via Wilderness, Spottsylvania, Cold Harbor and Petersburg to Appomattox.

Manassas has been so very thoroughly described that we can mark it off as a back date, and hastily skim over its historic plains by a fast Pullman vestibule train into Washington City, to spend an evening and to get supplies for the further trip necessary for the "more-out-of-the-way" paths to Gettysburg that we shall follow.

While waiting for the train which will carry us to the Capital in less than an hour for less than a dollar, we can walk, promenade the long platform of the neat summer hotel alongside the tracks. Just down the track on the top of the little cut is the remains of the *first* earthwork *of the war*, erected by Beauregard to protect some guns bearing along the railroad tracks.

Fort Beauregard is on a hill on the other side of the town and there are some earthworks back of the hotel. During the war when I was in here on a Union scout, the only "town" consisted of the tumble-down railway depot. It has entirely disappeared. In the place of the army that thickly populated the surrounding plains, there has grown a neat little inland town, well supplied with churches, schools, stores and railway conveniences. It more closely resembles a western town, however, than a Virginia settlement. Around the neat station-house are piled, ready for the next coming trains, a jumble of large tin milk-cans. One of the industries of the place is supplying milk daily to Washington City.

I was fortunate in meeting here a former army comrade, Capt. Geo. C. Round, who married a most estimable lady and has resided here since the war. They most kindly entertained us at their comfortable home on the outskirts.

If any of the club should ever visit the place from Washington, Captain Round will be a most competent guide. He has made a study of the field and through his assistance we were able to obtain a complete set of the best views.

As previously mentioned, we have struck the trial of Braddock, who passed through here guided by Washington on the war path to Fort Pitt.

We will return to this neighborhood from Washington en route to Gettysburg.

In running into Washington from Manassas, we are following literally in the war path of our troops; though the trains make a little better time than our fellows did from First Bull Run. Subsequently, when the Army of the Potomac passed through here from Fredericksburg, en route to Gettysburg, as we are now traveling, I rode with the staff. General Hooker, then commanding the army, had established his temporary headquarters near here at Fairfax Court-house, or "Coat-ous," as they pronounce it I was sent into the city by train as a bearer of dispatches, carrying along with me an immense mail for the quartermaster and paymaster's office, which I was ordered to deliver personally and procure receipts. You know in army routine they both give receipts and take receipts in triplicate for everything. While we are gliding along comfortably seated in our parlor car, permit me to digress a little in the interests of the telegraphers of the war. The editor of the organ of the telegraphers says:

"A large number of gentlemen of more or less influence have made it one of the objects of their lives to persuade the United States Government to recognize the military telegraphers who gave such efficient service to the country when it needed that peculiar service. To them it has seemed criminal for the Government to refuse this recognition. The trivial reasons assigned by those in authority against the measure are unlike what should be the utterances of a Republic to its faithful sons. But the question has been often asked, why did not the military telegraphers, when actively engaged in behalf of the Government, compel it to recognize them, when their services were needed and praised by the people of the entire country? We are in receipt of the following letter bearing upon this point, which will be read and considered with much interest by all telegraphers:

"WASHINGTON, D. C., Aug. 30, 1889.

"J. B. TALTAVALL. *My Dear Sir:* I did not notice in the *Age* until too late that the military telegraphers were to hold this year's reunion in Philadelphia, or I should have been present. During the war I went in as a scout, tapping Rebel wires, etc. For this service I obtained a commission in the Signal Corps from President Lincoln. General Eckert, who was then in the War Department, objected to any of the operators being commissioned. He represented to Secretary Stanton that all the force would join the Signal Corps, and to prevent a strike General Eckert had Stanton issue an order prohibiting any telegrapher from being commissioned. It so happened that in my papers in the War Department in the descriptive list, under the head of occupation, I was set down as an 'operator.' That one word gave me a heap of trouble in those days. General Eckert brought Secretary Stanton's clerk's attention to it, and, in obedience to his order, a long red mark was made over my name—in a word, I was debarred and prevented, for the time being, from promotion for 'gallant and meritorious' services. My friends, J. W. Forney, ex-President Johnson and others took the matter in hand. Representations were made to Secretary Stanton that the subject would be discussed in the Senate when the question of other confirmations came up. Secretary Stanton was induced to make an exception, and my name went in. I was commissioned second lieutenant in the regular army, and President Lincoln had it dated back a year. I served to the end in the field as a scout, etc. I am writing all this to say that there is an inside history to the military telegraph corps that needs ventilation. It will be hard on General Eckert, but the truth must be told, and it will show that *he* is responsible for the present anomalous position of telegraphers who served faithfully in the army. What I desire now is to get all the boys interested in working up the bill which died with Senator Logan. As I am an old resident here, and in the newspaper business, I shall take delight in looking after their interests. Yours very truly,

"J. O. KERBEY."

"Mr. Kerbey is a well-known ex-telegrapher, both in Washington and New York and in the West. He was a prominent telegraphic figure at the Centennial Exhibition, Philadelphia, in 1876, since which time he has been more or less actively employed in the newspaper field. For three years he operated the leased wire of the Chicago *Inter Ocean*, and has recently written an interesting war narrative of 500 pages, 'The Boy Spy,' in which he gives some interesting war telegraph history, in connection with his own experiences as a scout. We have conferred with several military telegraphers on the point Mr. Kerbey brings out so prominently, and all agreed that the inside history had better now be made public. It would, they declare, lead to prompt and effective legislation, for the average senator or congressman very properly concludes that, if the telegraphers were worthy of being commissioned for the prominent part they took in the Civil War, that honor and duty should have been conferred upon them when the facts were fresh, and not delayed until years afterward. General Eckert is a member of the military telegraphers, but has never taken part in the deliberations of the association to any extent. It is due his old comrades to now have his position explained to them.—Sept. 16, 1889.

In imagination I take hold of the once-familiar telegraph key to have a talk with the "boys." I "call up" the thousands of offices along the railways all over the country, and, as each answers, I give the signal for "copy" or attention. I have not handled the key in some years, but have not forgotten the art nor lost interest in the artists. When an Associated Press reporter, I had the reputation of being a steady, long-distance sender whose Morse got to the end of the line in large quantities.

(I am not sending from copy altogether, but drawing from memory through my fingers' ends. I will ask you not to "Bk." or send me back. So here goes "copy" for the record.)

Without any desire to seek controversy with prominent officials of the telegraph companies, or any disposition other than a sincere desire to put on record the facts gained through a personal experience in the matter of the official recognition of telegraphers, I submit the following plain statement:

Being somewhat familiar with the process of legislation at Washington through my newspaper connection, I was asked to give my attention to the interests of a bill before Congress to give to the *telegraph operators* of the war some official recognition by allowing them brevet rank or commission as officers on the same line with Signal Corps or Engineers. No pay was asked, and of course the commissions were not to be in force, the primary object being to get their *names on record.* I have cheerfully done all that I could in furtherance of their desires, but suggested that the *military railroaders* should be included in the list.

Objection was made to this, not because the railroaders were not equally worthy of the same recognition, but it was found by the manager of the telegraph bill that such an addition would encumber the very few telegraphers asking the relief. In other words, selfish interests prevailed.

The Veteran Signal Corps Association by a vote expressed their opposition to having these telegraphers tacked on to the signal corps *now*, as they had not only refused to unite with these during the war, when commissions were offered them in that branch, but the officers in charge of the military telegraphers had taken advantage of their opportunities by being close to the War Department to annoy and embarrass the operators of the signal corps then working in the field.

The Veteran Signal officers do not offer any opposition to a proper recognition of the civilian telegraphers, but they do object in an official manner to the proposed method, and for the reasons stated.

Through some personal relations with General Logan, then chairman of the Senate military committee that had the bill before them, I became somewhat interested in the matter.

The prominent question that naturally arises, and will not down, propounded to me by some Senators was, if these telegraphers are entitled to the rank and privileges they now seek by legislation, were they not eligible to the same during the war?

Why was it not conferred then? In reply to this question I have given *my experience* to the committee without comment. They, like the operators who hear this, can form their own conclusions. One naturally seeks for motives in all matters of this character. Opinions and surmises can be as easily made by the reader as the writer.

My statement has been made that General Eckert personally procured an order from Mr. Stanton prohibiting any operator from being commissioned in the Signal Corps. This matter was tested over my commission so late as the year 1864, which date it is important to keep in mind.

It is obviously impossible to procure from any of the survivors of the military telegraphers any adverse testimony against the gentleman who was then, as now, their "general manager." A majority of them are yet in the telegraph business, or whose interests are closely allied with those of the great corporations. It is a question of self-interest, or perhaps of daily bread and butter. Their lips are sealed. I was for years under the same bondage, and discreetly held my peace. Now, however, I am a "free lance," and as I expect to die some day, I am simply putting the truth on record, without fear or favor.

What was General Eckert's motive in quietly procuring such an unjust, if not outrageous, order? My personal opinion then, which has been strengthened by a twenty-five years' association, was that he was prompted wholly by a selfish and grasping disposition to elevate himself at the expense of the operators in his employ.

General Eckert's friends will no doubt attribute his opposition to the rivalry then existing between the telegraph and the Signal Corps. Indirectly, that is correct, but in antagonizing the Signal Corps at that time, he knowingly worked against the interests of the telegraphers.

That this is true is established by the "inexorable logic of events," as the Signal Corps now have the record, the rank, and the glory of their service in every field, while the military telegraphers are begging Congress now for that which was tendered to them in 1861–62.

The Signal Corps is of prior organization to the telegraphers. In fact, it ante-dated the war several years. The chiefs of the signal bureau were therefore entitled, not only by seniority but in every other way, to the control of all the Government telegraphs during the war, in greater sense than it has since in operating the Government's military wires in connection with signals, etc. No one doubts but that in future wars the telegraphers and signalists under the present organization will control all military communications.

The signal officers were dissatisfied with the imperfect "Coffee Mill" induction or dial instruments they were compelled to use on the field, and desired to improve the telegraph branch of their service by adopting the Morse method in its place.

Telegraphing was only one and a minor branch of the duties of signal officers who are properly described as the eyes and the ears of the army, the telegraph being the tongue used to communicate their observations.

The present general manager of the telegraphs is known as the "Executive" of Jay Gould in controlling the consolidated lines of numerous opposition companies that this great "consolidator has caught in his net as little fishes, that he feeds to the voracious big sucker fish."

During war times General Eckert was strongly opposed to consolidation. He no doubt saw that in the event of the Signal Corps obtaining the control of the telegraph, he would lose his occupation as manager of the War Department office. Primarily, this was his motive in antagonizing the Signal Corps. He was enabled by virtue of his necessarily close personal relations with the Secretary of War, which were cunningly brought about by his fawning services in personally delivering the important dispatches received by the operators from the hard-working men in the front instead of using messengers. It will be readily seen that in placing himself between the telegraphers and the Secretary, he became a "vehicle," and was, of course, in a sense in a confidential relation with the Secretary. It was through such influences, and the misrepresentations to the Secretary, that he was enabled to procure such an arbitrary order as previously indicated.

Mr. Stanton's motive was to retain through this source the control of and personal supervision of all telegraphic communications of whatever character between the generals in the field and their friends in Washington or elsewhere.

I assert of my own personal knowledge that every dispatch sent from the field in Virginia passed through his hands, if he so desired or his friends thought advisable.

In the War Department the telegraph wires from *all sections*, whether North, East, West or South, were led into separate little instruments which recorded, when *necessary*, *every single* item telegraphed in any direction.

When General Hooker was out here at Fairfax the question of his being relieved of the command was being discussed in Washington.

As is generally known, there were all sorts of intrigues and plots being concocted, both in the army and at the War Department in Washington. Hooker's friends were, I believe, those of Secretary Chase, who was an aspirant for Presidential honors to succeed Mr. Lincoln's first term.

Stanton was, of course, interested for Mr. Lincoln's succession. *All political matter passing our wires from any direction referring* to Chase, as well as criticism of Stanton and Lincoln, was referred to Mr. Stanton.

Hooker and his friends in the field did not imagine when filing matter at a railroad station out here that their private and personal telegrams, addressed to friends, probably in New York or the West, *passed through the War Department*, were laid before Mr. Stanton and his friends; but this really was true, and sad is the fact, that the same secret espionage or censorship was extended over *every other prominent* man's telegraphic communications. McClellan and *his* friends suffered from this same cause.

In this way much, very much, of the true inwardness, not to say cussedness, is explained, that came between President Lincoln and his generals in the field.

It will readily be seen that in order to accomplish these ends and each serve his own purpose, Mr. Stanton decided it to be a "War Necessity" to keep the management of the telegraph independent of military control. And for him to give an order was equivalent to an act of Congress.

The records will show that in the judgement of nearly all the prominent generals in the field of war it was more of a "Military Necessity" to have the telegraphers under the control of the generals. President Lincoln, Secretary of War Cameron and Assistant Secretary Thomas A. Scott, early favored the formation of the telegraphers into a military organization, as the following official correspondence indicates.

Col. Anson Stager was the general superintendent of the Western Union Telegraph at the commencement of the war. He represented the interests of such capitalists as Amasa Stone, Ben Wade, Chase and others.

Upon the recommendation of these persons and none other he was selected by Col. Thomas A. Scott to take charge of military telegraphs for the Government.

Colonel Scott, as Assistant Secretary of War, directed Mr. Stager to submit a plan of organization, notifying him that the entire matter was in his hands and any recommendation he would make would be confirmed by the Government.

After consulting his telegraph interests it was decided that to offer commissions to operators would result in detaching from his Western Union lines the best men who would be tempted to come to the front and serve as officers. Rather than the business interests of his company should suffer commissions were not recommended.

A plan was submitted for a civil organization, restricting the pay of military operators for the same reason as influenced their rank.

These papers with Mr. Stager's estimate are accessible, in the War Department, to any proper person.

There was not the remotest suggestion for military rank. However, this question was forced upon these gentlemen's attention by Gen. M. C. Meigs who was then Quartermaster-General of the army, who declined to recognize officially such an organization and refused to issue supplies or money on the requisition of general managers and foremen of construction gangs. He intimated that he would be pleased to issue such supplies, etc., on the orders of the Signal Corps, as it was legally entitled to make such demand upon his department.

But this would not suit the "general managers."

Gen. Meigs is credited with helping them out of the dilemma by suggesting that the manager and operators in the field be commissioned as assistant quartermasters and he would in that capacity be enabled by law to fill their requisition and be empowered to deliver into their hands Government property necessary for their equipment and maintenance.

This suggestion was acted upon to the extent of issuing commissions to the General Manager only.

To further establish the point, that it was the desire of the Government to give the operators commissions, I submit copies of some official correspondence.

[*Copy.*]

WAR DEPARTMENT, Oct. 28, 1861.

Respectfully Referred to the President:

The Secretary of War believes it to be a necessity to commission telegraph operators as per Gen. Meigs' suggestion, but desires your views. Mr. Stager is now in charge of Government lines and is well calculated to perform the duties. His connection with all leading lines will be of service. *If you approve, arrangements will be made at once.*

[Signed] THOS. A. SCOTT,
Assistant Secretary of War.

Which Mr. Lincoln endorsed in his own handwriting, as follows:

I have not sufficient time to study and mature an opinion on the plan. If the Secretary of War has confidence in it and is satisfied to adopt it, I have no objections.

[Signed.] A. LINCOLN.

This was further endorsed

Approved by Secretary of War.

SIMON CAMERON,
Secretary.

In compliance with this, commissions were given to Stager as Colonel and Brigade Quartermaster.

There was no more law for Stager's appointment than for that of any operator.

In order to facilitate his business he soon found it advisable to ask for commissions for a few of his friends.

Eckert, who was made manager as late as July, 1862, and a few other Division superintendents, who were at home, were made captains.

The operators in the front who did all the work, remained mere civilian clerks to the quartermasters.

In most cases the operators were respected by the general officers to whose headquarters they became attached; but among the associates of the General's Staff he was without rank or consideration. To be sure he was given a seat alongside of an ambulance driver, but he suffered keenly from the envy and misrepresentation his false position gave him among the gentlemen at headquarters.

If these boys had been commissioned as Signal officers, they would have enjoyed the privilege I had as such of going as they pleased.

It is a fact that a second lieutenant on the staff of a General has all the independence without any of the responsibility of his General.

The specious plea of the general managers that the object in not issuing their commissions was simply to prevent "military control," will not suffice in the face of the well-known fact that Signal officers are of the General Staff and like the Quartermaster and Adjutant-General are essentially independent of Military Control except from *the headquarters.*

The operators, as a rule, in those days were boys and easily deceived by the plausible talk at Washington of an attempt of the Signal Corps to absorb them; or perhaps they were influenced by the promise of being kept "independent" of everybody, but the Washington office.

It will be seen by the most casual observer that Mr. Stanton, through channels *practically* kept a telephone at Army Headquarters, through which every "vibration"—and they were numerous and heavy sometimes—was transmitted to his private ear. In more senses than one the Army of the Potomac was tied to his office by a wire; when he pulled the string the monkey *had* to dance.

In war times there can be no such thing as being "independent" of the Military, as General Eckert and his operators, as well as Mr. Stanton, subsequently found out when they undertook to tangle General Grant up by their wire-pulling.

It will be remembered that the communications of the Generals in the armies of the East to those in the West necessarially passed through this War Department "telegraph mill."

The attempt of Mr. Stanton to revise or oversee the official correspondence from Grant in Virginia to Sherman in the West has become a matter of historical mention.

Colonel Stager, at an early period, retired from the actual control of telegraphy, though he remained in commission and was *nominally* the head of the service till the close of the war. All communications to the telegraph department were addressed to him, though Major Eckert was the manager at Washington War Department, and handled *all* such matter. This fact should be borne in mind in reading documentary evidence at War Department.

As indicating General Grant's views in support of my statement, I give herewith some characteristic correspondence that, in his own words, indicates General Grant's views of the "military necessity" of the telegraph being independent of the General's commanding in the field.

[Copy of Telegram.]

U. S. Military Telegraph Blank.

WASHINGTON, Nov. 14, 1862.

To U. S. GRANT, *Major-General:*

Some one signing himself "John Riggin, in charge of Military telegraphs," is interfering with the management of the telegraphs in Kentucky and Tennessee. This man is acting without the authority of Colonel Stager, General Superintendent of Military telegraphs, and *is an impostor.* Arrest him and send him north of your depart ment before he does mischief by his interference.

By order of the Secretary of War.

P. H. WATSON,
Ass't Sec'y of War.

Imagine the indignation of General Grant upon being handed such a dispatch by the operator at his own headquarters. It indicates that his headquarters' affairs had been reported to Washington without his knowledge; the telegraphers in his armies were acting as informers on his own Staff officers.

His reply in vigorous United States language shows his feelings.

[Telegram.]

SECRETARY OF WAR, Washington.

John Riggin referred to in your dispatch as an impostor is my aide. He has given but one order referring to telegraphing, and that was dictated by me. It was that private dispatches might be sent over the wires when it did not interfere with Military dispatches. Colonel Riggin is assigned the duty of looking over telegraphs in this department, a position which interferes with no present arrangement and is intended solely for my relief. Your agent has misrepresented the matter.

[Signed.] U. S. GRANT.

This correspondence probably caused General Grant and his Staff officers to investigate and ferret out the telegraph spy in their camp who reported direct by wire to the War Department, instead of through him. To be brief, word was passed along the wires in that department one ugly November day to the effect that a certain captain of Western Union Telegraphs in that department had been arrested and placed in a guard-house by orders of General Grant.

An official message, not done up in cipher, but plain so all operators could hear it, was sent to Washington officials to this effect:

Captain of W. U. Telegraphs *must go out of my department. My orders must be obeyed.* U. S. GRANT.

He did go out, on the day following, under guard, and if he had been sent back, Gen. Grant would have resigned.

Some of the operators along the lines were disposed to

resent this military interference with their "independence" and openly talked of striking or resigning. Grant heard of this and without asking for any bill of particulars or grievances issued an order to every commander in his department to "Arrest every telegraph operator who resigns or attempts to leave his post, or refuses to perform military duty." I think Mr. Somerville was arrested. This raises the interesting question whether the Brotherhood or Knights of Labor, of which the telegraphers are an influential factor, would, in time of war, come in conflict with the Military by an organized strike all along the line.

It will become apparent that the *telegraph* is as much a "military necessity" as any other of the important auxiliaries, all of which are essential to any complete system of warfare.

The War Department cipher, which General Eckert appropriates, as of his own and Col. Stager's invention, which is based upon the route system, was used first by Col. Myers, well known as "Old Probabilities" and first chief signal officer. The military operators entrusted with the key to this much vaunted cipher code were carefully selected and trained at the War Office in Washington before being put in the field. Their instructions were of the most positive character, *not to reveal to any one* under any circumstances the key. In fact, no written keys were permitted, each of the "cipher operators" was made so familiar with the system that the carrying of any written explanation was obviated. On one occasion Gen. Grant happened to be some distance from his headquarters, when he received a couple of long dispatches from Washington.

They were in regulation cipher of course, and as he was not accompanied by the cipher operator he could not translate them. He inferred from the condition of affairs that it was a most important communication—one perhaps involving the movement of armies, in which thousands of lives may be at stake—but he was helpless and mad. In order to prevent future recurrence, he instructed his Chief of Staff to inform himself as to this cipher. It is always understood that the Chief of Staff as confidential aide of the General always accompanies him. In making this demand on the operator, he explained his orders from Washington, but Grant insisted, and *that operator being a detached soldier*, he obeyed Grant's orders and under protest gave up the key to the Commander-in-Chief of *all the armies*. He reported the circumstance to Washington and *was at once dismissed from the military telegraph*. The key being immediately changed, Grant was again helpless. He, however, nobly protected his soldier operator and *demanded his reinstatement*, which was accorded, and Mr. Beckwith, the *soldier operator*, remained with him to the end. In communicating with Mr. Stanton, General Grant said: "It occurred to him that Mr. Eckert had his operators so trained that they were afraid to obey any instructions but those that emanated from him, etc." My record at the War Department will show that I was detailed at Cavalry Corps Headquarters from May 3, 1863, to June, 1864, or until acceptance of commission. At this headquarters, as well as at those of Hooker, and at different points, were detailed one or more of these "cipher operators," with whom I came in contact. I did not let it become generally known that I was an operator, because I knew that as long as they were in ignorance of this acquirement, I could unsuspectingly linger near the wires that run from Headquarters along the railroad to the War Department and could and did read the sounds of the instruments as often as I chose, or whenever I thought a little attention would result in any interesting developments. I translated the cipher and was familiar with its use, notwithstanding General Eckert's statement recently printed in a Philadelphia paper and copied largely, that his cipher had *never been revealed.*

"Gen. Thomas T. Eckert, who is a guest of the Continental, does not seem to have any particularly pressing business that calls him at this moment from New York to Philadelphia. There is no person in the world who has been more intimately associated than he with the development of the telegraph system. He was an operator in the early days of the Morse invention, and he was the man chosen under President Lincoln's administration to construct and conduct the telegraph corps of the War Department that was everywhere with the forces in the field. As an executive officer—he was made an Assistant Secretary of War—he selected and commissioned the Government telegraphers and invented the cipher in which all important messages were transmitted between the department and commanders of armies, corps and divisions and between the respective commanders. The cipher was a marvel. No man who did not possess the key ever interpreted it, and yet it did not appear at a first glance to be exceedingly complex. There is a story which runs that when it was first presented to Secretary Stanton, he was inclined to despise it as a clumsy piece of work. "Look here, Eckert," he said, "anybody can read that." Try it yourself, Mr. Secretary," responded General Eckert, as he laid the carefully prepared sheets before his superior officer. "Pshaw, that's no trouble," Stanton said, as he cleared a space on his desk and went to work on them. After he had covered a dozen sheets of manuscript with his guesses at the meaning of the cipher, his persistent temper rose high. The perspiration came out on his face, he ran his fingers through his mop of iron-gray hair, he glared through his gold-bowed spectacles and stroked his beard with extreme fervor. Meanwhile, General Eckert sat by, calmly waiting and expectant. If he felt a sense of triumph he permitted no symptom of it to escape him. Mr. Stanton was not the man to abandon any task until he was sure that he was defeated; but at the end of an hour he tore up his own papers, handed General Eckert's manuscript back to its author, and said: "I give it up, Eckert; and now you can tell me what all does it mean. General Eckert gave him the explanation, and on the following day this ingenious cipher was put into use The secret of it was never betrayed, and it was of inestimable value during the war."

I will, for the benefit of this war club, give a brief illustration which represents this much vaunted War Department cipher. If you will notice the next telegram you receive, most likely you will find precisely five words on each line. It is the custom of expert telegraphers to place five words on a line because it enables him at a glance of the number of lines to tell exactly how many words are in the entire dispatch. The "check" that accompanies all dispatches and the operator's count must agree. In this way he is sure of not having missed a word. Of course it will be easier to count lines by five and the fractional part being on the last line. Upon this basis the "route cipher" of the War Department was built. This system was devised because it was frequently necessary to telegraph openly, as it were, the exigencies of the war requiring an unlimited vocabulary, such as is barely possible by the usual arbitrary methods.

Five	and	arbitraries	form	simplest
detection	the	of	of	the
of	insertion	use	the	of
difficult	of	the	much	illustration
quite	blind	by	vaunted	an
becomes	words	war	war	as
system	and	the	office	only
the	prescribing	during	cipher	given
routes	of	government	used	is
intricate	innumerable	our	by	this

I have for brevity and convenience placed this in the order of columns. In transmitting by wire, or by letter or courier, there may be any number of words on each line. The party who receives the cipher will afterward arrange the colums after the prescribed key. In order to simplify it I have made the first word five, which we will say means that the matter following it is to be placed in five columus, as I have arranged it. The *route* to follow in reading has been previously arranged—in this case it is made almost too plain. To interpret: Read up the last, down the fourth, up the third, down the second and up the first column. In the war ciphers numerous "arbitraries" were used that made it more difficult; each general officer's name and rank was expressed in one word. Armies, cities, rivers, roads, etc., are also represented by arbitrary words. Numerals are so arranged that they can not be mistaken, a certain class of words being used exclusively for this. The time of day in half hours is given by boys' names for the morning and girls' names for the afternoon. Numerous changes in the routes may be made; some read diagonally.

The Signal Code of our Army is practically the same as that of the Morse or American telegraph system, which is composed of two of the simplest known characters. It may be recorded by a dot and a dash or received by ear by a short or long sound. Visual signaling by the flag is conducted on precisely the same principle, a motion to the right or left signifying a dot or a dash. At night, short or long flash or occultation. In rockets, by discharging a white and a red ball.

To form this now almost universal war alphabet it is only necessary to use any combination of these elements to form the Morse character by signals.

A . — B — . . . C . . . D — . . E . F . — . G — — . H . . . . I . .
J — . — . K — . — L —— M — — N — . O . . P . . . . . Q . . — .
R . . . S . . . T — U . . — V . . . — W . — — X . — . . Y . . . .
Z . . . .

It may be applied to the most sensitive of galvanometers; in fact, it has been for many years in use on the Atlantic cables, the message received being read by the right and left deflection of a needle, as the flags are read. When I was out here on this very track on which was standing a locomotive, *I used to whistle* to call in some telegraphers by way of a practical joke. A bugle may sound the alphabet by long and short blasts. Two signal officers or expert telegraphers may converse with each other by winking the right or left eyes, or, in the darkness, if they can but touch each other with the feet or hands, conversation may be carried on in absolute silence by the sense of long and short or hard and soft pressure; therefore when you play poker with a signal officer be sure that his feet beneath the table are properly insulated. Much of the phenomena of modern mind-reading or locating may be accounted for in this way. The deaf and dumb and blind may find in the invention brought out by our war a more satisfactory method of communication than that of their sign language. It is not, of course, to be expected that words are always spelled out; I have worked out a system of signal shorthand that enables accomplished signalists to talk at a distance as rapidly as if they were together.

The possibilities are wonderful, and the fact that all the governments of the earth have adopted the system of war signaling our war developed, proves its utility; but of this, more anon—perhaps. We are now running into the depot where Garfield was shot.

CHAPTER X.

WE will not detain the club in Washington; having only run in from the front on a sort of 24-hours' furlough to secure some necessary supplies, make a change in clothing, and to procure some refreshments.

Everything of interest about Washington has been so fully written up that there is but little to be added to the volumes that have been printed about the Capitol. The old boys of the war will miss many of the old landmarks, such as the guard-houses and the once too-familiar footsteps of the patrol of the provost marshal that we all had to dodge nightly when meandering through the dark ways of Hooker's Division. The old "Canterbury" theatre has disappeared, also its brass band accompaniment that paraded the avenue every evening, followed by a mob of contrabrands, its four pieces making more noise than Gilmore's modern band. In its place there are a couple of dime theatres, located on the flanks of the division, which, by the way, continue to do business at their old stands.

Judiciary Square, which is directly in the rear of the City Hall, at the head of 4½ street, was during the war almost entirely occupied with blocks of frame barracks, then used as one of the general hospitals. Some of these buildings remained after the close of the war, being used on one occasion as the place for holding an inaugural ball. Where these long, narrow frame buildings once stood, is now a beautiful park, the cosy seats and walks shaded by trees that have grown since the war on this soil made rich by the blood of many poor boys. On the northern side of this park and extending along its entire length of two full squares, attracting attention by its size, is a red brick structure, probably the largest public building in Washington, except the Capitol. It is supposed to be architecturally in the style of an Italian palace, but it looks like an immense machine shop or factory. This is the Pension office, in which the late inaugural balls have been held. We will step inside for a moment only; while we stand on one of the galleries and admire its beautiful interior, permit me to give you a few facts and figures for future recollection, from which each may form his own conclusions.

First offering a personal explanation, I was an employé in this Department for about three days, during which I had enough to satisfy me for the balance of my life. A closer study of the institution since, has served to further develop and confirm the first impressions. I should state that I spent a considerable part of the three months immediately following Mr. Harrison's inauguration about this big building, endeavoring to secure the employment which when found only lasted three days. Some of my friends seemed to think that I was not fit for any other duty but some sort of "Secret Service," and they imagined that the most available place for me was to look after "pension frauds."

On account of Civil Service rules, I was disbarred as a clerk, though no one questioned my fitness for the duties. Mr. Tanner yielding to the pressure of friends and desiring to relieve my necessities, graciously notified me one day that if I would accept a *subordinate* position temporarily he would see that I was properly "assigned" and subsequently "placed" where I could do most good.* I accepted and was at once "assigned" as messenger. I did not mind the subordinate position as long as there was any chance for advancement, but I did object suddenly and emphatically to the servile and menial duties required of messengers. I found that the principal use in life of a messenger in the Pension office was to wait upon a lot of young clerks—veterans asked to perform this service for school-boys. It was work that could better have been done by boys. I drew the line the first day at carrying water for a couple of airish old maids. I don't object to handing a lady a drink of water; but when it came to supplying them with toilet water, I kicked and appealed to the Chief; unfortunately he was a recent appointee from a New England State, who had

*"The *Tribune's* Washington correspondent, Maj. J. O. Kerbey, has been notified by his personal friend, Corporal Jim, now Hon. James Tanner, Commissioner of Pensions, that he will receive an appointment as a Special Examiner when these changes are made. Colonel Quay, Mr. Scull, and others of our State who knew Mr. Kerbey and endorsed him as a worker who wielded a sword in war as vigorously as he has a pen in peace, for the party, think that the author of the "Boy Spy" is especially competent to fill this position by reason of his familiarity with the "boys'" army methods in war and by a long training since as a searcher after "facts" for the press. There is an extensive field in the Pension Service, and Mr. Tanner is fortunate in having in his department a comrade who will no doubt use his abilities to help the soldier Commissioner to make a good record for the Administration. We understand the Major preferred a Consulate in the Pacific, but we are glad he will remain nearer home, and his duties will not be so onerous that the *Tribune* readers cannot occasionally hear from him. The pay is $2,000 per year and $6 per day additional for traveling expenses."

served the last six months of the War as a guard at Longbridge, and though the head of a division, he knew absolutely nothing of the duties, and being under obligations to his clerks, and anxious to maintain his popularity with the ladies, he misrepresented me to the Commissioner. I called on Mr. Tanner, and finding he had "shelved me" and had no intention of promoting me, I handed in my resignation in words more emphatic than elegant, but subsequently made a more courteous explanation to Secretary Noble.

There are employed in this building alone some 1,500 persons. If I were to venture an opinion here, it would be to the effect that one-half this number, under the management of a good business house, would accomplish twice as much work and for one-half the pay.

Altogether there are over 4,000 employés in the Pension service throughout the country. The expenses of the entire Pension establishment in 1888 was $3,262,524.67, and in 1890 will aggregate in round numbers $4,000,000. The pensions paid in 1888 were $82,038,386.59, or 31 per cent of the *entire expense* of the government in that year. In 1890 the increase in pension list will exceed considerably $100,-000,000, of course, also, with an increased ratio of expense. Pensions already paid exceed one billion of dollars. Pensions are now being granted to almost every applicant who can show any service or disability, however short or slight. In addition to this generous administration of the bureau, there have been passed 3,380 special acts that were not within the power of the commissioner to grant.

These are a few of the facts and figures which an old soldier of 1861 to 1865, who does not draw a pension though fully entitled to it, asks the comrades to paste in their hats and study over at leisure. The dependent pension bill has passed and will undoubtedly become a law, which adds limitless millions to the sum chargeable to old soldiers. This pension business is delicate ground, but I cannot, as a disinterested comrade, refrain from offering the suggestion to the *real* veteran "boys" to call a halt on this pension army that is marching under the leadership of the pension generals and guided by sharks, up the avenue bent upon a raid upon the Treasury. Recall, boys, the memorable spectacle of the grand review which we saw swinging up the avenue in 1865, without one thought of the treasury, their eyes only strained towards the generals on the reviewing stand.

Is it not degrading to us all to be called pension paupers? Does this latter-day raid not take the bloom off our glory and stain these once stainless flags? Don't let us *all* join this army of raiders—remember there is a hereafter, patriotism should not be so cheaply discounted and future generations must not be taught to look upon the old soldier as representing a mendicant statue, with a hat in hand, but instead, an erect, noble, manly warrior with a gun in hand. As a comrade I believe in the largest measure of justice, recognition and generosity to the soldier; to him every honor and every reward is due. These pension bills and all this agitation are not in the interest of the real soldier who enlisted early from patriotic motives and stayed late from a sense of duty and not for bounty, but in that of a remorseless, soulless lobby, who is using the soldier's name to rob the very government he fought to save. The sentiment is general that the soldier who helped to save the country is entitled to everything. But reflect, there have been other wars and other soldiers and other countries have been saved. Prussia's was created by Frederick, yet this entire pension list did not amount to a week of our expenditure. England fought Napoleon for twenty years, making a debt of three thousand million and her army did not demand extra thousands of millions for pensions. Germany has fought three wars since ours, yet her pension fund to-day is not quite nine millions a year. We are paying to our pension survivors a greater amount than is required to maintain a standing army in Europe. We believe in justice to the soldier, but it is not to be found in this rascally pension ring lobby. It is, in a sense, as much of a job of the ring as that to pay the Confederate loan previously noted. Nearly all sensible men concede that this money goes to pension agents, money sharks and professional soldiers, the robbery is being done by using the honored name of the soldier, because the scamps realize too well, that such a name may even atone for a crime. If the object is to disburse the surplus, the soldier is undoubtedly entitled to the first grab, but the objection to this argument is that it is sectional. The money goes East, North and West, and not South, and the South has been contributing her full share for years to increase this surplus. The Confederates get along without pensions and they returned to devastated homes and are now thrifty. It is said there are more pension certificates mailed to foreign parts, principally Germany and Canada, than go South of Mason and Dixon's line. In one regard the pension list is a benefit and it will do more to prevent future wars than Mr. Blaine's arbitration scheme.

These are a few abrupt facts for the consideration of old soldiers. I can only suggest the general remedy to the effect that all pension legislation should be made to deal directly with the pensioner and do away with all intermediaries. If the fees and emoluments that arise from the business of the pension sharks were cut off, the agitation would cease. I know there are laws and rules apparently restricting the attorney to a certain small fee, but we all understand fully that notwithstanding these guards hat legislators think they put around their laws, the agent reaps a richer harvest than the intended beneficiaries. There are many ways of evading these restrictions. No law can be enacted that will prevent a pensioner doing as he pleases with money after his warrant has been turned into currency. If some sort of a general law could be passed, paying pensions direct, monthly, through the Postoffice and War Department and abolishing all the present cumbersome *machinery* of the department, simply requiring of the applicant a local surgeon's certificate of disability, attested by the State or County official, where he is known, it would save millions in expense and wonderfully facilitate the payment of claims. In the aggregate the expenditure would not exceed that paid to the army of pension office clerks, but this will never be. This inside ring which thrives by this system is all powerful at Washington and they work in harmony with the outside ring or army of claim agents. It will be patent to the most casual observer that the pension business "pays," else there would not be so many engaged in it. It will also be apparent that the small fees allowed each attorney do not of themselves justify or account for so great an income in the financial standing of the brokers, who have no other visible means of support. The principal pension agents have silent partners who are employed in the pension office. The most careful management will fail to detect the general collusion of prominent pension officials with the attorneys outside. All dismissed pension employés immediately engage in the pension business. The chiefs of each division are appointed, and do not come under the Civil Service rules. They are, as a rule, selected by political preferment or from other influences. They know less of the duties than the sub-chiefs, and are, of course, subject to the policy of their "influence." In my very brief service in the pension office, *I detected a newly-appointed chief* in communication with the head of a prominent pension attorney outside, on the business of his office and making suggestions or giving official information. *I have the proof of it.* The thought occurs: if that could be discovered accidentally in so short a time, what a broad field there might be for further investigation! If the claim agent's profitable business could be taken away from him, there would be no incentive to the political demagogue to make trade and capital out of the business, nor for the old soldier to worry himself into fevers of restlessness and discontent. These agents mail broadcast throughout the land, at low rates of postage, weekly, millions upon millions of circulars, urging the soldiers to apply for pensions, offering him every possible inducement to do so, specifying increases, and, by exaggerated terms, outline the opportunities that these agencies afford *all* soldiers to easily secure a share of the surplus. In this way thousands of worthy soldiers have been induced to make application for pensions on account of disabilities that most probably result from their increased age, who would not otherwise have thought of it. No great injustice is done, perhaps, but once an old soldier gets his mind on a pension, it practically unfits him for work. They are led by these flowery circulars to believe that the Government owes them a living the balance of their days, which they are anxious to pay, and they put in their time waiting and waiting. I know of one pension office annex, as it is sometimes called, because of the private business being so extensive, that publishes a weekly paper wholly devoted to the agitation of the pension business of this one man. It is said that this paper has been sent out to the extent of 250,000 weekly—not as *bona fide* subscribers, but as "sample copies" to a "free list" of names obtained from the records of the Government of *all survivors* now known. To such an extent was this abuse of the sample copy law carried that, to my certain knowledge, the postal authorities felt compelled to take steps to prevent their service being loaded down with such *free advertising*. This is simply using the Government facilities to incite or encourage persons to file claims that may not be just nor proper, and which creates discontent among the people with the Government, where the promised relief is not granted, as the recipient of these papers are led to expect. This weekly trade paper for claim agents formerly enjoyed quite a large circulation. The cost of subscription being placed so low as to be within the reach of all. The apparent policy of its management being to afford soldiers an opportunity of "fighting their battles o'er"—its columns are opened to free contributions from all sections of the country. In this way barrels of material are gathered, from which selections may be made and printed without expense. On account of its free circulation the advertising space is of course valuable and eagerly sought and used by other unprincipled schemers. *No advertisement,* however, of a competing claim agent is admitted to its columns, but that class of advertisers which are rejected by all respectable publications find it a convenient medium to expose their loathsome and villainous schemes. Prizes are offered also, and in divers ways the management succeed in obtaining many applications for pensions, which, when granted, may come back to them through their variously advertised schemes.

There are now some twenty local G. A. R. papers being published throughout the United States. The ex-soldiers are not now dependent upon any one "organ." Neither are they under any obligations to the self-styled "soldiers' papers." On the other hand the proprietors and claim agents are indebted to the ex-soldier contributing of their all; which amounts, perhaps, to millions.

These hordes of claim agents are, in no sense, friends of the soldiers, except so far as it may promote their own purely selfish ends. A poor soldier would fare sadly at their hands if he appealed personally for enough to get a cup of coffee. I know something of this by personal observation; as serving to illustrate the point I mention an actual occurrence.

A soldier who contributed some material for a certain soldiers' paper enjoying a large circulation among veterans, was having some hard luck for which he was in no sense responsible, either from bad habits or management, appealed to the wealthy claim agent who was a director in a bank in which a note for the small sum of $30 was due, asking the favor of an endorsement for an extension, explaining that unless it was granted he, the soldier, would be legally notified to vacate his house, his family being practically put upon the streets. Sufficient money to secure the endorser would be due and in their agent's hands in a few days. This "friend of soldiers" refused in most ungentlemanly terms to even "consider" the matter. In a few days following he generously and publicly contributed $100 to a Post charity as an advertisement. He did not imagine the "poor soldier" would ever be able to give him the benefit of this advertisement.

In my newspaper scouting through the late Confederacy in late years, I have met in a business as well as in a social way, quite a good many prominent ex-Confederates, with whom I have talked freely about the war; more especially in regard to the personalities of the leaders of both sides. In discussing the death of "Stonewall" Jackson I found there was a remarkable reticence in regard to it and a disposition to quietly change the subject. On several occasions, on referring to the rumors of his having courted death, I was met by the retort: "Didn't your Secretary Stanton commit suicide?" While I have always resented the imputation, it has occurred to me that some one who knows should forever put to rest this impression, which has become quite general throughout the country, probably because of this appearance of mystery and studied avoidance of any discussion of the manner of Mr. Stanton's death, as in that of Jackson's. At the time of the sad occurrence I was employed in a confidential capacity in the telegraph office in Washington City. I confess that, from some private telegraphic correspondence that passed through my hands at the time, I gathered the impression that Mr. Stanton had in a fit of mental aberration done something that at least was an indirect cause of his death. The rumor that was carefully suppressed then was that he had cut his throat with a razor, the wound being of such a dreadful character as to cause almost instant death. The fact is significant. No one was permitted to *see Mr. Stanton* after death, which occurred in the double brick house on K street, opposite Franklin Square, now owned by Senator John Sherman. My purpose in referring to it is not to re-open any old wounds, but to afford the proper person an opportunity to dispel the cloud of mystery that hangs over our War Secretary's death. He is buried at Oak Hill, Georgetown. I would suggest that the G. A. R. do this great man the honor of removing his bones to Arlington, where they might appropriately rest under the shadow of the stone columns that once stood as portals to the old War Department building and that have recently been placed over the gateway at Arlington.

It is well known that Mr. Stanton made many enemies among his own people during the war, and subsequently he had his trouble with President Johnson. Upon General Grant's ascendancy to the White House, the ex-Secretary desired, and his friends expected, him to be made one of the Justices of the United States Supreme Court, as a just reward for his services. That he was entitled to the honor and fully capable of filling tne position was not questioned by even his enemies; but for some reason President Grant hesitated in making the appointment, which fact, it is supposed, bore heavily on the mind of the great Secretary, as savoring of a country's ingratitude, and may have, with other troubles, tended to unhinge the great mind. The nomination was made, however, a short time before his death, but it came too late, like the promotion of many others of our war heroes.

It is sad to reflect that so many of our war generals' lives after the war were made miserable by the seeming neglect and indifference of the Government to their great services. It is said General Meade died of a broken heart, and we all know the gallant Warren suffered keenly from his degradation by General Sheridan—he requested that he should not be buried in his uniform.

General Hancock's grave, in the corner of a little churchyard in Norristown, Pa., is unmarked by even a simple headstone, and weeds almost conceal the low green tent under which the great hero of Gettysburg sleeps. McClellan, Hooker, Pope, McDowell and Burnside, who were commanders of the Army of the Potomac, are dead, but who can tell where they sleep the sleep that knows no waking?

Among the survivors are some who have suffered a living death for a quarter of a century, like Patterson and Fitz-John Porter.

In this connection permit me to call attention to a remarkable instance of a country's ingratitude to a war hero, who yet lives a slow-torturing death, right under the shadow of the Capitol. Gen. Alfred Pleasonton—my dear old General, on whose staff the records of the War Department will show I served until June 30, 1864, or until promoted—walks the streets of Washington, a lonely, almost forgotten poor old man, but retaining his old-time military bearing and courteous manner. Though poverty-stricken and almost in destitute circumstances, he remains the gentleman—one of those quiet, elderly, distinguished-looking men who would attract attention in any crowd, whatever may be his condition. He is always neatly dressed, his face cleanly shaved, with the exception of a gray mustache. No matter who may address him, whether a tramp, or a newsboy, or a senator, he will rise to his feet and remain standing at "attention" while conversing; yet this great old hero is to-day a beggar, almost an abandoned outcast, disheartened, his life bitterly soured because of neglect.

It makes me sad whenever I see Major-General Alfred Pleasonton about the hotel corridors that he haunts here, for there is a grand memory of his war history that is fascinating to any man who answered to "boots and saddles," and drew rein and saber during those dreadful days of the Rebellion. The sadness comes from the knowledge that the man who, first of all Generals in the Eastern army, made the cavalry a power, and accomplished the work that mounted forces are supposed to be used for. Gen. Pleasonton—"Cavalry Pleasonton"—is so often confounded with his brother, Gen. Augustus H. Pleasonton, that I will explain here that the subject of my sketch has no middle name—just Alfred, a king of cavalrymen.

Alfred Pleasonton was born here in Washington nearly sixty-five years ago, while his father was one of the treasury auditors, and in 1840 went to West Point under an appointment at large from President Van Buren. He duly graduated in 1844 into the 2d Dragoons (now the 2d Cavalry), and from that time until his resignation from the army in 1866 his record was an important part of the history of the mounted service.

The Rebellion had not progressed very far when Pleasonton, then promoted to major, was made a general officer, and went to the Army of the Potomac as a Cavalry Division commander, and in June, 1863, succeeded Stoneman in command of all the cavalry of the Army of the Potomac.

At the fateful battle of Chancellorsville he was in the right center of the field when "Stonewall" Jackson passed close around our front to fall upon and drive the 11th Corps from the field, and it was he who discovered the movement and held the Rebels in check for twenty minutes, until troops came to close the fatal gap on Sickles's right that Hooker had left open. There was no infantry available, but Pleasonton hastily gathered several batteries and got them to work to check the well-conducted Rebel advance, and then, when all seemed lost (to gain the imperatively needed time), called the bravest major in all his command and hurled him on the Rebel front with a battalion in as desperate a charge as that at Balaklava, that is so famed in song and story. The gallant boy-major, a Pennsylvanian, and more than two-thirds of his gallant officers and men lay in front of that fringe of pine saplings when the help came that held the line, but the day was saved for all that. I have heard that when the young Major got his order he drew saber, rode up to Pleasonton and, saluting, said: "Good-bye, General; I'll hold them whether I come back or not." I have seen General Pleasonton's blue eyes very suspiciously moist when that has been talked of in his presence, and I've heard him say: "It had to be done, no matter at what cost, to save 10,000 lives, and the Major was the only man in all the command I could depend upon thoroughly to do it."

When the cavalry was organized into a corps in June, 1863, he was placed in command with Buford, D. McM. Gregg and Kilpatrick as his division commanders, and the work done in less than a month made him a major-general and changed the general opinion as to the value of cavalry in field operations. The Gettysburg campaign showed how far superior Pleasonton was to "Jeb." Stuart, the Rebel commander, in the duties pertaining to cavalry service, for he was outwitted and outfought through all that campaign; but it remained for the famous cavalry duel at Brandy Station, a month later, between those two leaders to demonstrate the all-around superiority of the Union over the Rebel cavalry. There Stuart held a knoll from which the ground sloped easily away on every side, and the broad surrounding fields were yet crossed by fences, between which ran narrow lanes, through which, in one instance, part of our force was obliged to charge in column of fours for lack of time to throw down fences. Not a piece of artillery was used on either side, but after a time Pleasonton drove Stuart completely off the field, and the Rebels never again won a general cavalry engagement in the East.

Pleasonton in 1866 was offered the colonelcy of one of the new infantry regiments, but with a cavalryman's disdain for such service refused the offer and indignantly resigned. When General Grant became President, he made Pleasonton collector of internal revenue for that district in New York City that included then Wall street and all the down-town banks and brokers' offices, in which was collected the largest revenue of any district in the whole country. Later on Grant called him here to Washington and made him Commissioner of Internal Revenue. No matter what may be said otherwise of Alfred Pleasonton, no man ever dared even hint at his dash as a soldier or his unswerving integrity in official life. Commissioner Pleasonton found that a great railway corporation had been evading its taxes, and he proceeded to make it pay a number of millions it owed. He began by grabbing every locomotive that ran into the chief central town on its line (after he had exhausted every other means in his power to compel payment), and within a few hours the road found itself almost crippled, while the danger of total stoppage was increasing. A wild appeal for compromise was made to Pleasonton. "Pay up your dues to the United States." Specious representations were made to President Grant, and despite Pleasonton's protests, General Grant suspended the order so as to allow passenger traffic temporarily. Pleasonton resigned the same day, and refused all further offers of political preferment. The House passed a bill to make him Colonel on the retired list, cutting him down to Major—the rank he held when the first volunteers were sent to the field twenty-seven years ago. Men who have been dismissed the service for various military offenses are restored by almost every succeeding Congress, with the rank they would have held had they remained continuously in service, and it seems as if General Pleasonton might have been granted that rank, notwithstanding his recent mistakes and bitter speeches, resulting from his neglect.

Recently I met Gen. Pleasonton in the reading room of Willard's Hotel, saluting in the old style, and introducing my little boy Fred to him with the remark: "My boy, this is my dear old army father, Gen. Pleasonton, the man who told us what to do in war and we had to obey, if we knew it killed us." He greeted my little boy so pleasantly and talked so kindly of his father, that I confess to a few silent tears over the interview. As he seemed to be in the mood for talking over old times, I reminded him of a conversation I once heard between himself and General John Buford, in which they were discussing the question of Buford's promotion to be Major-General, with Custer, Kilpatrick and Gregg. "Yes," said the General, "I remember that talk distinctly; I kept telling Meade he had better hurry his own promotion, because, you know, we were all expecting the Western fellows would come in with Grant, and as they were Stanton's favorites they would rank us out of our old commands. Meade was an easygoing fellow, you know; we used to call him an old woman, and some of them nick-named him 'rabbit ears.' Well, he always said that he had already made the recommendations and done all he could in his official way to secure the promotions; but you know Meade was not the man to press such matters, besides the War Department was always working against us of the old Army of the Potomac. Stanton was afraid of us Union Generals who happened to be born South. I am a native of the District here and Buford was born in Kentucky."

I interrupted here, saying: "Buford was as staunch a loyalist as Thomas or any other Southern man. I belonged in his brigade, and was attached to his headquarters long enough to become satisfied of this fact, and like everybody else, became quite attached to the genial old Kentuckian."

"Well," said Pleasonton, "Buford died here in Washington of a broken heart. This is the way it happened," said the General, as he drew up closer to me and began to tell the story in an earnest and half-confidential manner: "You know, of course, how dear to the old soldier of the Regular Army is the question of rank. It is a subject ever uppermost in his mind and heart. Whenever Buford and I got together long enough to talk, we would get on this subject of rank and promotion. I told him that I had officially notified Meade that he was entitled to his two stars for his Gettysburg fight, the first day alone, and said Meade always agreed with me as to that. One day, when talking together, I said, jokingly, 'Say, Buford, whenever the Government at Washington hears that we are dangerously hurt and are sure to die, they will give us our rank.

They are afraid to trust us Southern fellows too far.' Buford laughed good-naturedly about this at the time, but he never forgot it; and he got full of rheumatism down on the Rapidan; kept brooding over the matter. So one day I told him to go up to Washington and put himself under the care of the doctors.

"My idea at the time," said the General, "was to have Buford in Washington, where we had arranged that our friends in Congress would get to meet him personally. He was too much of a soldier to hunt up political influence himself, so Meade, Gregg and some more of us put up this scheme; for we all knew if the President could but see and talk with him it would overcome Stanton's suspicions, for to know Buford personally was to love him.

"Well, I had on my Staff a Surgeon who was one of those good-hearted, earnest fellows, who wanted to do all he could, but at times allowed zeal to override discretion. I sent this doctor along with Buford because he had some political acquaintance—none of the rest of us had. Buford got to Washington, and, instead of hunting up his friends, shut himself up in his room and was soon down sick in bed. He was away from the army and lonely. There was nothing serious the matter with him. The doctor attended him occasionally, but put in most of his time at the Capitol among his own friends, or getting up delegations to call on the President in the interest of Buford's nomination. One day it occurred to this fool doctor to tell the President that Buford was liable to die. Either the President or Stanton inquired particularly as to Buford's chances of recovery, and also as to the prospect of his dying.

The doctor had heard my joke to Buford, and his pleasant way of taking it made the doctor think that to exaggerate his illness would hasten his promotion. So one day, with this purpose in view, he rushed to the War Department in great distress and told the President and Secretary that Buford would surely die. He told me subsequently that he did not say he would die, or meant that it was likely to occur soon.

"The President, after conversing with Stanton, authorized the Surgeon to say to Buford that he should have his rank at once. Without any other thought than that he was doing a kindness for his General, the energetic little Surgeon rushed to Buford's house, unceremoniously entered the sick man's room and blatantly announced the good news to him.

"The doctor told me with some show of feeling when I questioned him regarding this," said Pleasonton, "that Buford looked at him from his bed in a dazed sort of way, and without uttering a word of thanks, turned his face to the wall. He imagined the General was so overcome by the good news that he had simply turned his head to hide his overflowing feelings of gratitude, and, therefore, did not disturb him for a while.

"When he went to him a few moments afterward, he found that General Buford had died a Major-General.

"I knew Buford intimately, and there never has been any doubt in my mind that the thought occurred to him at the time he was so depressed in spirits that the doctor had satisfied himself and the President that his case was hopeless, and the President had agreed to gratify his wish at the last hour. So he turned his face to the wall and died without saying a word."

But we will have to hasten on to Gettysburg. As we ride out toward Fairfax C. H., allow me to tell you a short story, which has the unusual merit of being something new about Gettysburg, bearing on the disputed historical question of securing the position there, which it is conceded was, in effect, making the victory possible. This was recently told to me by General Pleasonton.

Everybody knows that Pleasonton commanded the cavalry of the Army of the Potomac during this campaign; that he had for his subordinate division chiefs such gallant men as Custer, Kilpatrick and Buford, of the First, Second and Third Divisions, which, by the way, gained for that army much of the glory it achieved, for a great portion of which General Sheridan gets the credit now.

Pleasonton says that he had the positive evidence that Lee was making for Gettysburg during this Antietam campaign of the previous year; that, in anticipation of this, he sent a Prussian engineer officer, who was on his Staff, whose name is entirely too long to recall, with a squadron of cavalry up to Gettysburg in 1862, and that officer made a topographical map of the country, which is on file to-day among McClellan's papers.

Looking at the matter in the light of professional soldiers, Pleasonton and McClellan concluded that Lee had wisely selected Gettysburg or some adjacent point for a battle-ground, because all the roads to Washington, Baltimore, Philadelphia and Harrisburg, as well as toward the South, centered or crossed there. It was, on this account, strategically a good point for rapid concentration, which is one-half of every battle. Besides this, he could there fight with the South Mountains like a great wall at his back, the Potomac on one flank and the Susquehannah on the other. In cases of disaster, the round passes of the mountains would protect his retreat.

Now, Pleasonton asserts that, with this knowledge obtained the year previous, he, as chief of cavalry, sent Buford out to Gettysburg to secure the position outlined on the topographical map, in anticipation of Lee's intended concentration there.

However the statement may be disputed, we all know that Buford did go out there with his cavalry, and, after a careful and personal examination of the country, he took the necessary precautions to hold the ground until the Army of the Potomac should come up.

It is well known that it was Buford's cavalry that brought on the engagement the first day, and, with the assistance of Reynolds' Corps, the cavalry first drove and then held in check the advance of General Lee's army of veterans.

I said to Pleasonton: "Why do you never attend any of the numerous army reunions and recite these things? When Sickles mentioned your name at the Gettysburg reunion, recently, as being as worthy of promotion as were Napoleon's Field Marshals for your work, then it raised a small tornado of applause among the old boys who listened."

"No," said Pleasonton, in his quiet and modest way; "I never go to such places; they are only graveyards to me. Some of my best friends on both sides were killed there.

"It's just as Sickles says about Gettysburg—those Pennsylvania fellows who are booming that town don't want anybody but their own crowd to have anything to do with Gettysburg."

"But, General, you must remember that it was the Pennsylvania generals, Reynolds, Hancock and Meade, who fought that battle."

"It was Buford and Reynolds, my boy, who saved that day and made the victory possible;" but they seem to have overlooked a couple of other Pennsylvania men, two of our cavalry boys, Gregg and Rodenbough.

If we were not in so great a hurry to reach the battlefield of Gettysburg, it would have been more agreeable and entertaining to the Travel Club to have driven from Washington via the upper Potomac road outpost, the Chain Bridge, Great Falls and Cabin John bridge, enjoyng the beautiful and romantic scenery of this historic locality.

There are some interesting legends associated with this river road.

On the southern side of the aqueduct bridge, curious, if not supernatural, sounds are heard on quiet nights. These resemble so nearly the roll of a drum that it has given rise to the belief in the minds of some of the contrabands living near by that the noises there are produced by the ghost of a Federal drummer boy who ran away from his home and was drowned at this point while crossing in the darkness. There is no doubt about the noises, and their mysterious origin is a cause of wonderment to intelligent people therabouts.

Immediately above the bridge will be seen a group of three large rocks arising from the middle of the river, on the surface of which grow some beautiful aquatic plants. These are universally known as the "Three Sisters." The story told to the crowds of young people who daily enjoy the excursions up and down this lovely stream is that General Braddock and his friends had captured or stolen three beautiful Indian princesses which they held as hostages. These high-toned young ladies, preferring death to imprisonment and the society of these English gentlemen, bound themselves together, after the manner of the "Three Graces," each holding a stone in hand as a sinker or anchor, plunged into the stream and were drowned at this point. Their bodies were never recovered. The following morning those three rocks appeared above the water to mark their watery graves.

There is no doubt about this story, as the rocks may be seen by anyone who may be incredulous about it.

We will get off the train at Fairfax Station, where conveyances meet us, and as we drive the four rough miles to General Hooker's headquarters at Fairfax Court-house, permit me to tell you something funny about the Rebel money. This was an actual occurrence and tends to illustrate the low estimation in which our soldiers in the field held Confederate money. Perhaps not one of the boys ever imagined a time would or could come when any value could attach to Confederate bonds.

"I believe that I can honestly claim to have made the

biggest bet on record in a poker game," said an early veteran of the war, who was one of a recent group of comrades engaged in a social game of "draw" in Washington. "How much was it?" asked another player who had just thrown down his hand with the exclamation that it was "Only nine high." "Two million dollars" said the old soldier placidly. A series of "whews" came from the rest of the party, but the Washington veteran in poker was not in the least disconcerted. "It's a fact, as sure as you are living sinners," he exclaimed, "and if you will listen I'll tell you how it came about." For a minute or more the game was suspended, while the veteran talked: "We were in winter quarters, in 1862, near White Oak Church, Virginia. Each regiment took its turn in doing picket duty, and it was the good luck of the corps to which I was attached to have captured a paymaster's wagon, containing I can not say how many million of bills and bonds." "Oh, I see," interrupted one of the group, "it was Confederate money." . "Your head is level," replied the veteran, "but still it was money, and gave the boys who made the capture the opportunity for playing the heaviest game of poker ever heard of. The ante was $100 and there was no limit, hence you may conceive there was some lively betting.

"In the fray something like $5,000,000 of the stuff came into the possession of myself and my three tent mates, and as soon as we got back to camp we started the game. I had fairly good luck at the start, but after awhile the paste boards went back on me and I rarely got a pair bigger than deuces. This went on until my pile had been brought down to about $2,000,000. There was a $1,000 jack-pot and when I picked up my hand I found I had the invariable deuces.

"The man next to me opened the pot for $1,000. The next man and myself saw him and then we drew. Each of the others took three cards, but I contented myself with one. When it came my turn there was $2,000 to put up, and without lifting my hand I raised the last better $2,000,000. This drove the man next to me out and left the field clear for myself and one opponent. He deliberated a long time, counted over his pile, which contained just a little more than the amount of the bet, and then threw up his hand.

"When I looked at my cards I found that I had not bettered my two deuces. My opponent threw down a pair of kings.

"I ascertained later that at that very time certain Southern sympathizers in Washington and Baltimore were paying 5 cents on the dollar for Confederate money, and I wanted to kick myself for not having known it sooner.

"I have understood that agents have been quietly gathering up the bonds for some years."

CHAPTER XI.

FAIRFAX C. H. and vicinity, once populated by 100,000 of the Army of the Potomac, would now seem like a deserted village to any of the old army boys who might revisit the place. We will only tarry here long enough to take a photograph of the spot once occupied by General Hooker as the headquarters of the Army of the Potomac, from which so much intrigue relating to his removal from the command was concocted.

At this point we again take our horses and ride along over the same old war-path we traveled with headquarters in 1863.

On this occasion our path is a pleasant one, following the old pike leading through Aldie and the gap through the mountains to Winchester.

It was along here that I had the thrilling experience with Mosby's guerillas.

On my return from Washington, I brought back with me quite a heavy official mail for cavalry corps headquarters. At that time Pleasonton happened to be at Aldie, leaving quite a gap between there and Hooker's headquarters at Fairfax.

I supposed, of course, this road leading to our front was safe enough. Being well mounted, I dashed on ahead of the ambulance, which was carrying the mail.

This old pike, as you will observe, is laid out on straight lines. The early surveyors of roads worked on the bee-line principle, going up hill and down dale, without any regard to the theory that it might be the nearest, as well as the best way, to go around a hill instead of mounting it, thereby avoiding useless grades, and often contending with obstacles in the path that might easily have been flanked.

From the top of one hill the discouraged traveler sees the long and narrow road ahead of him, stretching for miles over other hills and through swaths of forest.

On galloping out here in that beautiful June evening, I observed ahead of me some distance what I supposed to be a wagon-train, turning off for evening camp. Riding along leisurely until within gunshot, my attention being attracted by some signs of activity, which is of so unusual a character about packing wagon-trains that my curiosity was aroused. Noticing a house off the road a short distance, I rode into the yard to make some inquiries. A bareheaded woman with a baby in her sleeveless arms kindly handed me a drink of water. I asked her in a careless manner: "What is going on up there in the middle of the road?"

"They done captured all them wagons."

"Who captured them?"

"Why, soldiers, of course."

"Yes, but what soldiers?"

"Why, Mosby's men, sah."

That was enough. I had run right into a gang of mounted guerillas, and had in my possession a number of important papers about our army. I pulled my little fatigue cap over my face, took a short hold of my bridle reins, turned my horse's head into the road, and, instead of turning up to walk into the trap, as they had expected, I gave the poor horse an inch of spur at every jump as I turned back.

As soon as my reverse movement was discovered, a volley was fired at me; guerillas came after me, not so well mounted as I, yelling and firing at me on the run. It was a pretty race for about two miles along this straight line. I won. If I had not, this absolutely true story would never have been told. When I got back to headquarters and reported to the Chief-of-Staff, he at once sent out, under my guidance, the cavalry escort, composed, I think, of Rush's Lancers, or "turkey-drivers," as we called them. Before we reached the place we heard the sounds of explosion, and soon saw rising above the treetops great clouds of white smoke. The officer in charge of the escort halted his men and observed to me: "No use in going out there; those fellows have got more than they bargained for, if they set fire to those wagons supposing they were destroying stores—it's an ammunition train." So we waited till the clouds rolled by, and late in the evening reached Aldie and reported to General Alexander, Chief-of-Staff, to whom the recital of my adventure seemed to be very amusing, as he laughed heartily.

One of the curious things to the young generation about our war stories is the apparent indifference amongst comrades to the fate of their companions. They look upon death, perhaps, as a sort of blessed relief from some of the horrors of army life. When I read nowadays of the burial of a G. A. R. comrade with appropriate military honers, the brass band accompaniments, the firing over the grave by the "awkward squad," and witness the tenderness with which the remains covered by the "Old Glory" are handled, my mind unconsciously reverts to a soldier's burial on the field.

It may not be a good thing to put in cold type, but it did seem to me that in a great majority of cases there was more eagerness to relieve the dying soldier of any valuables he might have than to offer him physical comfort or religious consolation. Most of the dead soldiers would be found with their pockets turned inside out. Of course, it is understood that in every regiment there were a few unprincipled wretches who stealthily pursued these ghoulish practices.

The poor fellows of the cavalry advance, who died in the very front, and sometimes beyond the front, in the dangerous cavalry skirmish line, are sleeping in the lonely almost lost graves scattered "on the advance line" all the way from Fredericksburg to Gettysburg. There are hundreds of these lost graves of forgotten heroes. In truth, our "war path" might be appropriately marked by an almost continuous line of monuments. One of the most painful remembrances of the cavalry soldier's burial is the sight of a dead comrade laid over a horse like a bag of potatoes, a companion leading while another holds in place the dead man. Ambulances could scarcely be used on these mountain roads, and, besides this, the cavalry were generally out of reach of them when needed.

The cavalrymen of the Army of the Potomac will recognize all this country. It was their ground and right nobly they earned their spurs here. It was Pleasanton's Cavalry that reported to Hooker the daily movement of Lee's army in its march to Gettysburg. The cavalry of the Confederates, under command of J. E. B. Stuart, were somewhere in our rear on a raid around our entire army. But Pleasanton paid no attention to them, as he said "Oh, I don't want any stern chase after 'Jeb.' I have something more important in my front here."

Stuart's raid was a failure and the movement a source of much annoyance and embarrassment to General Lee. It is seldom that a poor scout gets any credit for his dangerous work, yet Generals Lee and Longstreet officially report that to the individual effort of their scout Harrison is due the entire credit of performing alone the service that was expected of General Stuart and his cavalry corps. It was the scout Harrison who first reported to General Lee, when at Chambersburg, the important information that Hooker was on his rear and had that day crossed the Potomac. The intelligence caused General Lee to change his advance movement, and probably saved the city of Harrisburg, Pa.

The services of the scout are thankless but valuable. His life is always in jeopardy, as I know by bitter experience. There is in some minds a vague impression that the work of a spy, or a scout, is dishonorable, or that the service necessarily implies treachery and deceit. This is so only in the same degree that the strategy of a general is treacherous. Strategem as an art of war is considered to be honorable, yet it is seldom, if ever, applied without resorting to the aid of the scout. A spy or scout, therefore, may be inspired by as patriotic motives as the general and army whom he serves. It is the motive which should give character to any service. With me, this secret service was in no sense mercenary, and became in a manner almost involuntary. I never received one cent for it, but obtained that which is more lasting and which I value more highly than gold as a reward, and that is a commission signed by A. Lincoln and E. M. Stanton. As a special reward this parchment was antedated a year, to March 3, 1863. So that in fact I was an officer in the regular army while wearing the uniform of an enlisted man. My service was almost altogether of a special or detached character, as a telegrapher, signalist and scout at headquarters.

On this ground, and not that I make any pretensions to superior attainments, I base any claim for having had the opportunity of having seen as much of the war as any other person. I went as I pleased, enjoying all the privileges of a headquarters man, and perhaps I was a keen observer.

We will ride leisurely over the good road from Aldie through the beautiful pastoral scenery of Loudoun County to Leesburg. We might halt a short time in this old Virginia town, deviating a little from our route to visit Ball's Bluff, the scene of the battle or massacre at that point. It is not an agreeable affair to dwell upon. We hurriedly ride down to the Potomac, the beautiful Upper Potomac, which has been to so many a Rubicon and a river of death and oblivion.

We cross at Point-of-Rocks, a most picturesque place. The ferryman with his overhead rope and current for motive power points out the piers of the old bridge burned by the armies which has never been rebuilt. It would be impossible for me to make a pen picture of the grandly beautiful and historic spot. Nearly all the old boys will remember the precipitous hills, the rocky cliffs under which the canal and railroad curve. A little ways up the river are the mountains about Harper's Ferry. I sat on the edge of the boat as we slowly crossed the stream, taking it all in again, perhaps for the last time.

For the boys and girls and those of the club who have never seen this country, Willie Hazard and I secured, from our own camera, a number of the most striking views.

From the Potomac river to Frederick, as it is called in Washington and Braddock's Journal or "orderly book," is a half-day's uninteresting ride. The scenery, as viewed from the top of the mountains over which the road leads us, is grand, but the roads are so execrable that we can not enjoy it, so we hurry along in a sort of sullen silence toward Frederick.

The near approach to this, one of the finest old towns in Maryland, is suggested by the frequent appearance of toll-gates, a feature we had not met in our previous week's travel.

The roads, however, are improving, so that we cheerfully pay this Maryland protection tariff on Inter-state commerce. Here we find farms in the most improved condition, elegant homes are scattered along the great highway, giving us the pleasing impression that we have come into a more cultivated civilization.

At Frederick we drive to the City Hotel, at which

headquarters were domiciled in June, 1863. This was an old-fashioned country tavern, the best of its day, in the rear of which was an immense yard with stables, where the farmers were accustomed to keep their horses. It was a hostelry that afforded, as the sign said, "Entertainment for man and beast."

The headquarters horses filled the yard and stables while the officers filled the house and were in turn filled by the landlord barkeeper.

It was the Sunday before the battle. Custer was with us. Right over the street from the hotel was a drug store, the name on the sign I remember distinctly as being Schley. The family, as was usual in such country towns, lived above the store. During the Sunday we stayed there, Custer, the handsome, dashing, boyish-looking general, with long hair and short jacket, sat by the window of the hotel parlor, which was also upstairs, and carried on a flirtation with a couple of young ladies who were at the windows opposite. He became so much interested in this new-found delight, that he had apparently quite forgotten all about his cavalry, which were scouting around somewhere on the South Mountains. I was quite interested too, but was not able to find out how it all ended. So on the occasion of this, my first revisit, I at once looked for that sign, almost expecting to see the same pretty faces of the young girls, after twenty-five years, again. But I was disappointed in this, but in the innocence and guilelessness of an old boy heart, I began to ask the hotel clerk about the whereabouts of the Misses Schley. I supposed, of course, that Frederick hotel clerks were like all the others of that class, and knew everything. I related to him and the crowd about the desk, the story of Custer's flirtation, until my humorous recital was made suddenly sad by the gentlemanly clerk's reply to a question as to her present whereabouts coupled with the suggestion that I'd like to make a call on the lady.

"Yes, sir, the Miss Schley that was is living in this house now. She is my wife, sir."

CHAPTER XII.

WE are now on the war-path within sound of the booming of Buford's guns that opened the ball at Gettysburg. We will hurry the club along over the roads from Frederick, via Emmettsburg, stopping long enough to take some striking views of the points that every one who was "thar" will recognize, such as the toll-houses near Frederick, the rómantic points on the mountain road beyond Emmettsburg.

Gettysburg has been done and overdone so thoroughly that your guide will spare the club any infliction of his own experience. Volumes, yes, libraries that may be measured by the cubic foot, have been written about Gettysburg. Monuments have been erected, indicating the location of almost every Federal regiment that was here engaged, and at the dedication of each and every one the orators, poets and glee clubs told the assembled survivors many things that had not entered their minds before.

I admit that I have contributed my mite to the mass of contemporaneous history that has been printed about this great battle.

I have no desire to fight it over again with the club, and refer to the innumerable guide-books, so-called histories, and modestly suggest that the unpretending story of the observations of the "Boy Spy" be included in the study.

In all the war literature, I have yet to see discussed the fundamental question, "What can a soldier see from the ranks?"

The youth of to-day reading or studying war articles, as published, without first knowing the rudiments of war, the conception of space and numbers in a great battle is confined to a very small limit, his general idea of a battle such as Gettysburg is confined to the limits of the blocks of the small village where all of it could be seen without difficulty.

My definition of a line of battle to the Travel Club, in as few words as I can express it, would be a continuous double line of men, the length of the line depending upon the number engaged. There are supporting lines in the rear of this main line and these are shifted to the different parts of the field where they can do the most good, as is demonstrated as the battle progresses.

The main line is interspersed with the artillery, supported by infantry or dismounted cavalry.

A full regiment of infantry in line of battle will occupy, say, a thousand feet. A brigade of five regiments will cover about a mile in length. So it will be seen that an army like that of the Federals, comprising a force of 100,000 men, will be in a crowded condition on a battle line of ten miles. The area at Gettysburg during the three days' manœuvres was something less than twenty-five miles.

Waterloo was the shortest line in proportion to the number engaged. Napoleon had two miles, Wellington a mile and a half, 72,000 men on each side.

From this density came the carnage 60,000 dead, or 41 per cent. At Gettysburg the official reported casualties aggregated 55,000.

I have only attempted in the "Boy Spy" papers to

tell what I actually saw of Gettysburg. Being on detached service at headquarters, I went as I pleased wherever it was safe to go, and I think I saw as much of Gettysburg as any other one person.

When you read or hear of any of our large battles written by a soldier in the ranks, you can just put it down that he is writing or talking about something of which he could not possibly be cognizant from his own observation. Of course, they can tell, in a general way, something of the result, but they have only eyes for that which is immediately in their front, and mighty little opportunity or inclination to study the field, which is frequently covered by smoke under which reigns confusion worse confounded.

I have been asked frequently, "What were your sensations in a battle? Were you frightened the first time you got under fire?"

I always reply unhesitatingly that I was scared the first time and every other time, too. I never heard a shell screech in the air that I didn't want to go home, or a bullet ping, but that I wished with all my heart, I hadn't come. The war always seemed to be a failure to me and I wanted to quit after every fight. We seldom had the satisfaction of seeing the Rebels run.

The "Boy Spy" observations at Gettysburg were published first in the war papers of the Philadelphia *Press* and subsequently collected and edited and flavored to suit the tastes of a trade pension paper, published weekly in Washington. When this true story of the first days at Gettysburg was submitted to them, it was rejected with the observation of the editor: "It bears the ornate marks of truthfulness; but we do not care to print any such reflections on General Howard, because, you know, he contributes to our paper."

I may here state that these papers were "revised" to suit certain selfish ends, the work being done by a cashiered army officer, now a newspaper hack who finds employment at this place. The Gettysburg matter subsequently appeared, somewhat modified however, provoking no end of controversy.

I beg to present to the club and to put on permanent record the autograph letter of that fighting old hero, General Doubleday, which so completely and voluntarily sustains my statements that Howard was "rattled," as at Chancellorsville, and did not take any steps to stop the retreat or secure the position until General Hancock came upon the field.

Since the publication of the "Boy Spy's" experience and observation at Gettysburg in July, 1863, referring more particularly to the little personal fight, or battle, of the first day between the two Union Generals, Howard and Hancock, on Cemetery Hill, almost every issue of the paper has contained some adverse criticism or defense of General Howard. These contributions have come from all sections of the country, but I observe that, without exception, they emanate from the 11th Corps soldiers. This fact of itself will be sufficient in the minds of all the old Army of the Potomac boys, but as the editor has so generously appropriated column after column to the friends of General Howard to fire back, I have thought it advisable to give them a cavalryman's parting salute. Perhaps the following personal letter from General Doubleday, who succeeded General Reynolds upon the latter's death, in the command of the 1st Corps on the first day of the battle, relating to the interview between Howard and Hancock, will be more satisfactory and conclusive than could be supplied by any other authority, living or dead. The letter of itself is a most interesting criticism of General Howard's conduct as the commanding officer on the field.

A diagram in the old General's handwriting shows the contrast between the arrangements ordered by Howard and Hancock. This contribution to the "Boy Spy" papers not only fully establishes the position I take, but is an important historical paper, bearing on the much-discussed question as to "Who was the hero of Gettysburg?" It proves conclusively that Hancock, not Howard, saved the position and saved the day, the Army of the Potomac, Philadelphia, Baltimore, Washington and the Nation. Hancock's ride to Gettysburg, though not done up in song, poetry and painting, as was Sheridan's, yet in its results was far more important than Sheridan's at Cedar Creek.

MENHAM, MORRIS COUNTY, N. J., August 14, 1889.

CAPTAIN J. O. KERBY.

My Dear Sir: I received your article yesterday and read it with much interest. I thank you for the kindly feeling it manifested towards myself, and it doubtless is a true picture of what you saw and heard. I did not know that I had italicized my language in passing through Gettysburg to the extent you indicate, but I must have expressed myself in forcible terms.

As you say, General Howard was unwilling to recognize Hancock in any other light than that of a volunteer aid to himself, and Hancock did ride over and confer with me. I was only too glad to have something done that would tend to preserve the position. The only order Howard had issued was for the 1st Corps to form on the left of the main gate of the cemetery and the 11th Corps on the right. Let me illustrate by a diagram. If this idea had been carried out, nothing, in my opinion, could have saved us from capture. Now, compare this arrangement with what Hancock did. I sent Wadsworth to the right and Buford was directed to make the appearance of a long line on the left by moving up and down. This induced the enemy to think that we had been reinforced and that he occupied the whole ridge.

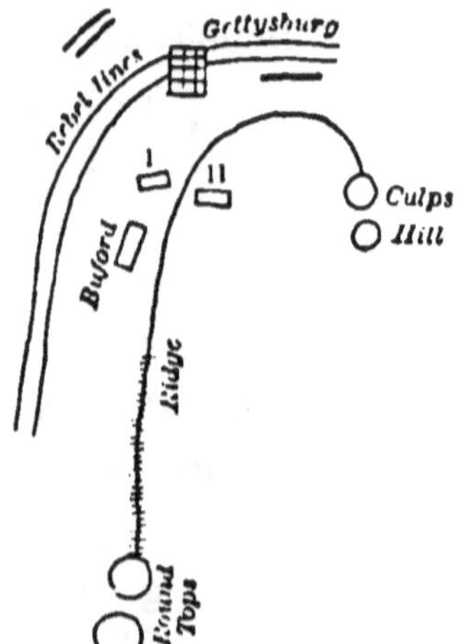

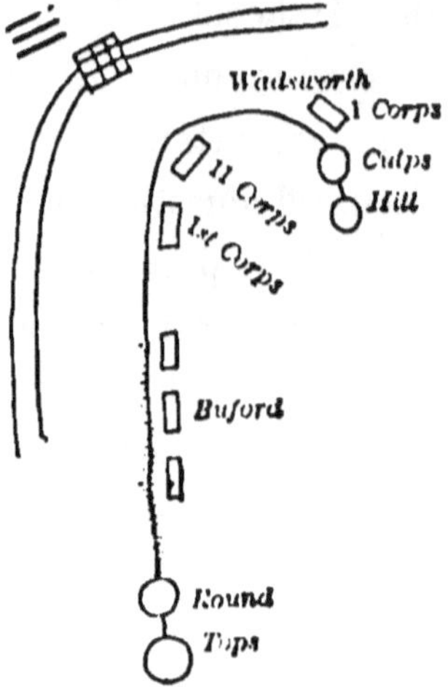

I always wondered why Devens' brigade of cavalry, which was on the right, did not make greater effort to keep the enemy out of the town, as they were following up the retreat of the 11th Corps in that direction, but Devens' report, which has only recently been published, explains it. He says he could have driven the enemy out, or at least have stopped their advance, but just as he was about to do so Howard's guns on Cemetery Hill opened a severe fire against him, and he concluded that the enemy had taken the hill and were assailing him on both sides, so he gave up the town and retreated. This was the second time that day that the cavalry suffered from the fire of our own guns.

Yours Very Truly

Abner Doubleday

I have told the truth about Gettysburg, but not the whole truth.

In a subsequent letter from Gen. Doubleday, not for publication, he says: "You appear to have been the only witness to that scene who was not either a Staff officer of Howard's or Hancock's, and you have, no doubt, told a straight story. You know Staff officers will lie for their chiefs."

I have no reply to make to the personal abuse of the numerous 11th Corps contributors. There is but one word to be said to these comrades, and that is: Howard said in defense of his conduct that he could not trust his men out there. Now, put that in your pipes and smoke it.

I have often thought that Darwin's theory of the "survival of the fittest" was controverted by army experience. The best soldiers were killed, or have died. It seems that a majority of the 11th Corps are still alive, judging from the newspaper fights of survivors. I can afford to say this: I was not an 1865 soldier, nor a substitute—not even a bounty man. I went in as early as April 10, 1861, and was at Montgomery, Ala., and at Fort Pickens, Fla., in active service before a man was enlisted; therefore, the "Boy Spy" claims to be the first soldier. I stayed till the last, and I do not now get a pension, though I am entitled to it, but I shall never ask it; and I've been about as close to the enemy as almost any soldier could get and come away again.

In this connection, I may show to the club also the private autograph letter from the widow of the dead hero, bordered in deep mourning. His words were prophetic in the light of subsequent events.

NEW YORK, 9 West 31st Street, Nov. 20, 1889.

MAJOR J. O. KERBEY.

Dear Sir: Two days since your very kind note with enclosures was forwarded to me here from Washington City, for which I thank you very much. To-day your interesting book, "The Boy Spy," reached me safely. It is needless to add with how much eagerness I turned to the pages containing your observation of men and events as they appeared to you upon that famous battle-field of Gettysburg during those memorable three days in July, 1863. Words are inadequate to convey to you the gratitude that filled my heart as I read of the well-merited praise which you have kindly bestowed upon my brave, good husband for the service he rendered his country on that battle-field. A day or two before my husband left us for his "eternal home beyond the skies," an officer requested a paper from him, in order that he might reply authoritatively to an article which had appeared from the pen of General Howard upon the same subject. Said he: "Those gentlemen are not writing my history—but their own to-day. The time must come when the truth will be told." *His words were prophetic.* Each year brings him nearer to the people, and they seem to understand him better—strange to say. I hope most earnestly your delightful book will have untold success, as it so well deserves. The frank, bright style of the narrative is truly very taking. Believe me, most cordially yours,

MRS. WINFIELD SCOTT HANCOCK.

I have no personal feeling or interest in the matter, except to record the facts as observed by myself.

Politically, I am a Republican, and voted in my State against Hancock for President, but I can tell the truth about a Democrat sometimes, if I am a newspaper fiend.

Lest my Republicanism should be questioned and a partisan bias be attributed to some historical facts mentioned in this brochure, I beg to establish my political preferences by references from "away back."

HE APPRECIATES THE VETERANS.

Gen. Harrison's Pleasant Letter to Maj. J. O. Kerby, of Johnstown.

Special to the Commercial Gazette:

JOHNSTOWN, PA., Nov. 5.—A pleasant letter from Gen. Harrison, which will be of special interest to all the old Harrison voters, was received by Maj. Kerbey, the Washington correspondent and well known to G. A. R. men as the author of the "Boy Spy." A few days ago, Gen. Harrison was sent the following items clipped from the Johnstown *Tribune:*

"Mr. G. W. Kerbey, the veteran agent of the Pennsylvania Railroad Company at Wilmore for the past thirty-eight years, cast his first vote for Harrison in 1836, and in those early days, when Mr. Harrison and his Presidential party were driving Westward over the old stage pike, Mr. Kerbey acted as one of the mounted escort tha accompanied the party from St. Thomas to Loudon, Pa., as far as the foot of the mountain, where he, with others, shook hands with the grandfather of the present candidate. Since then, Mr. Kerbey has consistently voted the Whig and Republican tickets. He now has three sons and one grandson living, all of whom will vote for the present grandson of the elder Harrison, namely: Joseph O. Kerbey, Thomas S. Kerbey and Edgar T. Kerbey. The grandson is Mr. George N. Kerbey, a chemist of Pittsburgh. Mr. Kerbey is also a great-grandfather. George N., the son of J. O., though quite a young man, is the father of a baby-boy, who will perpetuate the proud distinction of this truly Republican household. Agent Kerbey is, therefore, the father of quite an extensive Republican district. Mr. Kerbey enjoys the distinction of being the oldest agent of the Pennsylvania railroad, and perhaps, one of the oldest employés of the entire system, being appointed by his schoolmate and friend, Mr. Thomas A. Scott, when he was assistant superintendent at Pittsburgh."

A LETTER FROM GEN. HARRISON.

His Appreciation of the Old Tippecanoe Voters in Cambria County.

The following autograph letter from Gen. Benjamin Harrison, the Republican nominee for President, was written to Mr. J. O. Kerbey, of Washington, who is in the State campaign using his pen to the interests of the party.

INDIANAPOLIS, IND., NOV. 1, 1888.

J. O. Kerbey, Correspondent Press Gallery, Senate, Washington, D. C.

MY DEAR MAJOR: Your favor of the 28th with the Johnstown *Tribune*, has been received. I have read both with interest. I wish you would say to your good father that I appreciate very highly both his kind recollection of my ancestor and his friendly disposition toward me. The respect of these venerable men, who have not only witnessed, but of themselves done so much to promote the development of our country, is very highly prized by me.

I shall be glad to have the pleasure at some time of meeting your father. Very truly yours,

[Signed] BENJ. HARRISON.

Though General Harrison had been a very busy man those last campaign days, he found time, amid all the bustle and excitement consequent upon the reception of hundreds of delegations and bushels of mail, to sit down and write the above very pleasant letter, which applies to all old Cambria County Harrison voters equally as well as to Mr. Kerbey; and Mr. Harrison did not write for effect, either, for he knew that good old Pennsylvania was safe enough for him.

This is enough for one day at Gettysburg.

Of the second day, I can only record that as a newspaper man, I accompanied President Cleveland on his first visit to the field and subsequently attended in the same capacity the grand reunion on the twenty-fifth anniversary; also, when Gen. Sickles labored to explain how he won the battle at Gettysburg by being defeated on the second day.

The impression I had gained about headquarters at the time when there was always so much intrigue among the comrades, was that Gen. Sickles had played a risky game in the hopes of achieving some glory that would give him the command. It was the general talk about headquarters that he had made a serious blunder, and if he had not lost his leg, he would have lost his commission. This comprises our story of the several battles of the second day.

To most students of war history, the impression is imparted that the principal fighting at Gettysburg was that known as Pickett's Charge, which was, in fact, simply the fire-works closing a series of battles during the preceding days.

As the Northern and Federal side of this event has already been so well told, I have thought it might add interest to the subject to present some new facts from the Confederate side.

A short time ago, through some newspaper connection, I was accidentally put in communication with a gallant Confederate newspaper comrade whom I beg leave to introduce to the Travel Club, as my friend, Capt. W. R. Bond, of Scotland Neck, North Carolina, editor of *Roancke News*, a clever Rebel, and, of course, a courteous Southern gentleman, some time an officer of the Brigade Staff of the Army of Northern Virginia, who will speak to you for himself and his tar-heel comrades.

I will now relate a Rebel's story of Gettysburg.

"Longstreet's assault, or what is generally, but very incorrectly, known as 'Picket's Charge,' has not only had its proper place in books treating of the war, but has been more written about in newspapers and magazines than any other event in American history. Some of these accounts are simply silly, some are false in statement, some are false in inference, all in some respects are untrue.

"Nine brigades, formed in three divisions, were selected for the assaulting column. One of these was worthless, five had been reduced to skeletons by the hard battles of the two preceding days. Three only were fresh. The field over which they were ordered to march slowly and deliberately was about 1,000 yards wide, swept by the fire of 100 cannons and 20,000 muskets. The smoke from the preceding cannonade was their only cover.

"We all knew, when the order to go forward was given, that Cemetery Ridge was not defended by Mexicans or Indians, but by an army, which in large part, if not for the greater part, was composed of native Americans. An army, which, if it had never done so before, had shown in the first and second days' battles not only that it could fight, but that it could fight desperately.

"'As a rather extreme sample of the thousand and one foolish things which have been written of this affair, I refer our youth to the article in the *St. Nicholas* some time ago, in which, in comparison, language something like the following was used: 'Those on the left faltered and fled. The right behaved gloriously. Each body acted according to its nature, for they were made of different stuff, the one of common earth, the other of finest clay. Pettigrew's men were North Carolinians; Pickett's were superb Virginians.'

"To those people who do not know how the trash passing for Southern history was manufactured, the motives which actuated the writers, and how greedily everything written about the war was read, it is not so astonishing that a libel containing so much ignorance, meanness and prejudice as this could be printed in the *Century* papers, and believed by the Northern readers to be either entirely or partially true. It looks like an almost hopeless task to attempt to combat errors which have lived so long and flourished so extensively. But truth is a trap-gun before which falsehood's armour, however thick, can not stand. One shot, or two, or three, may accomplish nothing, but keep on firing and it will be pierced at last, and its builders and defenders will be covered with confusion.

"It will scarcely be disputed that the Confederate Army of Northern Virginia shed more blood than all the other armies of the Confederacy combined, and I reckon your gallant Army of the Potomac, which confronted us so tenaciously for years, can say the same of your side.

"Of the twenty-seven regiments which had the most men killed in any battle of the war, all but five belonged to our army; of these, three were from Tennessee and two from Mississippi.

"Again, of the twenty-seven of those whose percentage of loss was greatest, a very different thing, all but five belonged to our army; of these Tennessee had four and Texas one. Virginia, North Carolina and Georgia each had about the same number engaged at Gettysburg, and here soldiers of the old North State met with a greater loss of killed and wounded—for North Carolina troops did not attempt to rival certain Virginia brigades in the men captured—than did those from any other State, and nearly as great as that from any two States.

"The first Confederate soldier killed was a tar-heel, who fell at Bethel. The last blood was shed by Cox's North Carolina brigade at Appomattox. Why the troops which shed the first blood, the last blood, and the most blood, should be selected by the Northern writers as of inferior or common clay seems like a problem hard to solve, but I will attempt to explain it.

"The world at large gets its ideas of the late war from Northern sources. Northern historians, when this subject is peculiarly Southern, get their ideas from such histories as Pollard's, Cook's and McCabe's, and these merely reflected the opinions of the Richmond newspapers. These newspapers, in turn, got their supposed facts from their army correspondents, and they were very careful to have only such correspondents as would write what their patrons cared most to read.

"During the war, Richmond, judged by its newspapers, was the most provincial town in the world. Though the capital city of a gallant young nation, and though the troops from every State thereof were shedding their blood in her defense, she was wonderfully narrow and selfish. While the citizens of Virginia were filling nearly one-half of the positions of honor and trust, civil and military, Richmond thought that all should be thus filled. No soldier, no sailor, no jurist, no statesman, who did not hail from their State was ever admired or spoken well of. No army but General Lee's and no troops in that army other than Virginians, unless they happened to be few in number, as was the case of the Louisianians and Texans, was ever praised.

"A skirmish in which a Virginia brigade was engaged was magnified into a fight, an action in which a few were killed was a severe battle, and if by chance they were called upon to bleed freely, then, according to the Richmond papers, troops from some other State were to blame for it, and no such appalling slaughter had ever been witnessed before.

"This indiscriminate praise had a very demoralizing effect upon the Virginia troops. They were soon taught that they could make a reputation and save their skins by being always provided with an able corps of correspondents.

"The favoritism displayed by several superior officers in General Lee's army was unbounded. But then we know that the slaps and bangs of a harsh step-mother may have a less injurious effect upon the characters of some children than the excessive indulgence of a silly parent.

"The war histories teach that in Longstreet's assault, his right division (Pickett's) displayed more gallantry and shed more blood in proportion to the number engaged, than any other troops on any occasion ever had. Now if gallantry can be measured by the number and percentage of deaths and wounds and by the fortitude with which the casualties are borne, then there were commands engaged in this assault which displayed more gallantry than Pickett's.

"Who knows anything of this battle to whom the name of Virginia is not familiar?

"To how many does the name of Gettysburg suggest the name of Tennessee, Mississippi and North Carolina, who suffered terribly and their courage remained unimpaired? There were two Mississippi regiments engaged, which had between them 109 men killed on the field. Picket's dead numbered not quite fifteen to the regiment. The five North Carolina regiments of Pettigrew's Division bore with fortitude a loss of 229 killed. Pickett's fifteen Virginia regiments were fearfully demoralized by a loss of 224 killed. Virginia and North Carolina had each about the same number of Infantry engaged in this battle. There was 375 Virginians and 696 North Carolinians killed.

"In some commands of our army the habit of 'playing possum' prevailed. When a charge was being made, if a fellow became badly frightened, all he had to do was to fall flat and play dead until his regiment passed. Afterwards, he could say that the concussion from a shell stunned him. Troops addicted to this habit stood higher at home and abroad, if their correspondent could use his pen well, than they did in the army.

"Was it arrogance or was it ignorance which always caused Pickett's men to speak of the troops which marched to the front on their left as supports?

"An order was issued that they should be supported by a part of Hill's Corps, and these troops were actually formed in their rear but subsequently placed on their left before the charge was made.

"Our army could fight: could and did fight and conquer without their assistance. They and their whole corps did comparatively little fighting at Second Manassas. Neither they nor any part of their corps fired a shot at Chancellorsville, and it is no exaggeration to say here, that Pickett's men did not kill twenty of the enemy at Gettysburg.

"The front line of troops which does the fighting is always known as 'the line.' The troops in the rear to give moral support and practical assistance, when necessary, is in every known body of troops called the supporting line or simply 'supports.'

"Pickett's division had Kemper's on the right and Garnett's on the left with Armisted's marching in the rear of Garnett's.

"Pettigrew's formed one line with Lane's and Seale's brigades of Pender's Division under Trimble marching in the rear of its right as supports.

"How many supports did Pickett's people want?

"The Federals are said to have occasionally used three. Even one with us was the exception. Ordinarily, one brigade of each division was held in reserve while the others were fighting in order to repair any disaster.

"To show how a falsehood can be fortified by art, I saw

at the Philadelphia Centennial a very large and really fine painting representing some desperate fighting at the so-called "Bloody Angle." Clubbing with muskets, jabbing with bayonets and firing off cannon at mighty short range as the order of the day. Of course, I knew that the subject of this "historical picture" was founded upon a myth. I had always been under the general impression that while many of Pickett's and a few of Pettigrew's men were extracting the extremities of certain under garments to be used there as white flags, not a small part of them were keeping up a scattering fire.

"While before this picture, a gentleman standing near me, exclaimed: 'Tut! I'll agree to eat all the Yankees Pickett killed.'

"Entering into a conversation with him, I learned that he had been at Gettysburg, and had fought in Gordon's Georgia Brigade, and that he did not have a very exalted opinion of Pickett's men. As our Georgia friend was neither remarkably large nor hungry-looking, several persons stared at him on hearing his remark. That he did exaggerate to some extent is possible, for I have since heard that among the dead men in blue, near where Armisted fell, there were six who had actually been killed by musket balls.

"Pettigrew's North Carolina Brigade carried into action on the first day, 2,200 officers and men and lost in killed and wounded 660, or thirty per cent.

"After every sharp fight, when another is expected, a certain number straggle or play sick, even among the best troops. Say that fifteen to the regiment or sixty for the brigade were absent from these causes, then there were carried into the battle of the third day 1,480 and their loss was 445, or again thirty per cent.

"In Colonel Fox's 'Chances of Being Hit in the Battle' he gives a list of twenty-seven Confederate regiments which had the most killed and wounded in any battle of the war.

"The 26th North Carolina (the common clay) heads this list at Gettysburg with 588. Not one regiment from Virginia, of the finer material, is named in this list of twenty-seven. North Carolina comes first in the list with six of these regiments and Mississippi next with five, and two of those five met with their loss with Pettigrew at Gettysburg. The North Carolina Brigade had, in killed and wounded, 1,105, which is an average to the regiment of 276. This North Carolina Brigade met, on the first day, the famous 'Iron' Brigade, which was considered the flower of its corps, and many old soldiers say that your 1st Corps did the fiercest fighting on that day that they ever experienced. These two brigades, fairly matched as they were in the war, like two game-cocks in the pit, did the bloodiest fighting in the war. The records show this, and yet with the records accessible to all men, Swinton, a Northern historian, in the brilliant description that he gives of the assault of the third day, says: 'That this grand Heth's Division, commanded by Pettigrew, were all raw troops, who were only induced to make the charge by being told that they had militia to fight, and that when the fire was opened upon them they raised the shout "The Army of the Potomac," and broke and fled.'

"Are Pickett's stragglers responsible for this statement?

"Pickett's left and Pettigrew's and Trimble's right reached the crest. Men from five brigades entered the lines, but, in the nature of things, not a brigade on the field was in condition to repel a determined attack. When two regiments of Stannard's Vermont Brigade moved out to attack our right and enfilade our whole line, Kemper's Virginia regiment did not chance to meet them.

"Pettigrew and Trimble suffered most because longer under fire and having to march farther.

"Both Northern and Southern historians have, without exception, perhaps, down to the present time given not only most conspicuous prominence to General Pickett's Division, but, generally, by the language used, have created the impression among those not personally acquainted with the events of that day, that Pickett's did all the hard fighting, suffered the most severely, and failed in their charge because not duly and vigorously supported by the troops on their right and left. It might with as much truth be said that Pettigrew and Trimble failed in their charge because unsupported by Pickett, who had been driven back in the crisis of their charge and was no aid to them. With equal truth it may be termed Pettigrew's charge instead of Pickett's.

"I have always thought that Pickett's Division was the most indifferent body of troops in General Lee's army.

"The fifteen regiments, according to Longstreet, carried into the charge officers and men, 4,900. It is most probable that they numbered over 5,500.

"The 'brave and magnificent,' when they experienced a loss of fifteen to the regiment, became sick of fighting, as their number surrendered shows.

"One regiment of the 42nd Mississippi 'Cowards,' after it had met with a loss of sixty killed and a proportionate number wounded, concluded that it was about time to rejoin their friends. Another regiment of 'Cowards,' the 26th North Carolina, after it had suffered there a greater loss than any of the 2,700 Federal and Confederate regiments ever had, came to the same conclusion. The five North Carolina regiments had more men killed here than Pickett's fifteen regiments had.

"The surrender of soldiers in battle is often unavoidable, but I never knew a body of troops, other than Pickett's, who prided themselves on that misfortune. Nearly 2,000 of the 'brave little division' ran away from Gettysburg. They were demoralized and ready to run, and ran and kept running till the high waters of the Potomac stopped them. As they ran, they shouted that they were all dead men, that Pettigrew had failed to support them and that their noble division had been swept away. The outcry they made was heard in all Virginia and its echo is still heard in the North.

"After we recrossed the Potomac, it was ascertained that Pickett's 'dead men' had drawn more rations than any division in the army. Their subsequent behavior up to their defeat and rout at Five Forks, showed that they never got over their experience at Gettysburg.

"Of course there were exceptions, but the general rule was that troops who suffered most, themselves inflicted the greatest loss on the enemy and were consequently the most efficient. It was the custom in some commands to report every scratch as a wound and in others to report no man as wounded who was fit for duty. The most accurate test for courage and efficience is in the number killed.

"Now, I would not have it inferred from anything I have said that I intend to reflect upon all the Virginia Infantry. The fact, that from Fredericksburg to the close of the war, among the dead upon the various battle-fields, excepting that of Gettysburg, comparatively few representatives from the Virginia Infantry were to be found, is not always necessarily against their credit. It was not for them to say whether they were to advance or be held back. Their duty was to obey orders.

"Not long ago a New York magazine contained an elaborately illustrated article descriptive of the Gettysburg battle-field. As long as the writer confines himself to natural scenery, he acquits himself creditably; but in attempting to describe events he flounders fearfully. Of course, Pickett's men advance 'alone.' 'There was a terrible hand-to-hand battle at the Bloody Angle. Doubleday's troops lost twenty-five to forty per cent., and the slaughter of the Confederates was fearful, Garnett's Brigade alone having over 3,000 killed and captured.' This is Northern history. The facts are, as I have endeavored to show, Pickett's men did not advance 'alone;' there was no terrible battle inside the enemies works; Doubleday's troops did not lose their twenty-five to forty per cent. Not one regiment in Doubleday's or Gibbons' after the shelling lost one-fourth of one per cent. Garnett's Brigade carried into the fight less than 2,000 and brought out a very considerable fragment. It did have 78 killed and 324 wounded. With singular inappropriateness, Webb's Philadelphia Brigade and several other Federal organizations have erected monuments to commemorate their gallantry upon the third day's battle-field. It would appear that they should have been erected upon the spot where this gallantry was displayed. It does not require much courage to lie behind a stone wall and shoot down on the enemy in an open field and then to run away as it and other troops in its vicinity did when that enemy continued to approach. But while it does not add to their fame, it is not to their discredit that they did give way, for, however much discipline and inherent qualities may extend it, there is a limit to human endurance, and they had suffered severely. Webb's Brigade in the three days having lost forty-nine per cent.

"If there ever haveb een troops serving in a long war, who never on any occasion gave way till they had lost as heavily, they were superior to any in Napoleon's or Wellington's armies.

"The loss in the British Infantry at Salamanca was only twelve per cent. That of the Light Brigade at Balaklava was only thirty-seven per cent.; that of Pickett's only twenty-six, and they were ruined forever. It is true that the North Carolina Brigade of Pettigrew's Division, both on the first and third day, lost thirty, or, in all, sixty, per cent. in the battle of Gettysburg, and a Mississippi brigade nearly as much; but both of these organizations were exceptionally fine troops, and it is almost certain that even their spirits would have been appalled had their loss reached seventy-five or eighty per cent. And yet one of these brigades had a regiment, the Twenty-sixth North

Carolina, which, with morals unimpaired, met with a loss of eighty-five per cent. Governor Vance, now the honored senator from the old North State, was its first colonel. Whether any other regiment in our army could have done this, I know not; but this I do know, that if there was such another in either army, or in all the armies, Northern or Southern, it did not equal the 'common clay' of the old North State."

"They digged a pit,
They digged it deep;
They digged it for their brothers.
But it so fell out that they fell in
The pit that was digged for th' others."

And now, thanking our Rebel friend for his interesting and instructive story, we will take the Club away from Gettysburg.

Practically, the war closed at Gettysburg, July 4, 1863, with General Grant's capture of Vicksburg and Pemberton's army on the same day.

Here the anaconda of secession met with its death-wound. The backbone of the serpent was here broken. Its head and tail lived for over a year after; and, though dangerous if approached too closely, it was, in a manner, altogether helpless and at the mercy of the great crowds that had been gathered about to witness its death-throes. Generals Grant and Sheridan stoned and hammered it to death as it tried to escape through the wilderness of Spottsylvania, Mine Run, Five Forks, Petersburg to Appomattox; but, practically the continuance of the war after Gettysburg and Vicksburg was in the nature of a crime. It is said General Lee would have been glad to have made terms at this time.

I have frequently heard 1864 and 1865 soldiers criticise General Meade and the Army of the Potomac for not following up General Lee after Gettysburg, with the statement that if Grant had been there, Lee never would have gotten away. To this I reply, why did not General Grant follow up General Lee at once when he took command? He waited almost a year before following him, until his army was recruited and he had three to Lee's one and everything he desired in the way of support before he moved on Lee at the Wilderness.

We will escort our Travel Club over a line of Lee's retreat from Gettysburg, driving along the old pike, through the mountains to Chambersburg, Pa., thence to Hagerstown and the Potomac at Falling Waters. At this point we again strike General Braddock's war trail over which he was guided by Washington along the route since known as the National Pike, leading westward through Cumberland, Maryland, to Fort Necessity and Fort Duquesne, or Pitt, at the confluence of the Alleghany and Monongahela, which form the Ohio river, where now stands Pittsburg. Within a circle of say one hundred miles around Washington City, may be found pretty nearly all the important historical places of the nation.

Beginning with the early settlement at Jamestown, we have the Colonial period, as well as the Revolutionary, from the signing of the Declaration at Philadelphia to the final surrender at Yorktown. Also the birth-place, home and tomb of Washington and of many other prominent leaders in the debates of Congress; the duelling-grounds at Bladensburgh; the sacking of the Capitol by the

British in 1812; Fort McHenry in Baltimore; and later, the principal events of the War of the Rebellion were enacted between Richmond and Gettysburg, nearly all within the radius of 100 miles. In coming years, the students of history will visit the bloody war trail that we have been traveling over, the Peninsula, Richmond, Fredericksburg, Chancellorsville, Wilderness, Spottsylvania, Appomattox, Manassas, Antietam and Gettysburg.

As we drive over South Mountains we see, in the distance, the Heights at Harper's Ferry, which, by the way, is another of the many historic points about here. It was the scene of John Brown's raid, the first of the war. The fact that General Lee, then a colonel in the U. S. cavalry, was the officer in the command of the Government troops there is generally lost sight of.

All the Army of the Potomac will recognize the pictures of this picturesque place. Most of us have been here several times. When General Banks was in command here, his army was so often advanced down the valley and compelled to fall back again to this base that the boys called it "Harper's Weekly" instead of Harper's Ferry.

My mother was born on what subsequently became the Antietam battle-field, while your guide first saw the light close by on the north side of Mason and Dixon's line in Pennsylvania, almost within sight of the historic ground hereabouts, and is, therefore, somewhat familiar with the country from which he has wandered far; but his mind returns to the old ground, led, perhaps, by some trace of that instinct which the lower animals, even fishes of the sea, follow, the philosophy of which has not been clearly established.

I was a scout through this country during the first of the war, when Patterson's army of three months' men was encamped here, confronting Gen. Joseph E. Johnston. I recall, as if it were but yesterday, my hunt for headquarters, to which I had been ordered to report. Soldiers, —gay and happy boys of 1861, apparently out for a holiday,—were to be seen everywhere, strolling about the roads in squads, or lounging under the shade of trees, or filling arm-chairs on the neighboring house porches. Toward sundown the great attraction to the many lady visitors that crowded the camps was the dress parades. Seemingly, the adjacent swards became alive with marching troops forming for the parade, each preceded by a band. It appeared, from the noise, as if every company had a bass drum in those early days. A Rebel officer once told me that they were able to make a close estimate of our force by the number of bass drums they heard.

One of the most impressive scenes which I have witnessed was that of the chaplain's prayer at dress parade during those early days.

Imagine a regiment of a thousand men in line, fully equipped, standing at "parade rest" alongside of this Rubicon, or river of death, under the shadow of the great mountains about Harper's Ferry; their uncovered heads reverently bowed, their jaunty little fatigue caps hung on the muzzle of their guns; the band plays "Old Hundred" or the "Doxology," and, perhaps, hundreds of voices involuntarily join in the singing of this grand old hymn that is sung in Heaven. In the field the chaplains did not make so much of a show, though they were sometimes quite useful otherwise. They were entitled to a horse, and on this account were generally appreciated on the march by some lazy or tired line officer, who affected sickness that he might operate on the parson's sympathy and borrow his horse. In camp their greatest labor was spent in efforts to prevent falling from grace in the wicked society of their mess.

The chaplain was the regimental postmaster. In addition to this handling of the mail, he was supposed, also, to be a sort of professional letter-writer for those who could not write their own letters to fathers and sweethearts.

In those days our letters came in gaily illuminated envelopes. Flags and mottos almost covered them. A popular style of envelope, in the early days, showed a cannon, in the northeast corner, belching forth fire, the cannon ball in sight, while the cannoneers, with remarkable indifference, stood at attention. They were always addressed to Company, Regiment, Brigade, Division and Corps, so that wherever we went the letters, like Mary's lamb, were sure to follow. On one occasion, while executing a rapid change of base, our mail facilities became demoralized, and for some days we did not get a letter. At every opportunity the boys, who had become quite nervous over the prolonged delay, would appeal to the good chaplain for a letter from home. Failing to get it, they invariably began to fire questions as to the cause of the failure or endeavor to get some explanation. It was, of course, part of the business of the parson to comfort and encourage the men. He did all he could in this direction, but, in the army, patience soon ceases to be a virtue, even with preachers. The chaplain became tired of answering so many questions. The same stereotyped reply, day after day, "I do not know anything about the mails," finally irritated him so that he shut himself up in his tent and refused to see anyone. He was advised to place a printed notice on his quarters to the same effect, so that all anxious inquirers could see for themselves and not annoy him. He finally procured the board top of a cracker box and, with a piece of charcoal from his camp fire, wrote in plain letters the following notice, and nailed it to a tree in a conspicuous place.

"*The chaplain don't know anything about the mails.*"

A wag coming along, observing the sign and also the piece of charcoal, which he picked up and dryly added this amendment right under the chaplain's words:

"*And don't care a damn.*"

As I previously explained, the narrative of some of the actual experiences of a boy during the war was published, generally at the time of their occurrence, notably in the New York *Tribune*, Philadelphia *Press* and the paper of my home at Pittsburg. Subsequently, these were collected and, with some additions, appeared in a weekly trade paper in Washington City, devoted to the pension business of a claim agent. They paid liberally for the weekly installments, the oral agreement being that the story should be printed in book form, and that I was to be paid a royalty per copy. The matter became popular among the old boy readers, who, no doubt, realized that the writer was "thar or tharabouts." They declined to publish it in book form and with the usual dog-in-the-manger policy attempted to prevent others from doing so. I was not at all ambitious to have my name appear in the matter; in fact, it was my especial request, for business reasons, that the boy should remain "incog." and only be known by his *nom de plume* of "O. K."

To my surprise, after he had obtained nearly all the copy and the first instalment appeared, the editor declined for "business reasons," to permit even my *nom de plume* to appear at the head of my own articles. He did not, as he said to me, claim any rights as author, and I do not wish to be understood as charging so brilliant a writer as that editor with an attempt to rob a poor soldier boy of the little glory attaching to the original of the story; but the facts are indisputable that a majority of persons were, by inference, at least, led to believe that the story originated in that office. Of course, this claim could not be openly established and was subsequently abandoned, when the testimonials and corroborations began to come to the office by thousands from influential sources. I was in no way recognized by the editor or the proprietor of the paper; in fact, a systematic effort was made to ignore me, even to misrepresenting me personally to some old friend who called at the office of publication. I was generally informed by influential comrades that the same course had been pursued towards Si Klegg, Pittinger and others.

The matter supplied was hastily prepared amidst the duties of a newspaper worker, and, in the nature of things, were quite crude and imperfect. I was, in fact, indifferent and careless as to results. In the mercenary revision of such matter the editor took unusual liberties with my manuscript, to which I strenuously objected. And it has been my desire to correct, in "On the War-path," some of these revisions.

In this connection I beg to present the following from the *G. A. R. Record*, of Boston, as well as the letters of Gen. Fitz-John Porter and Col. Carswell McClellan, which explain and speak for themselves, without in any way affecting the truthfulness of the facts as originally stated:

68 West Sixty-Eighth Street,
New York, Jan. 30, 1889.

Maj. J. O. Kerbey, Washington, D. C.

Dear Sir: I am obliged for your letter. I can appreciate the situation in which you stood, when preparing your "Boy Spy," and the unfortunate influences you may have been under connected with the press.

I am not sorry for your work, so far as an injury to me—you injured yourself more than me, even in the minds of many of my enemies. I shall be glad to see your other work. I hope it will come before I pass to another sphere.

Your letter has been forwarded to Long Island.

Undoubtedly, as a telegraph operator, through whom, during the war, many important messages must have passed, you must have many points of interest; but you will have to be sure that your memory is correct when referring to authorities. Wishing you success, I am, Yours respectfully,

F. J. Porter.

218 Virginia Avenue,
St. Paul, Jan. 29, 1890.

Maj. J. O. Kerbey, Washington, D. C.

My Dear Sir: Yours of the 23d has been duly received, and I must thank you for having taken my criticism of the "Boy" in such good part.

I have not overlooked the fact that the blue pencil which "prepared and seasoned" your work "for a certain trade," is very evident. In truth, it is that very fact against which I would protest. To it is due most of the wrong done gallant men who gave their best days to the service of the country, and have, in return, received only censure from the "ignorant, intolerant judgment" (see Charles Sumner) of a public fed by a certain trade with food "prepared and seasoned" to suit the *trade ambitions.* (I refer, of course, to the trade politicians, and have no intention of being personal.)

That you appreciate this fact is evident from the pages of the "Boy," and I have already congratulated you thereon. Perhaps my studies of late years have made me somewhat sensitive as to injustice done to General Porter, but I need not to enlighten an old newspaper correspondent as to the avidity of the public for shams and prejudices, or repeat any of the trite expressions in regard to truth overtaking falsehood. The sale of a book is not always the best measure of its worth, especially as historic. Witness Grant's "Memoirs."

I take it, "The Boy," while not unmindful of the immediate returns received for his work, hopes in his work to outlive the mere present, and would not object to being received by future readers in company with —— and ——. Therefore I have ventured on my criticism of his work.

The original charge which Senator Logan attempted to revive against General Porter, in connection with the Patterson campaign, was based on the testimony of Col. R. Butler Price (Report Comm. on Cond. of War, 37th Cong., 3d Sess., Part 2, p. 187, et seq.) and the testimony of Col. Craig Biddle (same vol.), both of whom were aides on General Patterson's Staff, and neither of whom give any occasion for the charge their testimony has been distorted to sustain. The facts in the matter are all clearly stated by general Patterson himself, in a narrative of the campaign in the valley of the Shenandoah, in 1861

If you have not seen this, I have no doubt Mr. Fitzgerald can supply you, or tell you where you can find a copy. A brief outline of the whole matter is, that General Johnston, at Winchester, was, as he says in his report, "in position to oppose either McClellan from the West, or Patterson from the Northeast, *and to form a junction with General Beauregard when necessary.*" He could stay at Winchester *until he wished to leave, and then unite with Beauregard, tearing up the railroad behind him and laughing at pursuit.*

To order General Patterson to cross into Virginia and *detain* Johnston in Winchester to prevent his uniting with Beauregard, was, as General Porter once expressed it to me, like ordering a man to hold a dog by the tail when the dog was a long distance off, and running away. A glance at the map shows this.

General Patterson appreciated the position, and wished to cross the Potomac at Point of Rocks and take position at Leesburg, where he would be in position to support, co-operate or unite with McDowell, as circumstances might require. Instead, he was ordered to cross above, and advance on the Martinsburg and Winchester line. He was cautioned by the General-in-Chief to "take his measures therefor circumspectly; make good use of his engineers and other experienced Staff officers and Generals, and *attempt nothing without a clear prospect of success.*"

At Martinsburg, July 9, 1861, a council of war, composed of Colonel Crossman, Captain Beckwith, Captain Simpson, Captain Newton, Colonel Stone, General Negley, Colonel Thomas, Colonel Abercrombie, General Keene and General Cadwalader, *unanimously opposed a further advance on Winchester*, but, instead, advised the flank movement to Charleston, *which had been approved by General Scott.*

Captain Porter was not present at this council, and though the opinion of the members of the council was well known at the time, *five of the number were soon after made general officers.* Is it not then rather ungenerous to ascribe sinister designs upon General Porter's part, to a merely supposititious influence held by him over General Patterson?

From Charleston, *three days before the battle of Bull Run, twelve hours before Johnston commenced to leave Winchester*, General Patterson reported his condition to the General-in-Chief and asked, "Shall I attack?" *No answer was returned.* Two days later (July 20th), he telegraphed, "*With a portion of his force, Johnston left Winchester by the road to Millwood, on the afternoon of the 18th*, his whole force, 32,500.

With this information in hand, McDowell pushed out to Bull Run, *and General Patterson was allowed to receive his first news of the battle, which he supposed, from General Scott's dispatches, to have taken place on the 18th, through the newspapers on Monday, July 22d.*

This is a hasty and rather jumbled sketch, hinting some points well worth your looking up. The implication of responsibility resting upon Gen. Porter for malign influence upon the Antietam field rests on similar bald suppositions. The pages of Messrs. Nicholay and Hay's so-called history will not hold their own against the evidence of the Record and of notorious facts. I commend to your serious consideration the works alluded to by Gen. Porter in the printed letters to Nicholay and Hay enclosed in my last; and after you have carefully examined Gen. Patterson's side of the story of the first Shenandoah campaign, I think you will be willing to modify the views you have expressed through the "Boy."

I return Gen. Porter's note, as you may wish to keep it. I trust you will pardon the candor of my criticism for the sake of the intention.
Very truly yours,
CARSWELL McCLELLAN.

The critical letters of Gen. Fitz-John Porter and Col. Carswell McClellan, a relative of the Commander-in-Chief and a distinguished Staff officer of the Army of the Potomac, explain themselves and require no comment, except, that in presenting them to the club readers, it does not necessarily imply that they reflect my own opinions. Neither disputes my facts. It will be apparent to all that the only object is that prompted by an unselfish desire to afford to both sides a fair hearing. Readers may form their own conclusions from the facts stated.

I beg to take you all along on the flying trip I recently enjoyed in a Pullman palace car, from the Potomac through the historic, picturesque and once devastated, but now rich, Shenandoah valley. We will not have time to stop at Winchester, the Luray Caverns, the Natural Bridge, or to visit the graves of Lee and Jackson at Lexington, but hasten along through the thriving city of Roanoke, where we take the East Tennessee road, leading still on the "war-path," to the western armies.

At Knoxville, Tenn., I spent a couple of delightful weeks, revisiting scenes that were at once pleasantly and at the same time sorrowfully familiar to me. It may be remembered, that it was here, when this country was occupied by the Confederates, that the "boy" scout was kindly cared for, while sick, in the family of Col. Craig, then the prothonotary of the county. In this cultivated family, I was fortunate in meeting the charming young ladies mentioned in the story of the adventures of the "boy;" Miss Maggie, Miss Mary and the pert little Laura. They had only heard of me once, through "Belle Boyd," since my escape from Cumberland Gap. At this revisit after 26 years, it was my pleasure to meet all three of these ladies and a right royal meeting it was. All were married. "Our Maggie" to an ex-Confederate and a most genial gentleman. They have no children and travel considerably for their healths, spending the winters in Florida where they own an extensive orange grove and beautiful lake which has been named "Geno" in honor of the boy's heroine.

"Lake Geno" (so named by the owner in honor of the "Boy Spy's" war heroine, Geno Wells), is a beautiful sheet of pure, clear water, about thirty acres in extent, is the Spring Lake, or head of a chain of similar lakes dotting this entire region, varying in size from thirty acres to seven miles, which empty into the St. Johns.

Mary, the Rebel of the family is the wife of a Tennessee judge who was an ex-Federal officer and always a Unionist. They have quite an interesting family.

Laura, the little dark-haired beauty is the wife of a fine gentleman and now lives at Atlanta, Ga. Their only daughter Josie, a sweet girl of fifteen, resembles her mother as I once knew her.

The many pleasant days spent in this vicinity with Maggie by my side, driving in her own buggy, viewing the once-familiar scenes, will make some interesting chapters to be told in the sequel "Geno." The story could not be told under these covers.

This lady's poor health has somewhat injured her gay spirits. She, too, like Geno, lived between the lines and can a wondrous story tell of the war in the West that may equal "Geno" in the East. Though her wavy hair is slightly gray in front, she still retains the same pretty brown eyes and sweet Southern accented voice and manner.

We sang together the old songs, not forgetting "When you and I were young, Maggie."

I also visited the Brownlow house. Mrs. Brownlow still lives there.

My visit to Knoxville occurred during the glorious fall weather of 1889, about the time of the reunion at Chattanooga and Kenesaw which organized the Chickamauga association. It will be remembered that on this occasion the speech of Col. Will Henderson, an able lawyer of Knoxville, was delivered, in which he used the comparison since so widely quoted relating to the results of the war: "The war was of greater benefit to us than to you folks up north as it rid us of slavery and started our growth of manufactures." Or as the nigger, who had a law-suit about the ownership of a mule, which was decided against him, said: "You gained the law-suit, but I done got the mule yit."

Colonel Henderson was a gallant ex-Confederate. One of Miss Maggie's early friends and admirers.

It is proposed by the Chickamauga Association to ask Congress to appropriate $250,000 to purchase of the States of Tennessee and Georgia, 7,600 acres of land, embracing the battle-field, to be formed into a national military park to remain under control of the Secretary of War. It is hoped that the people of the East, notably of the Army of the Potomac, may be induced to emulate this worthy example of the Western army and ask Congress to add a little to the acreage of the Marye Cemetery at Fredericksburg, and, perhaps, purchase the strip of bloody ground thereabout, upon which not only the most blood of the war was shed, but that over which was shown the greatest heroism of the Anglo-Saxon race. This might be made to include the home and grave of the mother of Washington and become a shrine convenient to the Capital.

In this connection I beg leave to introduce to the club a Western Rebel who replies to some statements made by General Boynton, a newspaper warrior of Washington, D. C.

The Battle of Chickamauga Without Taffy, as told by an old Confederate, Capt. R. F. Powell, of Georgia.

I reproduce it simply for the sake of the historic incidents it mentions, and as a Rebel's conception of what he terms "an exposition of the wanton and base falsehoods that invariably characterize the Yankee historian's writings on these events." Captain Powell is a loyal citizen of the United States, but he thinks the time for apologizing and regretting things that can not be helped has passed, and his letter is written along that line. He says, among other things·

"General Boynton, a very pretty writer, has a very nice romance, which he calls facts, published in the Washington army paper, claiming the battle of Chickamauga as a great 'Union victory,' says the objective point was Chattanooga, and Rosecrans got there first.

"That reminds me of the little boy who ran home with another boy after him, his face scratched, his clothes torn, his hair standing on end, and, in fact, bearing all the marks of a boy who had been soundly thrashed.

"His brother said to him, 'Why, Ned, what is the matter? What are you running for?' Says Ned: 'Now, Bud, do you reckon I'm goin' to let that Jones boy hit me the last lick and beat me to the house, too? No, I aint.'"

After quoting from General Boynton, Captain Powell says:

"The first and most striking feature of the battle, as General Boynton represents it, is, that in every assault, in every death-grapple in all parts of the field, the Federals were always successful, and whenever there was a collision the Confederates outnumbered the Federals at least two to one; the Confederates were always fresh and the Federals always tired—and this is the case with every battle described by Northern writers that I have ever read. They may admit at the outset that their army is as large as, and possibly a little, just a very little, larger than ours, but where the battle rages fiercest, and deeds of heroism are performed, either by individuals or corps, it is always the same story—the single 'Yank' drives off three or four ambushed 'Johnnies,' one company of 'our boys' holds the position against a regiment of 'Rebs,' a regiment (always somebody's celebrated regiment) dashed at a brigade of Confederates and after a brave resistance on the part of the Rebs they broke and fled in the wildest confusion—and so on up to division and corps.

"Some of their most candid writers throw in a good deal

of 'taffy,' and speak of 'the splendid troops of Cheatham,' or 'Hood's brave veterans,' and others even admit that we had occasional spurts of 'dash,' and made some magnificent assaults, but such are never described without a sequel, and that sequel is always the same—a grand counter-move of the Federals ending in the total discomfiture of the brave, but unfortunate Southerners.

"The second prominent feature of Gen. Boynton's Chickamauga is his powerful effort to reconcile his statements. Crittenden's Corps occupied Chattanooga on the 9th of September and left a brigade to hold it, and yet it was not occupied by the Federals on the 20th, although the brigade was still there and no Confederate troops had been there since Crittenden took possession. But the weakest point in the article is his attempt to have Bragg outnumber Rosecrans all day Saturday by the arrival of Buckner's and Longstreet's troops, and yet he has Longstreet's fresh troops pouring in all day Sunday, and finally, he and Col. Duffield both agreed that Bragg's whole army of 65,000 men, half of them fresh troops, says Duffield, attacked Thomas's single corps late Sunday evening and utterly failed in the attack, and that Thomas held his position until dark. Now, if both armies had about or nearly the same number of men—as they say, about 65,000 each—and one-half of Bragg's army was fresh Sunday evening, late, then he had surely been fighting 65,000 men for nearly two days with 32,500 men, and during all that long and terrible struggle, Gen. Bragg was so fortunate as not to lose a single man, and had his entire army intact Sunday evening when he struck Gen. Thomas' Corps.

"The fact is, Bragg had fewer men than Rosecrans, and one-half of Longstreet's Corps was not in the fight at all, having arrived too late.

"The battle of the 19th was indeed a draw battle, but on the morning of the 20th the Federals seemed to have lost spirit, and were driven by the Confederates from the start, and we were only checked by the massing, on a high, double ridge, of Thomas' Corps and other troops that had not run away, to the number of 25,000 in all, says Colonel Duffield, a Northern writer of considerable prominence.

"It is true that several assaults on Thomas at this point were repulsed with considerable loss to the Confederates.

"I think the battle was ended about 5 o'clock P. M., by the breaking of Thomas' Corps and the surrender of 1,500 Yankees upon the summit of the ridge that Thomas had so bravely held.

"It is perfect bosh to talk about Thomas holding his position until dark, and then 'withdrawing' to Rossville. His corps was broken into atoms long before dark, and fled, totally demoralized.

"I can't remember the exact time, but I know it was long before dark, because I ordered my company to stack arms on the very ground occupied by Thomas' Corps, and exchange their Belgian guns for Enfield rifles.

"I remember, also, picking up a fine Colt's repeating rifle on the very summit of the ridge held by Thomas' Corps, inside their temporary works; also talking to the prisoners, and they were certainly very despondent, saying that Chickamauga was a dark day for the Union, etc., and this was long before sundown. There wasn't a Yankee soldier within ten miles of the battle-field at dark, except the dead, wounded and prisoners. We captured 30,000 rifles, sixty-eight cannon, and 10,000 prisoners. Great 'Union victory'!

"'The fact is, this 'old soldier' has told and read so many big tales of his own prowess and his daring attacks on 'great masses' and 'overwhelming numbers' of 'Rebs,' in which he was always victorious, that he has made his children believe them all, and he believes about half of them himself. Our side has been silent for a long time, and the witnesses are thinning out year by year, and it is time our people were putting in their testimony and placing on record for our children and children's children to read when we are gone. The 'Yanks' know, and we know, that we won four-fifths of the pitched battles of the war, and that in point of numbers their soldiers were three and four to one, their railroad facilities as twenty to one, their rations as twenty to one, their clothing as five to one.

"We had only one force to oppose to such fearful odds, and that was pluck, indomitable, unwavering pluck, and it took four years of steady fight for us to wear ourselves out whipping them."

It will be again understood that in thus presenting a Confederate to the club, I do not endorse the statements that he makes. It is simply a disposition to offer some new light on an old subject from the other side. As I have taken opportunity to introduce the same element in the East, I thought it advisable to stir up the Western boys a little.

Our own story of the war has been told and retold

thoroughly. No harm can come from a friendly discussion of the war with ex-Confederates, and much more good may result "fighting" them over with our former antagonists than in fighting them over among ourselves. The agitation will serve to bring out the true story from both sides.

We have nothing to fear, nothing to regret, nothing to be ashamed of.

And now we have reached our journey's end, and your guide, with hat in hand and a cordial hand-shake to each individual member of the Travel Club, reluctantly says goodbye, with many thanks for your kind attention and forbearance. I hope we may all meet around the winter's fireside, and, perhaps, hear the wonderful story of "Geno," a romance of secret service and secret love, during the war, that is, indeed, stranger than fiction.

NOTE.—I should be glad to meet in Washington any visiting member of the club, or to reply to any interrogation. A letter addressed to Washington will always reach me, wherever I may be.—J. O. KERBEY.

www.ingramcontent.com/pod-product-compliance
Lightning Source LLC
Chambersburg PA
CBHW032047230426
43672CB00009B/1497
9783744745079